GAYER-ANDERSON

GAYER-ANDERSON

The Life and Afterlife
of the Irish Pasha

Louise Foxcroft

The American University in Cairo Press
Cairo   New York

First published in 2016 by
The American University in Cairo Press
113 Sharia Kasr el Aini, Cairo, Egypt
420 Fifth Avenue, New York, NY 10018
www.aucpress.com

Exclusive distribution outside Egypt and North America by I.B.Tauris & Co Ltd.,
6 Salem Road, London, W2 4BU

Dar el Kutub No. 27121/15
ISBN 978 977 416 800 0

Dar el Kutub Cataloging-in-Publication Data

Foxcroft, Louise
        Gayer-Anderson: The Life and Afterlife of the Irish Pasha / Louise Foxcroft—Cairo: The
American University in Cairo Press, 2016.
        p.   cm.
        ISBN: 978 977 416 800 0
        1. Gayer-Anderson, Robert Grenville, 1881–1945
        2. Archaeologists
        930.1092

1 2 3 4 5   20 19 18 17 16

Designed by Jon W. Stoy
Printed in United States of America

For Pum's great grandchildren, Eliot D'Arcy and
Phoebe Solange Takara Gayer-Anderson

Contents

Preface

I
n a ramshackle barn in the Cambridgeshire village of Waterbeach, among rolled Persian rugs, sculptures, and *shisha* pipes, are many marbled boxes of curling letters and cards, a firsthand account of the opening of Tutankhamun's tomb, packets of sepia photographs of exotic locations and people, erotic drawings, and the poetry and psychic musings of Major Robert Grenville "Pum" Gayer-Anderson Pasha. But most wonderful of all is a copy of his unpublished memoir, "Fateful Attractions." In 2001, through an unpredictable chain of connections made up of friends, godmothers, and PhD supervisors, I met Pum's grandson, Theo Gayer-Anderson, who opened this remarkable trove for me.

The memoir, on which this book is based, was written in the early 1940s and looks back across an extraordinary life. It is a typed document of more than 130,000 words, arranged in four volumes and comprised of eleven parts and two appendices (one on the experiences of identical twins, the other on gifts and bequests to museums and libraries). Pum's twin, Colonel Thomas Gayer-Anderson, undertook some posthumous editing and a fair bit of censorship over the sex and drugs, though he was perhaps more exercised by his brother's grammatical errors.

In pursuit of Pum, Theo and I went to see Humphrey Spender, photographer and artist, in the bright modernity of his squat Richard

Rogers house and studio (the young architect's first commission, in 1968). In the early 1930s, Humphrey and his brother, the poet Stephen Spender, bought the Great House in Lavenham, Suffolk, from Pum and Tom. They became friends as well as neighbors. When I met him, Humphrey was in his nineties, but still tall, handsome, imposing, and in possession of many memories and yet more letters, photographs, and diaries. He also had an unpublished, candid roman à clef by Evelyn Wynn, the unfortunate mother of Pum's son and Theo's father, John.

Later that year, in the Bodleian Library, Oxford, I looked through volumes of poetry and folios of drawings gifted in the 1940s, including Pum's "Devious Devotions" and Tom's "He/She: The World's Sweetheart," dedicated to his twin. As I sifted through all these marvels, Pum gradually began to manifest himself: a thoughtful yet maverick adventurer, surgeon, soldier, avid collector, Egyptologist, dilettante, and a lover and preserver of beauty. Here was a man who had recorded five astonishing decades of travel, fighting, dealing, loving, and failing to love.

In February 2012, I made a research trip to Beit al-Kretliya, Pum's home in Cairo, now the Gayer-Anderson Museum. The rooms run together and are sober and charming, making the secret places and passages all the more exciting. The halls are tall, cool, and grand, and the outside clamor of Cairo seems distant and muted. Many of his pieces had been packed away because of the 2011 uprising, but to be in the ancient house Pum restored, to peer through the *mashrabiya* screens, to stand on his roof terrace overlooking the magnificent Ibn Tulun Mosque, was to reveal Pum in a far more visceral way and to make him all the more fascinating.

I am very grateful to Theo and his sister Chloe for their unstinting help and enthusiasm in the writing of this book. Thanks are also due to the late Humphrey Spender, and to Nicholas Warner and Salima Ikram, professor of Egyptology at the American University in Cairo, for their help and warm hospitality in that city. I am indebted to the staff of the University Library and the Fitzwilliam Museum, Cambridge, and the Wellcome Library and Collection, the British Museum, to Colin Harris, superintendent of the Special Collections Reading Rooms at the Bodleian Library, Oxford, to Carolin Johansson, Medelhavsmuseet, Stockholm, and to Tonbridge School, Kent. The Suffolk Building Preservation Trust gave me a generous research bursary, and Wendy Barnes, Martin Lightfoot, and the late Jean Beard, all from the Little Hall, Lavenham, Suffolk, were immensely patient and helpful. Thanks, too, to George Miller, Fiona Green, Justin Pollard, Jennifer Grove, Vic Gatrell, Patrick Walsh, Jonathan Burt, Mark Ellingham, and the late Peter Carson.

Introduction

Major Robert Grenville Gayer-Anderson Pasha (1881–1945) is best known as an Egyptologist who amassed an extensive and astonishing collection of antiquities, now spread across the globe. The most famous piece is the "Gayer-Anderson Cat," gifted to the British Museum in 1939, and one of its best-known objects. His pieces were his children, he wrote, Egypt was his flesh and blood, and the immediacy of his story is both startlingly candid and strangely modern. This book is based on his unpublished memoir, "Fateful Attractions," written shortly before he died as an exercise in self-knowledge and passed down in the family. It reads as part ripping yarn and part hastily reorganized stream of consciousness. Some of its fragments resemble the Egyptian artifacts that he discovered and pieced together, all carefully placed within a narrator's contemporary travelogue. This story is engaging and disturbing in almost equal measures, and the hero must be viewed through his times.

The major answered to different names: he was called "Nenny" as a child; "John" by his adult friends; and his identical twin, Colonel Thomas "Tom" Gayer-Anderson, privately gave him the acronymic name, "P.U.M.," though the meaning of this remained a secret between them. He is referred to as "Pum" throughout this book because it tells of his most private thoughts and experiences as well as of his

1

adventures and professional life. The title of pasha was bestowed on him in 1943 by King Farouk.

Standing just under six feet tall, he had broad shoulders, a long, high-browed, clean-shaven, open face with a fresh complexion, a large, sensitive mouth, and thoughtful, blue eyes. According to Tom, he was a kind, tolerant, humorous man. In his foreword to Pum's *Christeros and Other Poems* (1948), Stephen Spender declared that Pum was "never gloomy or sad; his inherited capacity for happiness, coupled with a keen sense of humour, prevented that."

Pum's life was a tightrope walk across the decline of an empire, teetering over the constraints and excesses of the early twentieth century. A respectable public persona masked an unconventional private life. He had to reconcile his occasionally cruel Victorian upbringing and, later, his given authority as a colonial government representative, with his quest for intimacy with the Arab people and his love of beauty and boys. His clandestine erotic and supernatural interests were counterpoint to the disciplined life of undemonstrative desire that he constructed for himself. Pum was intensely serious about his psychic abilities, and his writings reveal that indiscriminate mix of the superstitious, quasi-religious, and coincidental that so often reflected the late-Victorian and Edwardian cult of the paranormal. Forced through social expectations and personal vulnerabilities to keep up a respectable front, he recognized that his real desires were contradictory elements in his character that led him, successfully, to deceive his friends and acquaintances. Many of these people were extraordinary figures such as the eminent surgeon Arbuthnot-Lane, the anatomist D.E. Derry, T.E. Lawrence, Kitchener, Allenby, Conan Doyle, Eric Gill, Humphrey and Stephen Spender, Freya Stark, Glyn Philpot, Vivian Forbes, Reginald Brill, and Edna Clarke-Hall, among others. In his will, Pum bequeathed Egyptian rings to Eleanor Roosevelt, President Franklin D. Roosevelt, Winston Churchill, Field Marshall Montgomery, Crown Prince Gustaf of Sweden, and King Farouk of Egypt.

Born in Ireland, Pum's adventurous life began when he was only three years old. He and his siblings were uprooted to travel across a raw and often violent America, as his pioneering parents tried to turn a profit from the land boom of the 1880s. He learned, early on, to hide or camouflage those parts of himself that did not accord with his father's ideal of what a son should be. He kept his passionate feelings to himself, burying what he called the psychic, cosmic, and spiritual aspects of his personality. This emotional subterfuge was channeled into the writings and "doodlings" that he did alone at night all his life, and which are now held at the Bodleian Library, Oxford, under the category of "reserved material." His twin, it turns out, did the same, and there is an unsurprising connection and similarity between the brothers' works and minds. Erotica, crypto-religious philosophy, surreal cosmology, and a sentimental brutality are their hallmarks. Pum was in many ways a divided man, quite literally split in two: the twins' lives often ran in startling parallels, and he recorded actual and psychic instances where they seemed to merge into one creature. He was, he wrote, an "alloy" with his identical twin, and "an alloy of the sexes."

As a small boy, he had felt himself to be in a keen state of grace, safe within his own prelapsarian beauty, and he wanted to preserve it against the odds. But the inevitability of growing up meant that he had to seek out purity in unchangeable, extraordinary objects and in the succession of perfect young boys he cared for, educated, and launched upon the world. Pum assigned the virtue of beauty to things and people he cherished and so, he thought, rescued them from corruption and neglect. Eventually, through an ultimately disastrous arrangement with the discarded wife of an army colleague, he recreated that beauty and innocence in a son. But though he revisited his own longed-for perfection, he found it hard to love the real boy.

As a young man, Pum studied at Guy's Hospital, London, and became a surgeon before joining the Royal Army Medical Corps. Posted to the East, he worked on the Sudan Sleeping Sickness Commission, shot elephants, got lost in deserts, visited harems, adopted Arab life, wrestled Turks and crocodiles, smoked opium and hashish, fought at Gallipoli, boiled the heads of Nuba warriors in flowery glades for Henry Wellcome, and explored Tutankhamun's Tomb when it was opened by Howard Carter in 1923. Young men going overseas as British officials in the late nineteenth and early twentieth centuries were abruptly introduced to new cultures. Some of them, like Pum, found the sudden, apparent freedoms of thought and behavior astonishingly liberating and varied, and they received it all gratefully, occasionally fatally. Pum tried to experience as much as he could, from the clothes and food to drugs, sex, and superstition. He realized that he could allow his admiration and affection to cross boundaries of race and class in ways he had not thought possible before. He spent several decades in Cairo, he restored and lived in Beit al-Kretliya, a pair of eighteenth-century residential houses, now the Gayer-Anderson Museum, and dealt in objects of beauty, collecting for himself and others and selling his treasures to museums across the world.

The act of collecting and his love of beauty, innocence, and erotica formed the connective tissue to his life, while an outward show of duty and respectability gave it muscle and power. Yet Pum's obsessive love of beauty, in man-made artifacts and in the perfection of youth, was no passive desire, for he went to great lengths to seek them out, collect and admire them. There was a scopophiliac's clandestine pleasure in his wily acquisitioning and, most of all, in his need to rescue, order, and possess (scopophilia comes from the Greek, meaning "love of looking"). The adoration that he lavished upon his possessions, prosaic and pornographic, was, he acknowledged, an expression of sexual power. Freud argues that the impulse to collect is an anally retentive instinct connected with loss in childhood. Werner Muensterberger says, in *Collecting: An Unruly Passion: Psychological Perspectives*, that it is a response to the trauma of aloneness, need-driven and compulsively compensatory; drawing on fetish culture, it is phallic in the need to complete—the collector collects because of incomplete development. Philipp Blom describes this "strange and beautiful obsession" as a way to "overcome the limits of time and upbringing." In his book, *To Have and to Hold: An Intimate History of Collectors and Collecting*, he argues that the collector is attempting to find hidden meaning in the "multiplicity and chaos of the world."

As Pum's collecting became an ever more absorbing part of his life, other activities gradually lost their hold upon him. He promised himself a life of introspection, to be left alone to do what he wanted and not what others might want. He wished to live an unencumbered life, yet his obsessive collecting paradoxically weighed him down with anxieties. Pum's story of how he acquired his greatest treasure, the Gayer-Anderson Cat, a rare and beautiful life-size bronze, and of how he painstakingly restored it, smuggled it out of Egypt, and hid it in a well shaft in his Suffolk home to keep it from the Nazis, is full of pleasurable gratification, but also immense tension.

The friction between all aspects of his life—his Orientalism, collecting of antiquities, medicine, self-analysis, occultism, family dynamics, drugs, love, and war—is palpable, electric, and often troubled. They touch on questions of empire, on the survival of attitudes and identities transplanted abroad, on being British—his beloved mother, Mary, wanted her children to be "all-British"—and on negotiating the differences between East and West that still confront us.

1
Tutankhamun's Tomb and the Universal Love-Ray

Life, according to Pum, emerged by chance, through the "universal psychic love-ray." This fundamental idea was both plausible and desirable to a man for whom the grim realities of life demanded to be balanced by beauty, abstract and physical.

At night, alone in his bed, Pum scribbled away in his notebooks, producing page upon penciled page of ethical and religious philosophizings, all annotated with much crossing out and marginalia. He collected them into a volume called "Devious Devotions," now held in the Bodleian Library. Psychic rays are all around, Pum wrote, analogous to the communications that insects send out to each other with their antennae. But the life-giving love-ray was the most powerful; all other "psychic rays and emanations—those of heat, sound, radio activity, etc." were "secondary and complementary" to it. He imagined it as an emanation penetrating and permeating space, "striking off physical life as a spark, a flint on steel, when, where and however it encounters the rare conditions essential to its propagation." Earth was probably the "sole vehicle of life" in the universe, with a "billion homunculi at the moment of insemination struggling in the race to attain the solitary female single-cell, or ovum." Mankind, then, must be "supremely privileged beings, intruders who may by an accident have shared in this unique, brief (but a few billion years) episode, of consciousness, doomed though we are, as all life is, to extinction." This is a universe of "cosmic fecundity," where "the milky-way may be 'God's' ejaculation, seed-spend fructifying space."

What if, he asked, we were all "but things of thought, merely dream figures peopling someone or something else's dream, or maybe phantoms, daemons, that have materialized to actuality?" The truth might be "psychologically too vast, too omnipresent and out of focus to be distinguishable or comprehensible to us as such, just as our huge bodily proportions, motives, and motions are unobvious and inconceivable to the ant or fly." Each individual was surely a "cosmos within himself, each of his blood-corpuscles is a world in space, each is the apogee of his own creation, the hub of his own universe. In death his substance dissolves into all elements, permeating all times and states: *I am all*."

If space, time, and entity were the "Ultimate Truths," and each one of us came from and returned to a well-ordered cosmos, then this would alleviate Pum's sense of separation and rupture. To be whole was to be collected. To collect was to remedy.

*

In 1923, when Pum was forty-two, he experienced these truths and the "annihilation of time" in the tomb of Tutankhamun, newly opened by Howard Carter. He was a member of the official party at the private opening, stumbling down the slope into the hewn rock in the Valley of the Kings. For years he had dreamed and talked of the marvel of visiting an intact tomb and believed it was preordained that he should be there. He had received a personal invitation from Lady Evelyn Herbert, Lord Carnarvon's daughter, and as assistant Oriental secretary he was included in Field Marshall Viscount Allenby's Residency party.

But his journey to Luxor and the Valley of the Kings was jinxed. At the eleventh hour a series of incidents occurred that nearly prevented him from attending Lady Evelyn's alfresco luncheon party by the tomb of Ramesses VI. It was a mix of luck and disaster, and it appeared to Pum as though opposite forces were contending to determine whether he would be there. Firstly, the date and time of the reception were changed without his knowing. Only a chance remark by an acquaintance revealed that it was being held the very next day at noon, leaving him just an hour to catch the last train south. Catch it he did, but it was so delayed by an accident that at noon he had just reached Luxor and still had a long way to go to get to Thebes. When he jumped aboard the ferryboat to cross the Nile, he missed his footing and sprained his ankle badly. But as he limped painfully ashore on the other side, he saw to his intense relief that the Residency party had also only just arrived, equally late. He joined their cars for the last leg of the journey, six miles of rough desert road up the mysterious, coral-colored valley to the tombs.

The newly discovered tomb entrance was just a hole in the hillside, neatly shored up with dry masonry, recently built—"in such an obscure spot did that incalculable treasure lie." Around the entrance was a reserved circle beyond which was clustered a great crowd of inquisitive sightseers, tourists, journalists, and photographers. Within the circle stood the "hosts": Lord Carnarvon "looking tired and pale," Lady Evelyn, Howard Carter and his staff, and some personal friends of theirs—Egyptologists, diplomats, foreign and Egyptian ministers, and so on. Now there was only one remaining guest to wait for: the queen of the Belgians, who had traveled to Egypt especially for the occasion with a royal party including Prince Leopold, then a boy in his teens, the distinguished Belgian savant Professor Jean Cappart, and, as attaché, "Jimmy" Watson Pasha, whom Pum thought a delightful chap. While waiting for the royal party, in the crowd and heat, Pum passed the time with Carter and asked if he thought there were any other unrifled tombs to be discovered: "I hope to God not!" was the stern reply.

After all the bowing and scraping that greeted the arrival of the royals, Lord Carnarvon led the queen down the sharp incline into the tomb. The rest of the assembly began to queue up in pairs, formally, to wait for their turn to go in some twenty minutes later. As he waited, watching those coming up out of the tomb into the bright sunlight, Pum was reminded of the scene in J.M. Barrie's play *Dear Brutus* (1917) in which the characters "stagger back from an enchanted wood beyond the world, from what might have been to what is, and are so dazed by their experience that they struggle for something to grasp and cling on to: even a word with a concrete sense, 'A table, hold on to that; hold on to a table!' So, in this valley beyond the world did each guest emerge dazed and unsteadily into reality." Pum was paired with General Sir John Maxwell who had served in the Mahdist War, Sudan, the Boer War, and the Great War, and who presided over the secret military tribunals in 1916 that ordered the execution of fifteen leaders of the Easter Rising, changing the course of Irish history.

The time came for them to descend into the underground chambers. Taking off their hats and coats (Pum had to leave his makeshift walking sticks outside and hobble down), they "passed through that portal," sealed until then for over three thousand years, and stepped over the threshold into the tomb, "out of Time."

Going down a short incline they found themselves in an anteroom, a long, low chamber lit by electricity that had been rigged up for the guests. This chamber had been cleared of everything save a few large alabaster vases. At its south end, two magnificent life-sized black wooden figures of the young king seemed to guard the way into the burial chamber. They faced each other, identical apart from a detail of headdress, stepping out, staff-in-hand, life-like and imposingly resilient. Between them was a wide opening where until two days before had been the third and inmost sealed door of masonry, now completely removed. Through this portal gleamed one huge side of an extraordinary catafalque, a gorgeous surface of gold and turquoise-blue inlays. No one knew then that it contained three similar coverings one within the other, then a carved sarcophagus, and finally a coffin of solid gold in which lay the king's mummified body wrapped about with a fabulous treasure of jewelry.

Pum and Maxwell stepped down from the anteroom to the floor level of the burial chamber. The massive canopy almost filled the rock-hewn space, with only one or two feet separating it from the walls on each side, while its giant roof reached almost to the ceiling. So tight a space was it that the general got stuck as he tried to maneuver himself around the corner. Pum offered gallantly to pull him back, but the wedged man cried, "No! For God's sake, push me on!" and so he shoved and heaved the uniformed bulk through the gap, just a few more yards, toward the treasure chamber. The room was fenced in by a new barrier over which they leaned, as if over a garden gate, to peer into the inmost recess, "this holy of holies." Though the place had an indescribably time-worn appearance after thirty-four centuries, everything in it seemed to Pum's eyes untarnished, not a stain, not a scratch, not a spot of dust on the vibrant, shining gold and blue surfaces, as if it had been dusted and polished but a moment before.

In the center of the far wall was the unique canopic shrine, so complete and delicately made inside and out that Pum thought it "one of the masterpieces of the collection." At the time, the shrine was thought to contain all the king's viscera, but it was later discovered that the heart, a key component for the successful resurrection of the body, was missing. This and other anomalies, including the massive amount of resinous material covering the boy-king and affixing him to his coffin, and the fact that he was mummified with an erect penis, are still a mystery and the subject of much debate. Around the shrine stood four wistful little golden goddesses, their arms outstretched, appealing and protecting, as if, it seemed to Pum, they were whispering to him to hush and be careful not to wake the sleeper. Afterward, Professor Breasted told Pum that they had seemed to him quite gay, "like happy girls joining hands to dance around a maypole."

Just across the barrier, staring him full in the face, was black Anubis, watchdog of the underworld, life-sized and life-like, prick-eared and wide awake. Beside him was the cow-headed Hathor, gentle and shy. Both were magnificently carved in wood. On the floor between them stood a group of exquisite coffers, and stacked in one corner a pile of dismantled racing chariots. The remaining walls and corners were lined with sealed black boxes, on top of which were many charming models of brightly colored, full-rigged ships, which to Pum's mind brought an air of youthfulness to the place. Inspired, possibly by these "toy boats," the baby chairs and chariots, and especially the two adolescents guarding the way, he wrote home the next day: "I feel the King is a youth perhaps seventeen or eighteen years old." A later X-ray examination proved that Tutankhamun was just under eighteen when he died.

Their time in the tomb was up, and as Pum and Maxwell turned back they were shown the store or furniture room that opened up from the antechamber—a wonderful jumble of chairs, beds, and boxes of all sorts filled it from floor to ceiling. Now it was Pum's turn to grope his way out of the "wood beyond the world." Outside he found a table of cold drinks and sandwiches to help him pull himself together. Before they left for Luxor, the party was taken to see the workshop set up in the empty tomb of Seti II, deep in the cliff at the far end of the valley. Down both sides stood many deal tables and large wooden carrying trays, each occupied by an object in the process of examination or treatment—it reminded Pum of a hospital ward. As they drove back toward the Nile, the setting sun behind them, everyone in the party was silent and reflective. Luxor, when they reached it, was more crowded and excited than it had been since perhaps the days of the pharaohs.

Six weeks later, Lord Carnarvon was dead. Blood poisoning and pneumonia had killed him, but that didn't stop the rumors of the mummy's curse, a notion that had been around since the 1860s. "Egyptomania" had first taken off in Britain after Napoleon's invasion of Egypt in 1798 and his subsequent defeat, after which he had had to hand over all his Egyptian artifacts to the British. The curse rumors flourished after the earl's death, mainly because he had made an exclusive deal with the *Times* to cover the opening of the tomb, leaving all the other newspapers to capitalize on his death for their column inches instead. They gleefully reported that the lights of Cairo had flickered and failed as he died, that Carnarvon's three-legged dog Susie howled dreadfully and dropped dead—in England—and they blamed any and all subsequent mishaps and tragedies that befell many of those involved in the excavation on this new, sensational "Pharaoh's Curse." The tomb had been discovered at a time of political tension, when power was being handed over to the Egyptian national government, and riots, conspiracies, and assassination attempts on British officials were rampant. Colonial anxieties were displaced onto the curse—what might the unknowable "natives" know or do? In his own account, Howard Carter was dismissive of the curse rumors. He described the exhilaration of discovery as one of those moments when life may be vividly stirred. The true sentiment of the Egyptologist was not one of fear, he said, but of respect and awe, "entirely opposed to the foolish superstitions which are far too prevalent among emotional people in search of 'psychic excitement.'" Yet, Pum, self-avowedly emotional and psychic, did wonder about the curse when, soon after the event, two of his own servants were brutally murdered, and he himself narrowly survived two terrifying assassination attempts.

Pum discussed all this with Arthur Weigall, Egyptologist, stage designer, prolific author, and journalist, who had covered the opening of the tomb for the *Daily Mail*. He was a prominent member of the smart set of Egyptian society centered in Cairo and Luxor, had worked closely with Flinders Petrie, Howard Carter, and others, and was a friend of Ronald Storrs of the Arab Bureau of Intelligence. Pum was "a particular friend" of Weigall's and was said to be the inspiration for the hero of the author's novel *Bedouin Love* (1922). The two men met for dinner and talked of nothing but the tomb, trying to assimilate their experiences, which seemed to have "involved forces beyond their ken." When Weigall died some ten years later, the *Daily Express* ran the headline "Arthur Weigall, who denied Tutankhamun's curse, is dead," and this very quickly became "A curse killed Arthur Weigall."

Pum felt he had to revisit the site, this time accompanied by his mother, Mary, in 1932. Beneath the orange-pink cliffs they went to "beard Howard Carter in his tomb." It happened to be the archaeologist's very last day there, and they found him packing up some final specimens of desiccated eighteenth-century flowers and fruit from the burial to be dispatched to a botanical expert. His work almost over, Carter was in a good mood, pleasant and facetious, and he jokingly asked them if they would like to be present at Tutankhamun's funeral? Striking a match, he wafted some burning incense under their noses, the same that had scented the air more than three millennia before, here in this valley at the pharaoh's burial service. Pum was deeply moved, once again, by the collapse of time and a spiritual sensation of oneness.

He later described himself as having been only "vaguely devout" as a youth and adolescent, with an interest in religious ethics and an adoration of Christ rather than a love of him. As an adult he had become skeptical, and eventually profoundly atheistic, coming to regard traditional Christianity as false and exclusive. Christ, thought Pum, was not divine but a "noble example of super-humanity—such as were the Buddha, Socrates, Shakespeare, Einstein and others." He was "an inspired fanatic who laboured under delusions, even believing himself—probably at the instigation of his mother—for whom in later life he seems to have had little affection—to be the messiah." Further, subject to moods and hallucinations, Christ displayed an aloof personality, and his "unloved and love-less relations towards the rest of mankind concealed a coldly 'ardent' temperament that is forever seeking out and demanding love, only to receive adoration or devotion, sorry substitutes, in its stead." These characteristics bred in him an "irascible frustrated nature . . . vehemently believing in his 'mission'" to enlighten mankind, chastise and correct the Jews—he was pro-Arab, anti-Zionist—and "make amends to mankind for the sins of his presumed father." It is tempting to say that Pum modeled his idea of Christ on some of his own experiences.

It followed from reasoned thought, and possibly from Pum's experiences of war and human frailty, "that there is not and never has been a CREATOR [of] the UNIVERSE, call it God or The Infinite Mind or Nature or The Creator was never created but always existed, forever disintegrating into dust—background material as Hoyle calls it—and forever recreating itself and expanding (like the Hindoo [sic] God Vishnu) at an incredible rate."

He grew heavily critical of the Christianity he had left behind in England. The Bible, especially the Old Testament, was, he thought, "one of the most immoral books that can be placed in anybody's hands." There is "something incredibly sordid and petty about so much of [it], it reeks of flesh-pots and burnt sacrifice, sweet blood offerings and incense, the Roman Catholic Church and Jehovah." Schoolboys in their scripture classes spent all their time "furtively looking up the smutty bits—(Genesis xix and the like)—that have helped to make this book one of the world's best-sellers—such is the child's initiation, his corruption, if you will, from innocence." God, wrote Pum, needs "putting in his place!" now that the "age of religion is past." Civilization must concentrate on building up a spiritualistic life on Earth. It should heed the words of thinkers such as Einstein, who argued that it was above all the fear felt by primitive man that evoked religious notions, and Aubrey Beardsley, who remarked that "Nero set Christians on fire, like large tallow candles; the only light Christianity has ever been known to give." Pum also quoted Bertrand Russell, whose "own view on religion is that of Lucretius, I regard it as a disease born of fear and as a source of untold misery to the human race."

Christ had arrived, Pum argued, at a moment of spiritual, national, and class unrest, and he had appeared to offer a "supreme enlightenment to the ignorant masses." The chief value of his teachings was the growth of the "first organised socialist movement, the first decisive step in world history towards liberty, equality and fraternity, as well as the first revolt against gods [in] the mean little, tuppenny-halfpenny, pancake-flat world of those days." In this sense only, that of his being a supreme example of manhood embodied for his mission to Earth, could he be considered the son of God. Even so, according to Pum, Christianity became the "most disruptive element in all religious history." It is "entirely false and suppositious, with nothing real or divine about it [and it is] in fact merely an abstract atheism"—an idea that Pum believed was taking hold among more people every day. From its enlightened beginning, Christianity became "a stumbling block throughout civilisation, a deterrent to all progress, a blight on all joy and happiness, a waste of life here and now, a dread for the hereafter." Such a destructive faith, he wrote, was not and never would be "centered in love (beauty, mercy) as some would have us believe, but in sin (selfish fear and dread), and so in sex the source of all sin, since Eve first presented her forbidden fruit for Adam's delectation, the imp!"

Pum's version of the story was that a young Jewish woman, Mary, had become pregnant by a Greek mercenary and decided to "turn to profit this awkward predicament." When her son Jesus was born, she "doubtless inculcated the boy's sensitive mind with a belief in his own godhead, his mission on Earth, very much as Mrs. Anne Besant, not long since, tried and would have succeeded in influencing the young Krishna Muerti, doubtless in all good faith, to believe himself divine, a messiah, had that youth submitted to her insinuations." In 1909, Jiddu Krishnamurti was fourteen and living in India when he met Charles Webster Leadbetter, occultist and Theosophist, who believed him to be a future world spiritual leader. The boy was separated from his family, and Annie Besant, the radical socialist, secularist, and activist, became his legal guardian and uber-mother.

Accordingly, this false nature of Christianity meant that there needed to be, and could only be, a "new religion for mankind to be called UNIVERSALISM . . . a one-world religion, non-sectarian requiring no 'faith' because it is obviously sound and provable and traffics with real (overwhelming) love rather than SIN . . . . I BELIEVE in one all-loving, all-compassionate, all-understanding God . . . devoted to influencing, guiding, and helping mankind towards a stage of supreme love." But this god, thought Pum, would by no means be omnipotent; he would have no power over nature because that is entirely governed by laws of cause and effect. Rather, the godhead would be the combined and accumulated "essence of all the love and goodness of those human beings who have developed to a supreme excellence in the Spirit World." In this system, life on Earth was a "breeding-piece, a momentary break in our continuance, a change from our earthly to our ethereal bodies on a higher vibration in the Spirit World," a vibration that coexisted and interpenetrated Earth and its atmosphere. Man could not hope to understand or appreciate any of this until he had taken on his ethereal body, but he could communicate with the spirit world, and when he reached it he would be able to recognize those he had loved on Earth. Happily, "any psychic defects due to illness, accidents, amputations, etc., will have disappeared for those defects were only to the earthly body left behind."

Pum's atheistic imagination harmonized his Christianity, "if one can call it so," with an erotic paganism. In his preface to Pum's *Christeros and Other Poems* (1948), Stephen Spender remembered that a "keen interest in the riddle of life and death led [Pum] early to a study of comparative religions, and especially of pagan and Christian lore. There was a constant rivalry in his mind between a kind of modern paganism and Christianity, and he sought some blending of the two as a satisfactory compromise." But his speculations "bred within him a certain disillusion and frustration [that] doubtless reacted upon a sensitive and solitary soul to increase his introspective and fatalistic attitude of mind."

"Religious rituals, initiations, and the like," Pum argued, were

erotic manifestations inspired by, and inseparable from sex, often perverse in character. Celibacy, monastic life, etc., all tend to this. The subduing of the flesh, the wearing of sack-cloth, or else the rich female attire affected by priest and prelate, acolytes and choristers, at the altar are concessions to sex—the rod and the phallus are identified by the author, in this respect, as like implements of torture exaltation and resurrection.

Universalism's "touchstone of love" would be more honest, even though it might be considered by some to be sensuous and profane. To Pum, it could justify his "devious devotions." He insisted that only by acknowledging sex as truth and through the sex act could one find heaven, gain paradise here and now on Earth, "and in no other place or fashion. . . . Since there is no god and no future life, as the author presumes," paradise can only be attained through compelling coital heaven. "[It] is a fourth dimensional place and orgasm is the route to it." It is the resurrection. Heaven is orgasm's divine expression, "the sum total and climax of existence, the extremest ecstasy of life [and] the antithesis of death."

In an almost prosaic aside, Pum interjects in his own narrative the idea that "certain moslem [sic] sects deny women their paradise and to this extent they may be justified in that sixty percent of their sex are said never to attain the coital climax, being too loathe or lagging, so that 'left in mid-air', as the expression is, they never quite achieve heaven." For those not so denied, this state of bliss is "physically induced through the act of love no matter how essayed, engendered and accomplished, in kissing couples or as a solitary self-satisfaction, 'naturally' or 'unnaturally,' 'rightly' or 'wrongly.'" Pum wanted to believe that any and all manifestations of love were heavenly and, by extension, sacred. Every creature, every species, could ascend the "Angel-paths [and] golden-stairs," for "as Freud has demonstrated every subconscious thought and act leads up to and ends in love." Sexual love, Pum believed, was "the one essential act common to all creatures that alone renders existence endurable, makes life worth living."

2
A Family Abroad

Pum's father, Henry Anderson, was a difficult young man with a God-given capacity for upsetting all those who came his way. In the summer of 1876, the twenty-five-year-old had "appeared like a whirlwind" to Mary Morgan, who was just eighteen. In her diary she wrote that they "were quickly married within a few months" by her father in their small parish church on December 29, and "up till then I had had nothing to record but utter joy and happiness."

From that tumultuous beginning, Henry Anderson and his bride produced Violet, born in 1878—"How Henry loved her I could not possibly describe!" wrote Mary. "He would have kept her in his arms forever." Next came Reginald D'Arcy in 1880, "a fine child, but being more sensitive in both body and mind than the others, he will never be such a favourite, nor appear to such advantage as the Twins," who arrived last, in the following year. To have produced four children within the space of three years, though welcome, was somewhat embarrassing to a family that was by no means well-to-do. Besides which, in the nursery, though Violet received the twins as gladly as she might a brace of new dolls, their nearly two-year-old brother D'Arcy, until then monarch of all he surveyed, was extremely jealous and resented their presence so thoroughly that until he got reconciled to it he would have done them an injury if he possibly could.

Robert Grenville [Pum] and Thomas Gayer, identical twins, were born at six in the morning on July 29, 1881, at Listowel, County Kerry, Ireland, "a propitious hour," noted Mary. Pum arrived head first in the traditional fashion, and twenty-five minutes later came the contrary Tom, feet first. Their parents were not really equipped to appreciate all the interest presented by the two identical beings they had brought into the world. It seemed easier to think of and to treat them as two ordinary boy babies who had happened to arrive together, though the twins, as they grew, had an instinctive feeling of awareness and affinity toward one another: theirs was no ordinary sibling relationship. They looked so very alike that their mother tied a ribbon to Pum's wrist to enable everyone, including herself, to distinguish between them. "Our few physical differences," Pum wrote later, "come largely under the heading of those 'negative' mirror-image differences; for instance, at birth we each had a slightly enlarged costal rib, Tom's on his left, mine on the right side," and he thought that perhaps they had narrowly escaped being conjoined twins. "We both had also a small almost colorless but slightly raised mole similarly placed on one cheek, Tom's on the left, mine on the right." Born into duality, Pum struggled all his life with forming a distinct identity, making a mark, being recognized. Later, Pum wrote at some length in his memoir about his experience of being a twin, for good and bad. Throughout their lives, his and Tom's manners, movements, tastes, prejudices, idiosyncrasies, virtues, and vices would remain either the same or identically opposite, "which is much the same thing," and they were held together all their lives with an exquisite, sometimes troubling, balance.

Tom was known as "Gayer" and Pum, early on, as "Nenny" from Grenville. "Pum" came later, as did "John"—he had many names to go by—and most people close to him called him that, but Pum was his most private name used by his twin. The family was "all-British in composition but thoroughly mongrel," for which Pum declared himself thankful, "for I consider such a blend preferable to an unmixed descent."

The family was not quite obscure but was "for the most part undistinguished, just ordinary nice people, what were called 'gentle-folk' in the Ireland of those days."

Mary was of Welsh origin, a Morgan, and her family, too, had emigrated to North Ireland, to Belfast, while her kinsmen the Gayers were from Liskeard in Cornwall. Her father was a Presbyterian minister, the Reverend Thomas Morgan, and of him Pum wrote that "his career affords, I should imagine, an extreme example of staying put for, having taken his degree at Trinity College Dublin at twenty-four, he was called in 1850 to organise and become the first minister of a new Presbyterian congregation at Rostrevor, County Down. There he and his flock raised enough to buy land and build a small church and manse, and there he stayed, married, and begat and brought up his family of seven." He never moved thereafter, except for rare visits to friends, until he died in 1909. He spent sixty years in one house and occupied one living. The reverend's father had been a celebrated divine and powerful preacher in Northern Ireland, the Reverend James Morgan of Fisherwick Place, Belfast, and it may, Pum speculated, have been because of such a godly tradition and ecclesiastical environment that both Mary and Henry were "extremely lax in all religious matters; though outwardly conforming to the Church of England, they gave no real allegiance to any religious faith, and though their ethical and moral teaching was sound and thorough, it was never related in our minds with 'Religion.'"

Mary's grandmother Charlotte, with whom she spent much of her childhood, was one of the "six beautiful Miss Gayers" of old Dublin society. They were an established family; her grandfather was John Gayre of Dublin, who held office in the Irish Parliament, 1794–1802. The line could also boast Sir John Gayre, a merchant and member of the Worshipful Company of Fishmongers, of the East India and the Levant Companies, who was sheriff of London in 1635, lord mayor of London in 1646, and president of Christ's Hospital in 1648. As an alderman he was twice consigned to the Tower of London by Parliament for refusing to list the inhabitants of his ward who were able to contribute £50 or more to a loan for King Charles. Sir John sailed his own ships to the Barbary Coast and beyond and, in 1643, "travelling with a caravan across the deserts of Arabia he was by some mischance belated and cut off from his escort. At this moment a lion of tremendous size approaching him, death appeared inevitable. In great trepidation Sir John dropped on his knees in the sand and prayed to God for protection, at the same time promising the Almighty that, were he spared, he would endow the poor of his birthplace, Plymouth, with the entire proceeds of his venture and also inaugurate an annual service in his parish Church in London to God's glory and in thanksgiving for such a deliverance. Thereupon the prowling beast made off and Sir John was left unmolested until dawn, when he found his caravan." The "Lion Sermon" has been preached every year since, at lunchtime on October 16, and the story of Sir John's miraculous escape is retold at St. Catherine Cree's Church, Leadenhall Street, in the City of London. There is a brass plaque with a portrait of Sir John on it, and his remains were eventually buried there. A *New York Times* article of 1880 says Sir John left £200, so that the minister should have £1 and a further sum of £8 16s and 6d was to be distributed among the necessitous inhabitants. It also says he met his lion in the Turkish Dominions, whereas Hatton's *A New View of London* (1708) puts the event in Arabia. When Mary took her family to London they made a point of attending the service, dressed in their "gentlemanly blue suits." It was partly the pride that they felt in their romantic ancestor that led the family to adopt the name "Gayer" by deed poll in August 1917, but it would also help them distinguish between names should any of the boys be injured or killed during the Great War.

The paternal line came from Ardbreck, near Aberdeen, and they prided themselves on their motto epithet, "Stand Sure," said to have been gained in battle at Otterburn in 1388 and later placed in a "fabricated" family crest. Escaping the persecution of Catholics, the family fled to Ireland and settled there. Henry, born at Slaney Lodge, Baltinglass in County Wicklow, was christened Robert Henry Barré Phipps. His father, also Robert Anderson, was something of a maverick, too. He was friend and agent to the last earl of Aldborough, known locally as "the mad lord," and helped him with some of his more elaborate projects. They devised a flying machine in the form of a balloon with a light gondola slung beneath it and powered by "monstrous birds or bats wings," each quill of which was to be fashioned of chilled and tempered steel, to be manipulated by hand. They were so sure of their design that the machine was patented in 1854, and Aldborough bought a landing ground in Spain on which he built a charming pavilion for the convenience of his audience who would be waiting to see the machine make a successful descent. Robert Anderson went off to Spain to make sure that everything would be in order even before the machine had been built. Unfortunately, it never was. A devastating fire destroyed the earl's home, his plans, and parts of the machine, and he died shortly after the inferno.

The men of the Anderson family consisted of variously distinguished soldiers, sailors, and adventurers. Robert's one-eyed great-uncle, Colonel Isaac Barré (1726–1802), was a soldier, writer, statesman, and member of Parliament, whose portrait hangs in the National Gallery. He had fought on the Plains of Abraham under General Wolfe, was a close friend of William Pitt the Elder and pallbearer at his funeral, having served him as well as the Lords Bute and Shelbourne, and he had fiercely opposed the taxing of the American colonies. Barré is thought by some to be the author of the "Letters of Junius," a series of public letters written to inform the people of their historical and constitutional rights and liberties as Englishmen, and to let them know exactly where and how the government had infringed upon these rights. John Britton published *The Authorship of the Letters of Junius Elucidated: Including a Biographical Memoir of Lieutenant-Colonel Isaac Barré, M.P.* in 1848, though there are more than forty suggested authors including William Pitt, Benjamin Franklin, Thomas Paine, Catherine Macaulay, Edward Gibbon, and Edmund Burke. Another great uncle, Captain James Smyth of Carlow, was severely wounded fighting in the Indian Mutiny when, captured by sepoys, he was tied to the mouth of a charged canon but was fortuitously rescued before they could blow him to bits. An illustration of his terrible ordeal was published in the *Pictorial Times* in April 1846.

As a child, Henry acquired the reputation of being naughty and unsociable. This rambunctious boy did look up to his elder brother, Arthur, a slight and grave graduate of Trinity College, Dublin, who went to India as engineer-in-chief of the Bengal Dooars Railway but was drowned in the Teesta River on a tour of inspection. Henry was left bereft by this loss, but was not surprised by it because he had had a premonition—he was a "receptive." Pum believed that he had inherited this quality and thought it derived from the family's "wild Celtish blood."

Henry studied medicine but dropped out, dithered, and then threatened to run off to America at the suggestion of his piratical uncle Captain Fred Smyth. His parents were horrified and swiftly fixed him up with a job at the Bank of Ireland, hoping for a steadying influence, a regular respectable income, and a wife to complete the picture of stability. He actually won promotion but, as Mary recorded, he "always greatly disliked the routine work and time of his work in an office." She praised his energy, but knew that his peers resented him for not being a drinker and for refusing to join in with their "orgies." His character was "good and evil, inextricably mixed" but with "harmony and proportion missing," so that his great abilities had strange limitations. Looking back, she thought that "nothing was quite right or quite happy . . . he would not get on with other men [and] that fact repeats itself from first to last." It was Mary's capacity for happiness—the quality Pum thought he had inherited from her, "like a fairy gift"—and her devotion and loyalty that saved her and her husband from disaster. Pum says that his parents were happy despite his father's suspicions and stinginess, his exaggerated thrift, hypochondria, insomnia, and misanthropic ways—despite, in particular, the curse of "The Books."

The Books were an institution: Henry's grim, banker's obsession, ledgers of torturous household minutiae that were a damnable satisfaction to the patriarch, and an oppressive misery to everyone else. The day-book recorded expenditure down to the last farthing, the cash-book was totted up at the end of each week, the ledger had a balance struck on a monthly basis, the general balance sheet was drawn up every six months, and the Digest of Family Expenditure covered the exact outlay, under every possible heading except food and doctoring, for each family member. All the books unfailingly showed that the family was "ruined" or was destined for the workhouse. The grand finale appeared at the end of each year, accompanied by other accounts too intricate for any but Henry to fathom. He had held his wife responsible for presenting the monthly household accounts even though he considered her useless with figures and they were a "daily irritation" to her, "a weekly ordeal, a monthly torture and a yearly crucifixion" that "reflected dolorously" upon the children. Keeping the books had begun as a routine domestic necessity but had gradually developed into a complex obsession, "fiendish and damnable."

The tyranny of the bookkeeping may initially have been Henry's response to being forced into an occupation he hated, a way to control at least part of his life. He became restless and irascible and so made a fair fist of alienating anyone in the whole of his native Ireland who might offer him employment. Thus, in 1880, he took the opportunity to go off to Canada, paid for by the government there, to see the continent and to lecture about it back in Ireland for the benefit of interested settlers. He brought home "buffalo robes, white fox skins [and] curious and beautiful feather rugs made by the Indians," all of which he sold or gave away, to Mary's chagrin as she realized they were important relics. Excited by his short adventure, he was easily persuaded by Captain Fred Smyth, who had settled in Wichita, Kansas, to make another leap across the Atlantic. Known as the "Skipper," Fred was, as Pum remembers him, a "gruff, kindly, strong-smelling old salt" and a free-booter, all but a pirate, who happily showed the children his pistol and scattergun. Henry resigned from the bank and took off for Wichita only to find it was the most hideous spot: the climate was unendurable, the conditions crude, and the Americans hateful. He quickly returned, but found he had burned all his bridges, so with no prospects left in Ireland he borrowed money left, right, and center, and in 1884 packed up his young family to set sail once again for a country "but half civilised" to try his luck in the land-boom. It was "a great crisis in our lives," wrote Mary.

On board the SS Peruvian the whole family were desperately seasick. There were storms, icebergs, and whales. And there were clergymen—eight in all, two of them priests. One, a Dr. Wardrope, "creeps in the room next to ours, is so kind and good. He has taken such a fancy to the children, especially to the Twins. He asked for locks of their hair, which I gave him yesterday, nicely tied up." The twins were just three years old, but Pum remembers the voyage out, the great green waves that swept over the portholes, and his father in a long, white night-dress opening the little, round windows between waves to let in fresh air. The family story has it that a childless, wealthy "American-Indian Chief and his squaw" approached Mary and asked to adopt one of the little blonde twins, suggested his price, and promised an opulent future for the child. The offer was rejected: Henry was to make his fortune selling land, not babies. These were years of commercial pioneering, of chance and risk; people on the make had to be prepared to take care of themselves: Mary concealed in her bustle a small pocket revolver of tiny bore—The Bulldozer by name—known in the trade as a "stinger" rather than a "stopper," though there is no record of her having used it.

Passing the Statue of Liberty and disembarking into a confused crowd at New York's customs sheds, the children were crushed between bags and bustles, squashed onto trains, and finally brought to the new family home, a wooden house on the scrubby outskirts of Wichita. Mary wrote letters home—from Quebec and Cobourg in Canada, and later from Alabama, California, and Tennessee as they traveled through America—and was very angry with the Smyths for giving such a deceptively glowing description of Wichita. She found the women shrill and the men miserable effeminate creatures and thought that "regular" Americans were of the worst type, mean, common, ruffian-looking people in their "pig-pen neighbourhoods," and the girls went out with young men unchaperoned. The poor and servants were every-where, just as in Ireland, but, she observed, they were usually "Niggers, and are called Niggers, not colored gentlemen and ladies . . . [and] kept well in their place," and the common opinion was that if "left to them-selves they wd [sic] work none, live from hand to mouth, revel in dirt, laugh, sing and be perfectly happy always."

Henry began to do very well for himself in real estate, but his suc-cess didn't alleviate his grinding economies, and his "close-fistedness" and "slave-driving" continued to wear down his wife and children—on a bitterly cold Christmas Day in 1885, with all the children ill and whimpering, Henry maintained his economy measures and refused to light the stove. Pum could not understand why his mother never complained at her husband's atrocious behavior, why she didn't resist him or at least resent him. "Had she been more self-assertive, less even-tempered, less devoted, much might have been different," he wrote, but as his father met with no opposition he grew increasingly tyrannous.

Pum didn't wonder how life might have been had his father been more even-tempered, more devoted; Henry's behavior seems to have been regarded as a given. Eventually, when as an adult he continued to suffer the damaging effects of his father's treatment, Pum did ask his mother why she had submitted so totally to her domineering husband. She could only answer that she had thought it best at the time for the children's sake, and for Henry's, too, and "perhaps, even for my own." Her son accepted this as an example not of fearfulness but of wisdom and intuition, and he "was convinced . . . that her decision was sound and the course she took was the right one."

His beloved mother's submissive life was tempered, at least for her, by her religiously inspired reading matter, which included a heavily annotated copy of a fantastically popular narrative poem on ideal marriage and womanhood, "The Angel in the House" by Coventry Patmore (1823–96). Mary's copy was inscribed, "Missionary Ridge, Chattanooga 1887. Dear book, loved when I was very young and again in this far-off land."

"To him she'll cleave, for him forsake, He is her lord," wrote Coventry Patmore:

Man must be pleased; but him to please
Is woman's pleasure; down the gulf
Of his condoled necessities
She casts her best, she flings herself.
How often flings for nought, and yokes
Her heart to an icicle or whim,

Whose each impatient word provokes
Another, not from her, but him;
While she, too gentle even to force
His penitence by kind replies,
Waits by, expecting his remorse,
With pardon in her pitying eyes;
And if he once, by shame oppress'd,
A comfortable word confers,
She leans and weeps against his breast,
And seems to think the sin was hers.

Virginia Woolf satirized this image of submissive Victorian domesticity in her essay "Professions for Women" (1942): "She was utterly unselfish . . . She sacrificed herself daily . . . she was so constituted that she never had a mind or a wish of her own." The marginalia in Mary's copy of the poem revealed how much she expected from life, love, and her husband, and just how disillusioned and disappointed she must have been, how insufficient Henry must have proved, and how he must have failed her. Perhaps, her son ruminated, she had been sustained by her pity for Henry. She was a humanist in the best Renaissance sense, he thought, a hedonist in the best Hellenic sense, and a true Romantic—but by her own admission she had no friends, not a single one.

Mary had had "a blissful childhood" and had been "steeped and surrounded by beauty and love." She passed on to Pum her intense love of beauty, "of which I was always conscious, which was like the bread of life." The idea of beauty that they shared rested to some extent on sentimentality, on an aversion to vulgar reality, and it was otherworldly and out of time. Pum's childhood, in contrast to his mother's, was one haunted by "cheese-paring economy," as he called it, and it was this, he felt, that was the root of his adult craving for luxury and refinement. He wanted to live lavishly, romantically, and he sought out pleasures, comforts, and refinements where he could.

Henry's miserly and obsessive nature developed in unlikely ways. One was an unwelcome and cruel manifestation, what Pum thought of as a "truly Germanic, Frederick-the-Great-at-Potsdam" passion for drill, discipline, and instruction. Violet, D'Arcy, Pum, and Tom were on parade all day long if "He" was around—when Pum recorded his father's excesses he always did it with an ironic capital letter. On the dining-room door Henry posted a form with their names and with headings such as conduct, punctuality, and neatness, under which any offender was marked down—though never up for good behavior. Henry made wooden rifles for his children and marched them endlessly up and down the backyard, once into a waist-deep trench that he had purposely filled with rainwater to see if they would follow his command, which they did, with "the unreasoning submission" he had reduced them to.

He was proud of them and of himself, but Mary took a less positive view of her husband's ideas on child rearing. Pum later understood that, though they used laughter to dissipate their unhappiness, there was a "decided strain of sadism" in his father's treatment of them: the boys were made to box each other until their noses bled, in front of any visitor who happened to call so that they could see for themselves the pluck and stamina that Henry's mode of upbringing had produced in his children; they had to hit each other hard with sticks to avoid the charge of effeminacy, and if one of them disgraced the family by crying, he would put on a mean face and taunt them for their weakness. It was a sorry exhibition, thought Pum, and he realized even then that the visitors thought so, too.

Another of Henry's favorite Spartan recreations was to guard a small coin or lump of sugar with a cane in his hand and have the children take turns at a sound switching for trying to retrieve it. But the really serious "training" Henry inflicted on them in their last year of American life was when Tom and Pum were just eight years old: the truly terrible Self-Control Drill. Henry would "set them up in a row in front of him, saying and doing absurd or painful things. He would give a sudden shout, quickly raise a threatening hand, tickle our ribs, pinch us or pull our hair . . . in spite of which none of us must show the slightest emotion of any sort. If we flinched, flushed, giggled, gasped,

laughed or even flickered an eyelid we were shouted at and slapped."
After many such tests, Pum says that he and his siblings reached an
artificial state of almost complete self-control, and that this had a seriously evil effect on all their characters and later lives.

It was Henry, concluded Pum, who was the one most lacking in self-
control, not his small children. In the face of his increasingly violent
behavior, the acquiescent Mary would compensate with declarations
of maternal love. She would shower them with excuses—their father
was tired; if he was cross, it was because he loved them and wanted
the best for them. Because they were frightened of him, they all went
to their mother with their needs and achievements, and her love and
approval lessened their unhappiness. At bedtime she would smuggle
them up apples and biscuits, and one night as she tucked them in, Pum
asked her whether she loved him enough to eat plum cake off his bare
behind; her promise that of course she did was enough for him.

The contrast between his mother's devotion and his father's cruelty meant that Pum learned the art of camouflage very young, hiding
aspects of his true self. He grew up deeply regretting his emotionally repressed nature and linked it all to these childhood abuses. His
passions were subsumed by externals, buried beneath a hard crust of
ritualistic behavior and an obsession with orderliness. He and Tom
were destined to live highly successful public lives of duty and honor
while pursuing their clandestine pleasures with fervor and necessarily
fierce discretion.

One can only say that the family endured Henry, particularly
when it came to his regime of Spartanism. The children had no toys
because their father thought this would make them practical, self-
reliant individuals. It was a deprivation that Pum later considered
"an unwittingly excellent deprivation," as the children were drawn
together in their attempts to withstand the tyranny of their "red-hot,
gold-rimmed, gimlet-eyed" father, whom they secretly called Jehovah.
"As the Jews felt for Jehovah, as Jehovah behaved towards the Jews,
such seemed our parental relationship, our mutual reactions." Happily, though, the deity that was Henry, unlike the more conventional

Christian God, was absent for the greater part of most days. Still, there was no escaping his dominance as he assumed the proportions of an ever-angry family divinity. He was the very devil, too, for obsessively scolding and dragooning them: "Keep your head up D'Arcy," he would shout. "Put your cap on straight, Grenville. . . . Square your shoulders, Tom." Pum's own obsessions were to be less mundanely cruel, but equally pressing.

In the mid-1880s, aged about five, Pum and his brother had begun, he later said, to notice their "cocks," and it would be an unnatural and "strangely unimaginative and unemotional little boy" who didn't, he thought. They "surveyed themselves and others quite innocently but with surprise, curiosity and satisfaction at that independently living, moving, almost separate little entity." As they grew, Pum and Tom became more and more fascinated by their own developing bodies, measuring themselves and jotting down the results in notebooks, comparing the bulges of their knotted biceps, their chests, and the girth of their calves and thighs. The attraction Pum felt to his own body, and by extension to other little boys, began when he was a child himself:

Even at a very early age sprawling naked over others with that peculiarly helpless impotent satisfaction which puppies evince in a similar manifestation. I remember too, when I was perhaps seven . . . I was put to bed with a little boy of about my own age, and we sprawled over one another so that by morning we were very much in love with each other without knowing why. On erotic occasions in those very early years I was a prince who rode a horse and became the "Cynosure of every eye". They took me and lifted me off my horse unbuttoned and bound me to another unbuttoned little boy . . . else I was locked in a warm room and they stripped off endless delightful little-girl garments until I was naked . . . I would lie quite still in the privacy of my bed before I fell asleep under warm intimate blankets and sheets and very much in secret, feel myself all over—and I expressed it far later:

I feel myself how warm and real
The curves of my bare body feel
And I have fingers in my soul
That feel and find it beautiful.

He would think such thoughts in church or in the classroom, "doubt-less wearing that seraphic 'innocent' expression which tempts kindly old ladies to ask 'Well, little boy and what are your pretty dreams? A penny for your thoughts.'" Pum knew how to disarm people, to appear a paragon of late Victorian boyhood, though his secret feelings were constantly at odds with the strictures of family life.

Having ridden the land boom in Kansas, Henry moved his family on to Chattanooga, Tennessee, a "heavy unhealthy place" where the summers were stifling hot and damp, and the children fell ill again. Other dangers were waiting for them, too. Out in the wild countryside they came across a huge circle of white ash under a tree and Pum, barefoot and happy, ran to it and jumped into its center. But it was only white on the surface and he landed, ankle deep, in "a furnace of Moloch" (Moloch was an ancient Ammonite deity worshiped across North Africa and the Levant and associated with parental sacrifice of children by fire. In Milton's *Paradise Lost* (1667) he appears as one of the fiercest of the fallen angels: "First Moloch, horrid King besmear'd with blood / Of human sacrifice, and parents' tears.") The pain and shock were tremendous, and Pum passed out and was carried home by the other children. His mother wrapped his feet in swathes of cotton wool thickly coated in Vaseline—the universal family remedy—but no doctor was summoned, as Henry believed himself to have insufficient funds but sufficient knowledge left over from his days as a medical student to treat his suffering son.

Life continued a risky business, the land boom expanded, and Pum and his siblings began to prosper, unencumbered by schooling or shoes. The next move was to California, to a suburb of San Fran-cisco called Alameda where the unmade main street stretched down to the "crab-haunted" mud flats of the bay, and the children began their education at last. An English governess was hired, Miss Pratt, who taught them little but encouraged them to write, and Pum composed his first poem—a mournful deathbed scene of a child watched over by his silent mother and soon carried away to a better land by an angel. But Pum's "dear little mother," on reading his efforts, laughed. "She who would not wittingly have hurt me or any one of us for the whole world, laughed! laughed hilariously. . . . Little did she guess how hurt and offended I was." His brothers and sister joined in the teasing so that poetry became "a hidden and secret vice" for Pum, and he didn't admit to writing poems again, nor did he show them to anyone else until late middle age. He wrote them alone, secretly, in his bed, as though they were a sin, but they were also a constant pleasure and relaxation to him. Tom had his bedtime secret, too: he drew his fantasies and carried on drawing them into his old age. Both these activities centered around the twins' "similar predilections," but they did not reveal them even to each other until much later in their lives.

After California came Chicago in 1890, when Pum was nine years old. They arrived in the middle of a freezing winter when all those around them were dying of an influenza epidemic—hundreds died and the streets were blocked with funeral processions—and the whole family came down with it. Henry tried his best to feed his family while his wife was ill, but he was more successful as a land agent than as a cook.

When Henry had had enough of real estate and made himself some money, he impulsively decided to pack up his family and belongings and return to Ireland. In 1891 they traveled north, via Niagara Falls, where they hired a guide to take them directly behind the great green wall of thunderous water, a memory that remained fixed in Pum's imagination. From there they went on to Montreal, across Lake Ontario and up the St. Lawrence River, meeting "Red Indians," visiting lumber camps and the Thousand Islands. It was the most fabulous river trip, one Pum would never forget, though it would be eclipsed by his first journey up the Nile, from Cairo to Aswan.

3
To Be an Englishman

At home again in Ireland in the 1890s, the family moved from place to place looking for somewhere to settle. They stayed with the extended family, made up of Gayers, Morgans, D'Arcys, Barres, Pringles, and Andersons. They went from Rostrevor, in "the hole of the pit from which I was digged," Mary wrote, to Baltinglass, County Wicklow, and Howth, near Dublin.

It was at Howth, once a small fishing village and now a suburb of Dublin, that Pum had one of his earliest psychic experiences. The youngest and the darling of the six cousins with whom they were staying was a "pretty lad" called Guy, and at night the older children would gather around this sleeping boy and ask him questions. These he would answer correctly, wittily, and wisely, though they were often beyond his limited experience and he had no memory of them the following morning. Pum thought this a genuine psychic experience, where the questioner was receiving his own or someone else's, or even a collective, answer rather than that of a vacant immature medium such as the little Guy. It had, he came to think later, much in common with what was known as *mandel* (divination) in Egypt, during which a boy who is a virgin, or has not been burned by fire, bitten by a dog, or cut with a knife, gazes into a crystal or a pool of ink or oil and in a trance-like state would "see" whatever was asked of him.

Rostrevor was a poetic place of mountains, murmurous streams, and idyllic, mottled glades dropping down to the sea. It was sheltered, indolent, and dreamy, a land where the children could roam free, investigating the peat bogs, fairy rings, and goblin pits, and drinking the true elixir from a fresh spring tucked away among velvety mosses and primordial dripping ferns. At Rostrevor, Pum's maternal grandfather, the Reverend Thomas Morgan, a godly, idle, and selfish little man, lived in uxorious comfort at the roomy, sweet-smelling manse. He was tended to by a bevy of devoted females—his daughters and his wife, who as a young woman was known as the "Pocket Venus." Keeping much to himself and his books, the reverend habitually wore a black cleric's coat with a golden cross dangling from his watch chain. He was always the same, apart from the morning that Pum surprised him on the earth "privvy" in semi-darkness, book in hand, clad only in his waistcoat and watch chain. "Run away little man," he said blandly to the child, and the horrified boy did just that. A meditative man, he plucked at his eyebrows as he listened to conversation, but was uncommunicative and uncreative, save in the way of all flesh.

It was the Reverend Morgan who, in an uncharacteristically cold fury, put a stop to the notorious Self-Control Drill after an ill-advised impromptu display for guests on the vicarage lawn. A few days after their arrival and at the family sit-down tea, Henry lined up his children to show off their drill, ignoring his wife's protests. At first the audience was puzzled, then shock began to register. No one laughed. The reverend plucked at his eyebrows, then took off his spectacles. Inarticulate and shaking with anger, he made an effort to address his son-in-law, and, in front of everyone, in a low, harsh voice, he told Henry what he thought and that he must never again inflict this cruelty upon the children. The party melted away, leaving the children "quite pitying" their father, who had been expecting praise and was stunned to receive the opposite.

In contrast to the generosity and dreaminess of Rostrevor, the family trips to the Anderson grandparents at Slaney Lodge, Baltinglass, were practical, earnest, and dynamic. Arriving by train and met by the car—driven by the red-headed and bearded factotum in a cockaded top hat and dingy "Russian" livery, hiding his even more dilapidated wardrobe beneath—they were welcomed on the front lawn by the maiden-aunts, Emmie and Reby (Rebecca). Grandfather Anderson was now a frail man, though one of ability, but he had always lacked judgment and balance, much like his son Henry. Born a Roman Catholic, he died a Plymouth Brother having adopted and abandoned every intervening sect. Mary spent "many an hour with him talking of all sorts of things. His queer, narrow religion among them." He had put his whole trust in the Lord, but unfortunately found him sadly inadequate, though he felt it was bad form to mention it. Grandmother Anderson, a "little, parsimonious weak-eyed 'Holy-Ghost' of a grandmother," rheumatic, bent double, and a rigid Protestant, was estranged from her husband. Where once they had been energetic and loving, their strongly opposed religious views now meant that they each believed the other was heading straight for perdition.

All her life, Pum's grandmother, like his father, had feared poverty and had taken to squirreling away small sums of money in desks, trunks, secret drawers, and any remote crack or cranny. Now she struggled with her memory and her failing sight and, if she could escape the strict and jealous supervision of her elder daughter Emmie, was constantly poking about in the dark with her walking sticks, worrying and searching for her hoard. Her hearing was acute and if, when she was on one of her searches, she managed to catch hold of a passing child, she would cry, "Which one are you?" staring anxiously with vague eyes into theirs, alarmed and alarming. Tears rolled down her small face when she played the drawing-room piano after high tea—"Cherry Ripe" or "Drink To Me Only." Otherwise she sat and knitted garments for waifs and strays, which Emmie secretly unpicked at night, like Penelope's, so they were started again the next day and never finished.

Aunt Emmie was the grande dame of the house. She was tall, poker-straight and steel-stayed, with freckled skin, coiled red hair, and myopia. Her tight-lipped mouth turned down at the corners but could be redeemed by an occasional smile. She dressed in antique finery and looked like a barbaric parrot. With touches of bright color on her rings and bracelets and brooches of tiger's claws or dead relatives' hair, she wore a string of Chinese carved peach stones down to her waist and gave the appearance of a corseted savage.

On Sundays, the rigidly anti-Catholic Emmie took them to the Protestant church at Baltinglass where the unpopular parson, the Reverend Mr. John Usher, delivered his sermons (he was not much liked, according to the local magistracy in 1882, "largely due to the fact of his having fired off shots in the immediate proximity of a number of his parishioners"). The church organist played the one tune she knew, Chopin's "Funeral March," which she fitted admirably to all occasions by varying the touch and tempo (even playing it at the local dances), unless Emmie condescended to perform. No one in the family cared for Emmie; she gave the appearance of loving them in a rough, demonstrative way, tickling them till they cried hysterically and pinching their cheeks till they ached.

Emmie's drawing room was forbidden to the children unless she invited them in. It was grand and musty, filled with flowers, gilt chairs, occasional tables, and bric-a-brac jostling on every surface. Here she doggedly sought to improve her charges, reading them Blake's "The Tyger" as they lay on the floor amid a forest of furniture legs on ragged tiger-skin rugs baring yellow teeth and staring with glass eyes. Perhaps Emmie didn't have the effect she intended, for Pum's tastes in fantasy and the romantic began to show in his secret poetry writing, his nascent sexual daydreaming, and his fascination with beauty, particularly that of the "immature human form" which he was just beginning to be fully conscious of and which would "forever to be for me the acme of human beauty." The few mature men he had seen stripped had not attracted him, and his only experience of naked women was in the pages of the illustrated catalogues of the Royal Academy.

Some months after their return from America, Henry moved his family away from Ireland to Seaford in Sussex, where he had relations and hoped to find work. Mary wanted her brood to grow up in England, too; though she loved Ireland, she considered the Irish to be decadent and fretted that her children might become "degenerate" if they stayed. But this move, as with many others, was fraught with the worries of homeless discomfort, uncertainty, and the problem of finding suitable employment for Henry. He had limited qualifications, a difficult temperament, no friends, hobbies, or outside interests, and although he was reasonably well off at this point, he had his mother's abiding terror of poverty. He was anxious to return to America, but Mary was fed up with being pushed from pillar to post and didn't want her children to grow up as Americans. He considered farming, but ended up in the City of London as a commuting stockbroker. Luckily, he was offered a position as agent on the Carr Mill estate near St. Helens, Lancashire, by Mary's cousin Sir David Gamble. Terms were generous, a house was included, everyone was pleased, and Sir David was an affable man. Off they went, leaving the cold white cliffs and monotonous downs of the south to live on the banks of a large lake on the verge of Carr Mill Dam. The family spent three years there, an unprecedentedly long time for them to have stayed put anywhere.

The house stood in a landscape of spinnies and hills and an ocean of tall bracken for ten-year-old boys to hide in. Henry bought a penny-farthing, some "safety" bicycles with cushion tires (there was no end to the inventiveness of man, according to Henry), horses, a pony and a smart dogcart, and from somewhere he procured a Mr. Murtagh to run the stables. Murtagh was a "typical Celtic native," who boasted of his descent from the early kings of Ireland. He was cunning, plausible, kindhearted, and droll but an absolute terror when "he had the drink taken," attested to by his wife's broken nose. Murtagh taught all the children to ride, jump hurdles and ditches, and to hold on, shouting, "Howlt yer howlt with them knees, else tis the mud you'll be after kissin!" And often the mud it was.

Various tutors and governesses were employed to make a mockery of the children's education before they were sent off to public school. The first was a plump, freckled German, Fräulein Rinda. While she lived with them, Henry decreed that the children speak only German at mealtimes, with the result that they all learned to say perfectly,

"Another slice of bread, please" and "Pass the marmalade," but otherwise meals passed in silence. When Fräulein Rinda returned home to marry she was succeeded by a Miss Rowland, who was engaged to "a gentleman in sugar" who never actually appeared, but whom the children imagined buried up to his neck in a barrel of the sweet stuff. Miss Rowland was likeable but not lovable; she was short, dark, and stern, useless at languages but comfortable with botany. A daily tutor, the large, sleepy, and slow Mr. Gregory, instructed them in mathematics, classics, and painting, though he seemed even to his pupils to have little knowledge in any of these subjects. Thus, though the children knew something of Virgil and of plants, their ignorance on all other subjects was prodigious.

In the summer months a smart retired cavalry sergeant came twice a week to teach them physical development and deportment, chiefly by using lances and "singlesticks." Violet was excused from these "brutalising" exercises, but her brothers all whacked one another with gusto, protected only by flimsy wicker helmets. On overseeing one of these bouts, Henry decided that they weren't being forceful enough and, expressing extreme displeasure at what he considered their effeminacy, he challenged the sergeant to help him demonstrate how it should be done. The latter was somewhat disconcerted but started in on his employer enthusiastically and, before long, with growing fury. The adults lost their tempers and proceeded to give one another a terrific drubbing; the "science of the game" went straight out the window. The boys looked on horrified and excited until Henry called a halt to it. They must have been black and blue and the lesson Pum learned from the display was a qualified one: "never to cause others more bodily pain than necessary, nor to perpetrate any unwarrantable violence." Necessary violence, whatever that was, was permissible.

In stark contrast to this aggression, they went to genteel dancing lessons in Liverpool on Saturdays and boated, fished, and swam in the lake whenever they liked. Once, when D'Arcy was out on the water, the twins undid his painter and watched delighted as he drifted across the lake. He swam back to shore naked only to find his clothes gone.

Running back up to the house, across the lawn, and into the drawing room, he charged right into one of his mother's "At Home Days." The effect on the company was shocking, as was the punishment meted out by Henry later on.

The children would often row far out on the lake, over to a sodden skeleton-tree sunk vertically through the depths. Only its top branches reached up through the surface. Looking down, they could fathom the great boughs and a pallid luminous trunk disappearing into the water. Pum found the stillness, the deep, and the darkness appalling, yet he and his brothers were irresistibly lured to the spot. There, they would row to the middle of the lake and two of them would lean over the stern of the boat and grasp a branch, together giving the tree a mighty downward shove and sending it sinking through the water. Then they pulled away to wait. After a long time, slowly, silently, the tree rose up again in a terrible resurrection, pointing at the sky. They ceased this morbid play after the drowning of a young man called Salmon who had been helping to build a new boathouse in the hot July of 1892. Salmon had plunged into the water to cool down and became entangled in the clutches of another submerged tree. The children watched as his pale body was pulled out by his workmates, covered with their jackets, and rowed to shore. This first human death of their experience left them solemn-faced and scared.

Come that winter, they skated on the frozen lake surface, as black and smooth as obsidian. They waited until Henry deemed the ice would bear them and then ventured out nervously, for the ice looked like water still. Every day more and more people came to scratch the ice white, and all night long it groaned and shrilled as the ice expanded and vast cracks ran screaming from end to end. Weeks after the freeze began they plunged a hot poker through it to find it well over a foot thick and so clear in places that they could see the fish frozen solid within. Local men and boys came to skate skillfully on the outer rims of their iron-shod wooden clogs, and the miners ran whippet races across it. Then, one day, a quarter-mile course was swept and roped off and crowds of spectators leaned into one another to see young men gathered at the starting place, stripped completely naked apart from socks and skates, to race across the solid lake. Pum remembered it as being almost unbelievable that in the civilized and prudish England he knew, a dozen or more young, bare, athletic men would fly along with waving arms and vigorously pumping legs between two dense lines of onlookers of both sexes and all ages, regardless of the freezing air. At the winning post the racers skated straight into coats or blankets held out for them and then slid back to retrieve their clothes. The race happened several times during this fierce winter and each time Pum hurried there with great excitement, "enthralled by the free swinging beauty of the naked young men, the wide striding limbs, the rhythmic sweep of the arms, the eager thrust forward of their heads."

It was drummer boys, though, wrote Pum, who "were for me then and long after as I shall record—my beau-ideal of romantic youth and beauty." His intensely private and sublime musings on sex were sullied, however, by Henry's lecture on the temptations of school life, delivered when the family moved to Tonbridge and the boys started at school there in September 1894. Summoned to their father's study, they expected some task or punishment, but instead of his usual overbearing, irate self, Henry was oddly hesitant. After a good deal of throat clearing, he asked his sons whether they were familiar with kittens. Specifically, did they know how a cat had kittens? This question he framed as though he were exasperated at his own ignorance on the subject and needed enlightenment. None of them had any precise knowledge to share with their father. They knew that babies formed inside their mothers—D'Arcy had shown them a pregnant rabbit he had dissected—but they didn't really know how it came about. Henry proceeded with a confusing and alarming explanation that centered mainly on flowers but took in cats and dogs, too. Pum felt a certain pride that as a man, when the time came, he would be able to bring this thing off and produce kittens of his own with so little effort, even a little enjoyment—unlike the poor woman; the bother was all hers. Thus, he recalled, he gained his first and rather odd ideas about relations between the sexes, a matter that would later cause him to fall out badly with Violet when she took up the cause of women's suffrage. Unfortunately, Pum had also gathered that the man had to perform the reproductive act just the once in order to produce a baby, and he was thenceforth quite shocked that their neighbor, Mr. W., whom he had always considered to be a nice man, had thirteen sons and daughters to his tally. Surely four times would have been quite enough for a restrained gentleman.

This information imparted, Henry turned to "auto-erotic practices"—something they were familiar with—and how to avoid them by a devotion to sports, willpower, and cold baths. He had the Victorian obsession with health, purity, and cleanliness, particularly of the male body—the female body was a bit of a lost cause—an obsession reinforced by the provisions of municipal government and all sorts of fashionable bourgeois leisure. There had been periodic scares since the eighteenth century about the deleterious effects of masturbation. Renewed moral panic in the 1860s paid specific attention to the young and envisaged a fresh terrorizing catalogue of physical consequences such as blindness and insanity, as well as the usual fears of digestive and skin troubles. Hadn't the now infamous Dr. William Acton advised quoits as an alternative to masturbation? Panic over the solitary vice gained momentum from the 1880s, and it became a symbol of catastrophe: dangerous, cowardly, selfish, bad for team spirit, and a cause of national degeneration. This atmosphere fed the adult Pum's personality: his tendency to compartmentalize his interests and relationships; his strictly delineated public and personal lives; his abstracted love and admiration of young boys; and his obsessive collecting and transference of desire onto safely inanimate objects of beauty.

Henry had taken a position as partner in a well-to-do firm of stockbrokers, Lindow, King and Co., in the City of London, and was commuting once again. He did well at first—life at Carr Mill had suited him down to the ground and mellowed him somewhat—but he gradually returned to his harsh, bullying ways and miserliness. These character faults, along with his recklessness, led him into misguided speculation and dealing in dangerous loans. His temperament grew worse, he became even more demanding, intolerant, and violent, and he developed a fearful hypochondria. The children suffered; Mary worried and couldn't sleep.

For Pum, the crisis came through the barrel of a gun. In his parents' bedroom one morning with his mother and Violet, who were idly talking, he wandered aimlessly about, listening and ferreting, when, in the half-open drawer of his father's bedside table, he spotted a revolver. He couldn't resist it. He lifted it out and fingered it gently, then turning and holding it firmly, a finger on the trigger, he pointed it at his sister's chest not five feet from him. She looked up at him and said curtly, "Put that back, it may be loaded." "Of course it's not loaded," Pum replied and confidently, slowly, squeezed the trigger. Their mother turned and in a voice quite unlike her own she flung one word at him: "Don't!" At that moment the revolver gave a kick. There was a sharp report and a neat, round hole appeared in the windowpane beside Violet. Mary's cry had jolted Pum, shattered his concentration, and jerked his aim just in time to avert a catastrophe. With a face the color of putty, Pum looked in the bedroom mirror to register his shock. Mary banished him to his room. She broke the windowpane, cleaned the gun, and nothing was ever said about the incident. Pum's emotions ricocheted around his brain: overwhelming thankfulness, shame, terror. Years later he would still wake at night in a cold sweat thinking about what might have happened. His rashness outshone and made trivial every pain or misfortune that was to come to him.

At Tonbridge School the boys were put in the lowest forms, a shock to their parents who had thought their early education quite up to scratch. Violet attended the Select Academy for Young Ladies close by. Pum wrote later that one acquired little actual learning at school, an institution which merely provided a disciplined course to make boys, by nature carnal and lazy, conform to routine and work. Examinations were essential to back up the discipline. He thought that he and his twin had "average brains," that they had poor recall and a tendency to take themselves too seriously. At school, Tom was more mathematical and better at languages, while Pum was more literary and imaginative.

They were both slow readers and phenomenally bad spellers. Both were right-handed, manually dexterous, and artistically creative—Tom with pencil and brush, Pum with words. They found out, late in life, that in much of their work they were attempting to express almost the same ideas and ideals, and that they had strayed into each other's medium, though they would never have consciously competed with each other.

It was at school that Pum realized he and his twin were by no means ordinary boys. Each had gradually become aware of the power of beauty and was acquisitive of beautiful things, a devotion that increased until it formed the chief motive of their lives. Pum's passion for collecting, begun in America when he found lead bullets and chipped flint arrow-heads, was really ignited in Grandfather Anderson's sanctum, "The Office" at Slaney Lodge. It was an Aladdin's Cave of treasures and curios where Pum rooted about happily for hours. Here he uncovered ancient and peculiar objects, such as the snaffle bit made of an unfamiliar metal that he showed to his schoolmaster. "Send it to the British Museum," said the teacher, and the curators there wrote back to say that it was a Saxon piece and, if he wished, they would give him the astonishing sum of £5 for it. This was his first successful transaction with the British Museum and it started him off on a lifetime of dealing. Pum's collecting continued in a modest way with the standard fare of stamps, butterflies, and birds' eggs, but his heart was in gathering up beautiful objects—"curiosities"—chiefly antiques, wherever he could find them.

On one of his walks over the Medway he found, sticking out of the mud, a small, dark, unusual bone, heavy for its size, so he knew it to be a fossil. It had a double knuckle that he had never seen before, and he dug it out and took it back to show his form-master. On his advice, Pum sent it to the president of the Royal Geological Society, asking what it might be. It was, he learned, part of the humerus of what was then an entirely unknown type of pterodactyl, or "flying dragon." Professor Seely wrote a monologue and delivered a lecture on it at the RGS in London, which Pum and D'Arcy attended. The fossil was the first gift Pum made to a museum, institutions he regarded as "Valhallas of beauty," their only fault in his eyes being that they were proof of an ever-increasing deterioration of man's artistic power and manual accomplishments.

By 1897, when the children's patchy education was done with, D'Arcy had passed into the Engineering College of Cooper's Hill. He had intended to build bridges in India, but went into the Royal Artillery when a call for more officers for the war in South Africa led the College to offer commissions. Tom, at the age of sixteen, sat for the examination at the Royal Military Academy and passed it, to everyone's astonishment, scraping into "The Shop" at Woolwich and emerging as a second lieutenant in the Royal Field Artillery. Pum had been intended for the Royal Navy, but a change in the entrance age made Henry decide that his second son should become a doctor like his two uncles Morgan. Pum's career as a sailor with, he fondly imagined, a cutlass and telescope, was over before it began. Looking back, Pum thought that D'Arcy should have been an engineer, Tom an artist and architect, and that he himself should have taken up archeology and Orientalism and found fulfillment from the start. Violet went to the Slade School of Art; her education was like her brothers', with little knowledge of the usual and much grounding in the unusual. To Pum she seemed an awkward girl and socially inexperienced, but she was less snobbish and conventional than her brothers and found her feet in the world more speedily. To her mother, she was a "beautiful, gifted creature. . . . How few can compare with her. Artistic, poetic, literary, with capacity for every branch of life, ideas and practical, with a genius for friendship and a perfect temper and disposition . . . she *understood* everything and everyone." Violet, who was to marry Captain Thomas, R.A. (Tommy) in January 1910, was "swept away" later that year when she gave birth to a stillborn baby, "in one awful doom." Mary, echoing her son's divided self, mourned her lost and only daughter, saying that Violet "was my second, better, more gifted, more developed self."

4
Promise and Squalor

Though an intelligent, precocious youth, Pum had learned little at school, but it didn't stop him going in for the family trade of doctoring. When he was just seventeen, in 1898, he started his training at Guy's Hospital, London, and qualified five years later as Member of the Royal College of Surgeons (MRCS) and Licentiate of the Royal College of Physicians (LRCP), in the minimum time permissible and at the minimum age. For the first time he felt responsibility for himself and his future and discovered that there were advantages to be had if he worked hard; he applied himself with great diligence to his books, lectures, and demonstrations, to biology, anatomy, physiology, and chemistry. It was all-engrossing, and that in itself was a delight. This was the first time that work had gripped him and would, he realized, be essential to his future freedoms and adventures. His prime incentive was not the love of medicine but the urge to escape, be independent, his own man.

Pum discovered London at the turn of the century as a city of pleasure, leisure, and consumption. There was every sort of shop selling everything a man might desire; there were bars, theaters, restaurants, cinemas, and the exhilarating possibility for him to meet and mix freely with men and women of all types and social classes. At first he worked hard all week and played football and tennis on Saturdays. Then he met a girl called Maisie and they had one important thing in common:

a sense of fierce self-reliance. Maisie achieved her independence by, as Pum coyly put it, adopting the only profession she felt could give it to her. He doesn't discuss her occupation any further, but does say how he was nonetheless surprised, when out and about with her, at the bevy of acquaintances she had among rough, good-natured fellows, stockbroker's clerks, bookies, and the like. He knew her only as Maisie, or May, and she knew him as John. Pum was known to many of his friends as "John," a name he acquired at Guy's, from the song on everybody's lips at the time, "John Anderson, My Jo." This was originally a bawdy song about a young wife and her older husband, and was later adapted for Burns's poem on age and love.

Maisie lived in a neat, handy, two-room flat in an East End block with her permanent companion Fido, a spoiled little monster with a shrill bark that she affectionately called her "yap-dog." On Saturday nights she and Pum would go out to see a show, seated in the gallery or pit, then go for a drink or two at a second-rate bar—they couldn't afford a Soho restaurant. On one special occasion they attended a fancy-dress ball at Covent Garden, a weekly event in "the season," but one that cost a small fortune, the tickets being a guinea apiece, and Pum had to pawn his microscope to satisfy Maisie's longing to go. She outdid herself by constructing a costume she called "Poppies in Corn" that enveloped her body in an elaborate stock of real corn intertwined with artificial poppies. Her pretty face peeping out from the middle of it produced, Pum thought, a quite ridiculous effect. Silly and unbecoming as he saw it, it proved a hit among the clerks and bookies and with Maisie's girlfriends, who were, he carped, pleasant enough but vulgar, improvident girls of the popular barmaid type. Pum thought that these girls, including Maisie, had apparently all taken to prostitution quite naturally and of their own free wills. There is no suggestion that this may have been one of the only lucrative ways open to them to make a good, independent living, because women, thought Pum (along with the popular Kipling), "were all whores at heart." It was the greatest mistake to "fancy that the whole demi-monde has been seduced and betrayed to their 'pitiable' profession by heartless and profligate men," for such women could be as self-interested as any man, but if so, they could never embody Pum's ideal of beauty.

On Sundays, Pum and Maisie would spend the whole day lying around in bed, and he sometimes read to her the romantic poetry of Keats or Shelley, or they lost themselves in the Oriental fantasy and sensual delights of the *Rubaiyat of Omar Khayyam*. But occasionally, prosaically, they took a steamer to Greenwich and shared a pint of prawns at a little pub overhanging the river, or went off to the Crystal Palace or Hampton Court, as though they were just any other respectable courting couple.

Pum had lost his baby-pale, blonde hair to a deeper auburn color, and he wore it parted neatly down the middle. He was now a sturdy, long-legged, young man of twenty-three, grown strong and athletic; he played first-class football for Guy's and sometimes for the United Hospitals, Surrey County, and the London Scottish. To his evident pride the sporting papers described him as "promising," "dashing," and even "outstanding." Not only did this burnish his reputation as a sportsman but it also helped him considerably in obtaining successive House and Ward appointments. But more than that, this welcome praise saved him from what he saw as an incipient "inferiority complex" instilled in him by his father's cruel scorn and the increasing dominance of his twin, both of which he had just escaped.

Sporting success was an opportunity for adventure, too. The United Hospitals XV went off on a trip to Paris to play rugby against France at the Racing Club at Auteuil, and the game attracted a big crowd and a great deal of attention. Their team was virtually an international, far too good for the occasion, and the French began play with a tremendous zeal almost amounting to fury. Pum attributed their ferocity to a desire for vengeance after the Fashoda Incident of 1898, the climax of imperial disputes over territory in Eastern Africa between the British and the French. They seemed to have decided that the best tactic was to disable as many of the British team as possible, and they kicked wildly in all directions until several were lying on the ground more or less badly damaged. Pum sustained only a broken finger. The game was stopped, a conference held, explanations given, and they started afresh. Before long, the French were exhausted and the match became a travesty, though the crowd grew increasingly enthusiastic, especially the ladies, who pressed against the muddy and battered players of both teams when the whistle blew.

That evening they were done extremely well, as Pum put it, and were introduced to a less than elevated, subversively secret side of life. After bathing and changing they were taken off to dine at Chez Maxim, the champagne flowing liberally throughout the meal and the cabaret. One of their hosts, known as Oncle Vavaseur, the proprietor of several less salubrious establishments, took the young men off as his guests to one of his best brothels, to a room entirely walled and ceilinged with mirrors, where they paired off with girls. Most were naked in "the garb of little Eves before the Fall, save for shoes and stockings, but some, the more provoking, wore pants and shimmies." Pum remembers that in his drunkenness they had all seemed exquisite, as though this was something he would never normally have been tempted into.

The young men were returned to their hotel in the early hours and the next day were sufficiently recovered to be sitting on the deck of a Seine steamer by eleven o'clock, eating grapes invalid-fashion and spitting the skins overboard like so many accustomed debauchés. After a substantial lunch washed down with more champagne, they were escorted around the sights of Paris in a brake, and for the first time Pum saw Notre Dame, les Invalides, the Louvre, and finally the grim and renowned Morgue. Exhausted from all the exercise, dissipation, and drink, he couldn't quite recall his return home, but he was put on a boat, then a train, and finally decanted from a cab, apparently lifeless, at his parents' house in Blackheath. The cabby helped his mother carry him up the stairs to bed and, when tipped handsomely, added a reassuring, "He'll be all right, Mum, don't you worry!" Pum slept for twenty-eight hours and awoke fresh and happy to find his "little mother" gazing at him with relief.

Youthful adventures such as this were par for the course, but his passion for collecting set him apart from his peers. Walking near Guy's one day in 1903, he passed a group of workmen busy excavating the foundations for a new building just as they had come upon a plague pit, three or four feet below the road surface. Stained bones were everywhere, among them the outsized skull of what must have been an enormous man, which Pum purloined immediately to clean, varnish, and keep with his other treasures. There were also quantities of clay pipes, glazed earthenware, Bellarmine [salt-glazed stoneware] bottles, and some twenty pewter plates and dishes all piled up together. He managed to buy two plates for half a crown from one of the workmen; a friend with more ready cash bought the rest and sold them at a good profit to a museum. As was indicated by the bones, each plate had contained a helping of fish, telling the tale, Pum thought, of a dinner party put to flight by who knows what tragedy or terror. Each plate has a crowned feather ownership mark which he assumed to be an armorial badge or the sign of some tavern. They were gifted to the Museum of London in 1942, and are dated as early sixteenth century.

At this time, too, scavenging in the city streets, he picked up an exquisite life-size sketch of a man's head in oils on a broken panel for a shilling from a coster's junk barrow in the Boro'. On the back was a label saying it was a Van Dyck, confirmed later by experts. It now hangs on the wall of his final home in Lavenham, Suffolk. Pum was now an omnivorous collector. It became both a vice and a mania.

The Guy's Hospital regime gave its students the most up-to-date, modern medical curriculum available. In the 1890s the Rt. Hon. William Ewart Gladstone, then a senior governor of the hospital, had declared its facilities to be an aid to the personal and social elevation of medical students. Students were offered a complete training: materia medica and therapeutics; midwifery; gynecology and pediatrics; chemistry; dentistry; and experimental philosophy, comprising everything from mechanics and hydraulics to astronomy. Medical students in those days were extraordinarily busy, especially in their third year when they undertook ward work in the "Clinicals"—wards set aside specifically for their practice. It was in the Clinicals that Pum learned to diagnose disease and social class with equal proficiency. For three months he did obstetrics in the district, the borough, and was up at all hours of the night and day visiting the squalid, verminous, and unhygienic dwellings of the poor and destitute. "Often," he wrote in horror, "a whole family of six or more were living in a single room in unbelievable filth . . . terrible to me were the first shrill cries of the new-born coming into such a world, inheriting this squalor and destitution." For the first time, he saw real poverty and came deeply to pity the poor and unfortunate, but it made him decide once and for all against general practice and put him off obstetrics forever. These experiences also set him to thinking about Christianity, and he turned to agnosticism—which he considered had a more "cheerful" view of the world—setting him on his lifelong philosophical quest for a secular, non-sectarian Universalism based entirely on love.

Pum also did a course on fevers at an isolation hospital, and one on "mental diseases" at the famous Bethlem Hospital for lunatics—already by then known for centuries as "Bedlam." Here he recorded his encounters with the "idiots," including remarkable mathematicians who could do nothing for themselves. At Bedlam, the authorities kept a series of scrapbooks containing the patients' drawings and writings, and Pum found them often quite extraordinary, sometimes brilliant, generally obscene and always extreme. The drawings, he said, were "what we would now describe as markedly surrealist or ultra modern and most of them were sexual." Pum's, and Tom's, own later drawings—now in the Bodleian Library in Oxford—are just as these are described. Working at Bedlam proved to be a profoundly depressing experience for him. He felt that if he persisted in it he would lose his own reason, or at least become strange or peculiar, "as many young alienists did and do." It seemed to Pum, now that he had worked with these people at close quarters, that insanity was the most terrible of all afflictions. It alarmed him thoroughly, as if he "were approaching the great border-line from which, as from death, there is no return—so hopeless and miserable it all appeared."

Pum studied surgery under Sir William (Willie) Arbuthnot Lane, a champion of social medicine long before the National Health Service and a surgeon whose lectures and demonstrations in the dissecting room had been famous since the early 1880s. Pum attended one of the last operations carried out in the original Astley Cooper theater, built in 1867 (electric lighting had only been installed in 1896, two years before Pum arrived), with its six or seven tiers of seats, where the students rolled iron cannon balls around a specially constructed groove to drown the screams of patients undergoing surgery without anesthetics. *Guy's Hospital Gazette* records that the operating table was surrounded by a ring of seats and that on the floor-space stood the surgeons, apprentices, and dressers of the operating surgeon. The theater could get so crowded and rowdy that it was often very difficult to keep members of the public from pushing their way in to gawp at the medical procedures taking place, as though this were some bloody music hall. It was gas-lit, poky, and hot, the audience looked down on a wooden table at the center, up into dusty nooks and crannies, and across at a large portrait of Sir Astley Cooper hanging on the back wall. The whole performance seemed primitive and barbaric: the surgeons in their scrubbed mackintoshes, with their towels, boiled and wrung out in Lysol solution, the bearded assistants who prepared the instruments in a boiling cauldron, and the Puffing Billy, Lister's automatic carbolic sprayer, belching clouds of disinfectant steam over patient, surgeon, student, and gawper alike. Under Arbuthnot Lane's tenure, new theaters had been built in 1901, an aseptic ritual was introduced, and younger surgeons began wearing sterilized overalls and using sterilized dressings and rubber gloves. The old guard reluctantly abandoned their macs and only the most hidebound resisted the progress that accompanied Pum into the medical profession—Sir Henry Howse clung to his beard and antiseptic spray to the last.

Speed more than skill was the surgeon's chief asset before chloroform, ether, or any of the many marvelous hypodermic anesthetics arrived, when even the slightest operation was agony and the death rate was dreadful. Only once, and much later, did Pum witness preanesthetic surgery. He was in a remote village in Kordofan, a former province of Sudan, and there was a considerable commotion around a *tukul*, a bee-hive-shaped straw hut, where people were coming and going, milling around a large fire on which they were boiling jars and heating irons. He discovered that a man was about to have his leg amputated above the knee. Pum explained that he was a doctor and would take the sick man to the hospital if they wished, a three-day trek away. The villagers refused, wisely probably, because the man already had spreading gangrene from a severe septic infection caused by a hunting accident, and so it was left to the skills of the local medicine man. The patient lay across a bed, about three feet above the ground, supported and held by two companions, while behind him stood another with a heavy club in his hand. The injured limb was stuck through the straw wall of the hut from within, two more men holding it steady outside. Beside them stood a powerful fellow, executioner-fashion, with a Kordofan sword upraised—a reputed Crusader's weapon, long, heavy, and keen-edged. Nearby was the local imam, who conducted and synchronized the whole proceeding. On his word—*bismillah* ("in the name of God") given in a loud voice and repeated by all present—the patient was stunned by a sudden blow on the head from within the hut while at the same moment, outside, a mighty swing of the sword lopped off his leg. The spurting arteries were quickly cauterized, the bleeding stopped, and the surface of the wound sterilized by immediately ladling hot pitch over the stump. The whole thing was a revelation to Pum of speed and dexterity. He learned later that the man had recovered.

As part of his medical training, Pum was ward-clerk for a while to Mr. Jacobson, a "delightful and stimulating old-fashioned surgeon." He would ask his students, "What is my most useful instrument, Sir?" The answer was the index fingernail. And, "In applying carbolic, what sort of wood would you use?" It was cedar, and you fashioned it from an old cigar box. Jacobson was a thoughtful man, quite modern in some of his methods: he insisted that it was important to get to know the patient's family, husband, or wife, and to find out as much could be learned from them, though always indirectly. He made a point of having a good look at one sick woman's husband as he sauntered past "chasing his own centre of gravity, for he walked at an angle forward of the perpendicular as if about to fall over," and eyed him critically, nodding his head as if to say, "I thought so, I told you so," and muttered to Pum, "A scoundrel, Sir." The husband, realizing that he was being judged, became defensive and angry, but Mr. Jacobson had come to his conclusion and had made his diagnosis.

For a while Pum was dresser to the courteous and clever Mr. Chartris Simons, and soon after that was appointed Clinical Assistant (CA), an institution peculiar to Guy's and a sign of honor for one not yet fully qualified. Simons's clinic was housed by itself in a small two-ward building and had first choice of all the medical cases that came to the hospital, so Pum's experience there was immensely valuable to him. In the CA's room, above a cheerful fire, hung a murky portrait in oils of a man who looked just like a bearded farmer but whose name was long forgotten; he was said to have been an eccentric who had made a gift of his corpse for the advancement of medical knowledge on condition that his portrait hung permanently in the hospital.

When Pum qualified as MRCS and LRCP, he was appointed Assistant House Surgeon to Sir William Arbuthnot Lane, whom he knew to be a "marvellous, imaginative and progressive surgeon and a delightful often quizzical character." Arbuthnot Lane drew both praise and enmity from his colleagues: his radical advocacy of a healthy diet as a cancer prophylactic, for example, led him into conflict with the British Medical Association, from which he eventually resigned. He was an inspirational surgeon who raised Pum's interest in his art to outright enthusiasm and encouraged him with much praise and interest. He always seemed to ask his neighbor's opinion: "Do you?" "Don't you?" he queried, as in: "I never lift a knife under fifty guineas, do you?" or "I have a great belief in champagne. Have you?" Another of his house surgeons remembers him removing a kidney and remarking, "Such a dull operation, don't you think so?" Though seeing as the young man had been a House Surgeon for just a few weeks, he "was hardly in the habit of removing kidneys." Arbuthnot Lane had a sure touch and an uncanny skill in diagnosis: examining a case, he would say, "I can feel the appendix unduly swollen about four inches long and tilted up to the right. Can you?" Of course, wrote Pum, "you couldn't—but the operation would reveal that he had been quite right."

While practicing bone surgery with Arbuthnot Lane, who was supremely successful in setting simple fractures using wires and screws to keep the knitting bones in place, Pum developed a new mechanical device, which he called the "bone clamp." It was a steel contraption made in assorted sizes, consisting of two small double claws and spikes—the Bone and Madullary Spikes—for use with complicated fractures. Later, he was able to perfect his inventions in the armed forces with the cooperation of Messrs. Downs, a well-known London Surgical Instrument Makers, who manufactured them for him. They proved very successful and were an innovative novelty. The method then in vogue was to pierce the bone above and below the fracture, pass a length of silver wire through the holes, and then twist this tight and snip off the surplus, but with Pum's device the bones could be set far more accurately and healing was more rapid. He not only demonstrated his bone clamps and spikes, he also published and read several papers on them, attracting some fame in the surgical world. Occasionally, Pum could subsidize his income by earning a fee attending coroner's courts or by assisting his surgeon in private practice, and for the first time in his life he had some money of his own apart from the "miserable allowance his father had been characteristically niggardly in providing." He opened his first bank account and wrote his first check—he bought himself a dinner jacket.

Despite his successes, Pum often felt himself overworked and overanxious during his early career. Sometimes he descended into melancholy and despair, what he called his "complete and unreasonable despondency," which seemed to him to be out of all proportion to his circumstances. He felt it overtook him too often, particularly when he was faced with a multitude of tragedies, something that happened far too frequently. He recalled treating a dripping, half-drowned boy of twelve or thirteen who was brought to the hospital by two river policemen after he had jumped from London Bridge into the Thames. The boy couldn't swim, but had been picked up almost immediately by a patrol boat and given first aid. Later, in the ward and tucked up in a warm bed, the boy told Pum his story. He had been going out to work since he was ten years old, earning a small sum each week that he gave straight to his father to help support and educate two younger children. The boy's mother had died when he was little and his father, whom he loved dearly, looked after them all as best he could. Then, two weeks earlier the boy had been given a half-a-crown raise in pay, but had gone on giving his father the same amount as before, spending the extra on himself. His conscience began to prick him and soon he was seized by a terrible remorse, but now he was too frightened and ashamed to confess. The day before his suicide attempt, his father had given him a shilling as a rare treat and reward. He tried to refuse, he tried harder than ever to own up, but, no, Judas's thirty pieces of silver were all in that shilling. He had left the family lodging, weeping bitterly, and as a way out had thrown himself off the bridge into the river. He was detained for a week in the hospital and, to Pum, proved to be a charming boy, intelligent, serious, and reserved, as well as affectionate and brave, as his story showed. Pum recorded this story in his memoir, looking back across some forty years to turn it into a Dickensian morality tale of nobility and beauty, a sentimental lesson in how to be a man, honorable and virtuous. He could have filled a book with stories like this, he wrote, all tragedy or comedy, but ultimately triumphant.

To save a life, Pum believed, was always a triumph, and a life saved by a successful operation was the most thrilling he could imagine. His patients were like his children: he felt for them and worried over them when things did not go right. The nurses felt like this, too, he wrote, and the whole hospital system worked as a close team—the surgeon, house surgeon, unqualified dressers, and ward clerks all strove to work together in efficient harmony. The sometimes-strange experiences in the hospital were forever challenging Pum to think deeply of the value and meaning of life and what it implied, and his thoughts bred in him that cheerful and quasi-religious spirituality with cosmic overtones. It was an other-worldly forgiving and personal belief system, one that he would develop by and for himself and, consequently, one that he found completely satisfactory—unlike his troubled grandfather, who had looked to existing systems and never found one to suit him.

Arbuthnot Lane was renowned for his appendectomies, and when attending at one of these, Pum's life was changed in a drastic fashion. A young girl was admitted as an emergency and, though not particularly excited by the prospect, Pum turned up to see her. As he strolled across the ward to her bed, he saw, gay and animatedly chatting, a girl who fairly "took his breath away." She was the most exquisite creature he had ever seen. Her name was Kathleen Silver, she was sixteen years old, and, as he took her hand, he "felt completely overwhelmed as never before or since."

Pum was speechless. He had heard of love at first sight but had not believed it possible; he had "heard of overwhelming love [and] this was it." He knew then and there that he had never been in love before. It dawned on him that Maisie (and a few others, too—Olive, Meg, and so forth) had meant absolutely nothing to him. Still holding Kathleen's hand, he regained control of himself; neither she nor the Sister sitting by her bed seemed to have noticed what had happened to him. Kathleen did not withdraw her hand; reluctantly he had to release it.

Her operation was to be in two days' time and he was full of apprehension for her; thankfully it was a success, and Pum's relief was great. The next day he met Kathleen's mother, a charming matron, the widow of a civil servant, left to care for her only child. Pum could not stop himself telling the mother how attractive he found her daughter and she was not in the least surprised, saying most people felt the same. He entered a period of complete bewitchment; he had never been so elevated and overjoyed, so indescribably exalted, and at times so depressed and miserable. Never had he sighed and laughed so much, never had he experienced the "malady of love." He thought of nothing but the girl and spent all his spare time at her bedside, talking, laughing, "content to touch her, indeed irresistibly compelled to touch her, to look upon her, to be near her. . . . She was lovely in her budding womanhood and her face was of a sensitive, almost childish beauty. She was lively, intelligent and had read a great deal for her age and she wrote well too. Her voice was soft and full of character and, best of all, she seemed to like me."

When Kathleen was discharged, Pum moped and pined and grew uneasy, as nothing seemed worthwhile anymore. In his infatuation he turned to writing poetry again and he sent her his love poems daily. One, "Completion," tells her, "Yes, love, without thee I am incomplete," that she is a "very sacrament / A mystic wine to drink, a solemn bread to eat."

Their subsequent affair lasted over a year, during which they met often, went to tea or to her home in Forest Hill. Her mother, slightly alarmed at the intensity of Pum's ardor, took him aside to remind him that she was only sixteen, but still his infatuation grew. Over and over he told her how much he loved her. Sometimes he was allowed to kiss her, occasionally she kissed him, but he could never get her to say she loved him. He wrote to her constantly and at first she wrote back, tenderly and sweetly, but her replies began to dwindle. Soon enough he received the letter that told him she was sorry, she was deeply in love with someone else, someone a little less intense. He didn't reply, he didn't write again, he burned her letters and wrote more poetry:

Burning Love Letters
To KS
I untie the faded bands,
One by one love's missives cast
To the flames with shaking hands,
Sparing none from first to last.
*

For a moment I behold
Here a word and there a phrase
Seer to black then burn to gold,
Fall to ash and leave no trace.
*

Like a living thing each one
Burnt as a self-sacrifice

Psyche and pale Cupidon
Changed from love's to death's device.
*

Grimly, hopelessly, I see
The frail pages curl and twist
Withered skin of agony,
Letters that my lips have kissed
Crease and crack, then cease to be.
*

Letters that her hands have pressed
Burn away, are no more seen,
Cease for ever to exist,
Cease as they had never been.

Unable to be with Kathleen, he felt hollow and numb as though he had left himself behind with her, as though an irreplaceable loved one had died. His first real love affair had ended in exhausted disappointment and it had changed him permanently, utterly. Outwardly, he recovered himself comparatively quickly, but it was a different self and he kept his grief locked away. "So ended the only deep and true love-romance of my life!" he wrote. And it ended there: he had tried loving women, and failed.

Pum's unrequited love plunged him into further introspection, and he concluded that he would never again be able to fall fully and deeply in love with another person; he could only feel love for his mother from now on. Romantic love had "been extinguished and left him incapable of anything more than regard or an affection, perhaps shallow, even insincere." He decided to put all his emotional energy into objects of beauty and, in so doing, condemned himself to objectifying people, too.

In the notes he wrote compulsively at night in bed, Pum's lifelong self-analysis reflected Freud's ideas on "future inverts" in *Three Essays on the Theory of Sexuality* (1910). Freud wrote that he had "established the fact that the future inverts, in the earliest years of their childhood, pass through a phase of very intense but short-lived fixation to a woman (usually their mother), and that, after leaving this behind, they identify themselves with a woman and take themselves as their sexual object." The affair with Kathleen was a profound and defining experience in Pum's life. It pushed him out into the world, but also in upon himself. He would discover other kinds of love, other beauties, other obsessions, other conflicts. The idea of having a loving relationship with a woman—or worse, being married—became the stuff of nightmares to him. His deepest desires instead were bound up with the nobility of innocence, youth, boys, and beauty; these would be the focus of his sexual admiration and longing.

Disillusioned, detached, and too restless to settle, Pum, who as Assistant House Surgeon to William Arbuthnot-Lane had been encouraged to aim for a Harley Street career, threw it all away. It was 1904, a time of optimism and peace, of innovation in the arts, science, and technology, and Pum was twenty-three years old, newly qualified, and needing to get out into the world and have adventures. So he followed his twin, away fighting in the Boer War, by joining the Royal Army Medical Corps (RAMC).

5
Into the East

At first, army life expanded Pum's paranormal horizons rather than his geographical ones. As an army surgeon he was tied to the very physical worlds of the body and military life, but the psychic world, which had intermittently intersected with Pum's since his adolescence, now began to seriously distract him with spirits and hauntings. After a three-month course designed to teach him duty and discipline (even though billeted at St. Ermin's Hotel, Westminster), he was posted to the provincial army town of Aldershot to work in the fever hospital. One evening he was called over to see a little girl who was suffering from diphtheria and who might require an emergency tracheotomy. Having made an examination and concluded that her case was clearing up, he decided that an operation wasn't going to be necessary after all. Still, he was gripped by an uneasy feeling about the child, some psychic intuition that denied his a priori understanding of her case. So disturbed was he that he had a bed made up for himself in a room near her ward, at the other end of a long, brightly lit corridor. Giving instructions that he should be woken at once if he was needed, Pum took off his boots and jacket, lay down, and was soon fast asleep. Suddenly he awoke, startled; someone had shaken him and he heard a voice that repeated, "Come at once—come at once." Leaping out of bed, without properly dressing, he hurried into the corridor and there, in the bright light, stood a tall, pale-faced woman swathed entirely in black. This odd figure kept in front of him as they hurried to the ward, gliding and insistently beckoning him on. When she reached the glass door of the ward she stopped and peered in and then, turning a beautiful but haggard face toward him, she shook her head and without entering the ward slipped through a door to her left, letting him pass on. He had followed hard on her heels, and in a moment he was beside the child's cot. He saw at once that she was dead.

Agitated and distressed, he reproached the nurse, asking her why she hadn't called him earlier. "I didn't call you at all," came the reply. "The patient has just died of a sudden heart failure even before I could get to her bed, but I was about to call you. . . . Why did you come? How did you know?" Pum told her how had been woken and led there. "That's impossible," she replied. "I'm the only person here and I haven't left the room." Pum supposed it must have been the child's mother, but the nurse insisted that the mother was not present and, further, that the door Pum had seen her leave through was to a locked linen cupboard. The nurse produced her keys and they went to try it—it was just as she had said. Pum believed he had seen a ghost, the first of many, most of them crowded into a few years of what he called his tolerant and open-minded receptivity. He discovered that once he became skeptical, then the power, or privilege, of seeing the apparitions disappeared and his "psychic eyes" became dulled.

Henry had thought himself a sensitive, someone who believes they are responsive to occult influences, and Pum assumed he had inherited this facility from his father. His psychic capabilities, the apparitions he witnessed, were phenomena known then as the exteriorization of sensibility. The Society for Psychical Research (SPR), the first organization set up to attempt an empirical investigation of the field, was founded in London in 1882. Eminent men such as Henry Sidgwick, the SPR's first president and a Cambridge moral philosopher with a reputation for caution and skepticism, supported and gave credence to the movement, though he was anxious that it should not be seen as a front for Spiritualism or the occult. Alfred Russel Wallace, similarly, believed that psychic phenomena were facts, and if they did not accord with established scientific canons, then those canons needed revising—just as the established view of the Creation had had to be revised following his and Darwin's presentation of the theory of evolution. These men now sought to align the paranormal with recognized science in a sort of post-Darwinian grope toward meaning for humanity, beyond what now looked like just an animalistic, unspiritual dead end. They had their critics. Charles Kingsley charged the psychic movement with effeminacy and wrote about a new "mesmerizing, table-turning, spirit-rapping, Spiritualizing, Romanizing generation" of men, far from the male ideal of strength, duty, and stiff upper lip.

In 1906, by the time Pum arrived in Gibraltar, his first army posting overseas and the first stop on his road to the East, he was possessed by a heightened receptivity. He was twenty-five years old. It had been a dark and lowering day when he set out for Southampton, and as he and his fellows boarded their trooper a terrific gale was blowing up. In charge of the health of the "Reliefs" for the Rock, Pum was kept very busy, but even he was utterly overcome by a shocking dose of seasickness. Tottering to his cabin, he threw himself fully dressed into his bunk and remained there for three days and nights, suffering as he had as a tiny child crossing the Atlantic, but now without parents to care for him. On the fourth day the storm abated, and he crawled back on deck scarcely able to stand, emerging amid hundreds of prone bodies of young soldiers all spread out in the sun to recover. When they landed on the Rock, he was allotted rooms in a boarding house, the Maraquitas, overlooking the harbor, and here he began to immerse himself in Spanish life, eating good food, drinking wine, and learning to speak to the locals.

Though the everyday world was preoccupying to say the least, Pum had felt, from the moment he landed in Gibraltar, that it was a haunted place. The Maraquitas sat at a kink in a steep road that ran between two high walls, so that from the small balcony where Pum took afternoon tea, anyone passing down it seemed to appear very suddenly and as suddenly disappear around the bend. Every afternoon at four o'clock the officer in command of the Naval Forces on the island, an Admiral Chichester, walked past on his way to play cards at the club, dressed always in a tweed suit, smoking a pipe, and with a bulldog at his heel. When he contracted pneumonia, he was not seen for several days until Pum caught sight of him sauntering along his usual route. Pum was taking tea with a fellow lodger, a civilian named Jocelyn, and he remarked in pleased surprise, "There goes old Chichester; how quickly he has recovered." Jocelyn missed him, so quickly did the Admiral round the bend. That evening, before dinner, Jocelyn stopped Pum and told him he must have been mistaken about the Admiral for he had died at home that very afternoon. Pum was certain he had seen him but, he now realized, without either his pipe or his faithful dog. He wasn't alarmed by this; after all, Henry had had similar experiences, the most striking when he was visited by one of his brothers, a civil servant who had drowned while being rowed across the flooded Teesta River in Bengal in 1899.

Pum's next vision came in a vivid dream about D'Arcy: he was in great danger, clinging to a mountaintop, terrible anguish written across his face. The nightmare woke him, but when he fell asleep again, the vision returned. He told no one and then, a month later, a letter arrived exactly recounting the dream: D'Arcy, stationed at Quetta, wrote that he had gone out shooting alone on Murdar mountain, and when a partridge he had wounded fluttered onto a bare crag above a precipice, he had climbed down to rescue it. But the return to his position was much more hazardous, and he was forced to cling to an overhanging ledge, unable to move in either direction for hours. Pum felt that his brother's dread had transmitted itself to him and that it indicated a strong spiritual affinity between them. When D'Arcy later died on board his ship in the Great War and was buried at sea, Pum again experienced a powerful hallucination of his elder brother's demise before any in the family were notified of it.

Then, most startling of all, late one night Pum came face-to-face with his own disembodied spirit. He was woken about three in the morning by a knocking on the hall door directly below his window, a very unusual occurrence. When the knocking came again, he got out of bed, now thoroughly awake, and went across to the window. It was a brilliant moonlit night. Looking out, he saw the foreshortened figure of a familiar man who, when he raised his face and looked up, Pum recognized as himself. Oddly, it didn't occur to him that it might be his identical twin, and he didn't feel at all surprised to see himself at the door. Calling to the apparition to wait a moment, he quickly dressed and went down to let himself in. When he unbolted the door, he found the road was quite deserted and silent. He looked about for some seconds with a sense of disappointment mixed with excitement and an indefinite fear that his psychic experiences didn't usually provoke in him. He hastily locked up again and ran back to his room in a panic. It was possible, he thought, that the apparition had a "twin-ish" rather than a "self-ish" significance, but he felt sure he had seen another version of himself standing there—his second self—and that the disappearance was explained by the spirit entering or re-entering his body and being reabsorbed into his first self. He wrote a poem about it, "Self-encounter," which was published posthumously by Tom in the volume *Christeros and Other Poems*:

I met myself the other night
As I walked out beneath the moon,
We met, but 'ere I'd guessed aright
That it was I, my sprite had gone
*

My lips, about to speak to me,
Stayed silent and I saw no more
The thing I feared yet fain would see,
The thing that I had been before
Or later sure would be.
*

My hand, held out to take my own,
Fell empty at my inert side
And once again I was alone,
I of myself denied.
*

Then I was filled with sudden fear
Of that which was or might have been,

Of incarnation that appear
And second-selves that are not seen
Until the end is near.
*

So, in afright I turned and fled
From my own self, my heart achill,
For I felt sure I'd met me dead
Or seen that self death cannot kill.

Leaving the Maraquitas after these disturbing events, he went to lodge with other officers in a fine old house with a dark history. At the time of the Great Siege of Gibraltar (1779–83), when Spain and France attempted to capture the Rock from the British during the American War of Independence (the longest siege endured by British Armed Forces to date), this house, it was said, had belonged to two Jewish brothers, successful merchants, who lived there alone apart from a Spanish youth who attended them. During the bombardments they sheltered in a cave beneath the house where they stored their valuables, and the youth went out alone by day to look for food. One day he failed to appear in the market. At first, most people thought that the three had slipped over to Spain and safety, but before long the bodies of the brothers were discovered, without their treasures, robbed and murdered, apparently by the boy. The mouth of this cave had been closed by a stone slab with an iron ring at its center and had remained shut for over one hundred twenty years until Pum and his friend Captain Gorringe decided to investigate. Letting themselves down into the dank cave, they found an ancient, intricate system of tunnels branching off in all directions into pitch black, an endless series of large chambers and small grottos joined by narrow passages that were mere slits in the rock. Like Theseus, Pum used a clew of thread as he edged through this underground labyrinth. After three days and many balls of string, the friends gave up their search for an "end" and emerged for the last time from the warren, dropping the heavy slab back in its hole.

In his personal writings, Pum tried to absorb and make sense of his initial brush with new peoples and cultures and his sense of another, paranormal dimension. His attempts to align these spheres of experience and understanding sometimes resulted in a mishmash of idealism and prejudice. His notes on the Jewish "problem" illustrate one of the preoccupations of the period, the prevalent "state of the nation" anxieties, xenophobic and religious conflict. Here is his poem, "Deed-Poll," from one of his volumes of "Obsessions":

By deed-poll Myerstein the Jew
Has changed his name to Montague.
So Ethiope his skin, so pard
His spots may change—but it seems hard
The fine old name of Montague
Be used thus to unjew a Jew.

And a second poem, "The Jew":

Why is it the Jew is for ever taboo,
An outcast, the butt of mankind?
It's not that he slew Jesus Christ or would do
Down the devil, that nobody'd mind,
Nor because he's the chosen, the one-in-a-dozen
Jehovah's particular pet,
Though indeed it seems odd, that a common sense God
Should have mixed himself up with that set.
No, no, it's just this, the Jew was, will be, is
—Though he change his Jew name to Macpherson—
A Jew, and a Jew it matters not who
Is a perfectly poisonous person.

This poem has a note below it, written in pencil as if it were an afterthought, a further elucidation and justification for his bigotry, as though he had experienced a spasm of doubt. But it was merely a spasm: "There are certain brilliant exceptions, Einsteins, Disraelis, etc., to whom I apologise. Christ was but half a Jew so I make no apology to him—Dr. Wm Yates in his very perceptive book on Egypt 1843 (vol. II) makes this shrewd summing up of the Israelite: 'the Jews [of Egypt] are marked by that peculiarity which distinguishes them in every other country; squalor and raggedness in their persons, filth and nastiness in their dwellings, their morals are lax, and they are ready to engage in any business which the less vile would have a repugnance to.' In other words, rather than or besides being 'God's chosen people' they are 'God's bad ruin,' born bad and without even one redeeming feature that usually mitigates the evil of the ordinary bad man."

The young Pum was able to write off a whole race with little or no compunction, but he was usually very eager to be liked and admired by individuals. His facility for Spanish meant he was soon much in demand for medical consultations among naval and civilian surgeons alike. His boldness encouraged confidences. On one occasion he was called to tend the wounds of Chikita, a celebrated bullfighter, delightful and swaggering, whose body was pitted with the scars of his profession. Chikita told him of the infamous Kaid McLean and "his close friend, a certain O'Hara," who had served together as young officers but had got into some unnamed trouble so, threatened with court-martial, they had upped and deserted. O'Hara fled to Spain where he changed his name and became a bullfighter of some renown before he was gored and died in the ring, while McLean escaped to Morocco, where he eventually rose to head the sultan's army. Pum was to meet McLean at lunch one day; he was a thickset, middle-sized fellow with a close-cut Tudor beard who dressed as a Moor in burnoose and soft-tasseled tarboosh. With him was the sultan's physician, one Wilkinson, who had arrived in Fez on his travels and been taken up by the sultan there and then. Wilkinson told Pum he was on the lookout for an assistant and that he should apply, but it all came to nothing when the older doctor killed himself. Pum's career remained on track this time.

On a brief crossing to Morocco, Pum experienced his first intensely exciting glimpse of the East. In Tangier, Pum had been to the huge open "soho" (in Arabic, the *souk*, meaning "market") just outside the city gates, and had seen the men smoking hashish. With all their caravans unloaded, the bales of merchandise scattered, and camels continually chewing the cud, the servants, porters, slaves, and "camel-men" squatted in groups, prepared their food after sundown, and slept around the fires that dotted the black space like smoldering stars in the firmament. Here or there would be a hashish party of four or five men sitting around their small fire with a pipe about a foot long, its small clay bowl completely filled with pure Indian hemp. "Seizing a glowing charcoal from the fire with a small tongs or tweezers, the first smoker would set it to the primed pipe, then with a deep breath he would inhale and slowly exhale the smoke, this he repeated twice or thrice—then suddenly he would seem to grow limp and collapse, falling back to the ground—as he did so the pipe was taken out of his hand by his neighbour who did likewise till the pipe had been right round the circle, and in a few minutes the whole group lay there stretched out as if dead. In ten minutes or so they would rouse themselves and sitting up would all talk together, each recounting his adventures while under the influence." Pum noted that their "doped experiences are of an extremely exotic and amorous nature, and that the trained 'hashash' can conjure up at will whatever form of amorous situation he pleases." Later, he wrote, he became acquainted with a European addict who kept a volume of nude photos from which he made his selection and "on which he concentrated his thoughts and desires before drinking the smoke." The night scenes at Tangier, and all he heard then and later about hashish and its use, aroused in him "a keen interest in this drug with which of course I have since come in contact on many occasions, even in the Sudan where each petty sultan kept and used a hashish outfit."

While in Tangier, Pum was determined to travel down to Fez, the magnificent medieval capital of Morocco. Fez was then strictly out of bounds on account of the brigand chief Rasouli and the general unrest he was fomenting. Pum discussed his intention to go anyway with his friend Jimmy Long, a civil engineer, and they agreed to make the trip together instead of spending their three weeks' leave in Spain. Soon they were slipping quietly across the water in the wrong direction to where a dragoman, Mohamed, awaited them. In his pocket, Pum had a letter of introduction to none less than Rasouli himself, who apparently enjoyed a visit from the odd Englishman—not from Englishwomen though, for, as Pum put it, he was a "strong anti-feminist."

Leaving their Tangier hotel early one morning with their mule train of six animals and a rough chap called Hassan and his boy, they set out for the camp. Pum and Jimmy had been on the go for only a couple of hours when they heard explosions and fusillades. They decided to press on. But very soon, on emerging from a steep-sided gully, they found themselves in a standoff between the sultan's forces on their left and Rasouli's on their right. Each side had antiquated canons, and "round-shot bounded about them like cricket balls." It was as though Pum saw the whole thing as an imperial escapade of the public school sort. Their group was rounded up by "villains," shouting and brandishing weapons, and taken off as prisoners behind the sultan's lines. Hassan and the boy made a dash for it, accompanied by the mules and a ragged volley of musketry, and neither they nor the belongings were ever seen again. Mohamed the dragoman and one of the sultan's officers appeared to know each other and, after some tense negotiations, they were allowed to continue on their way. Immediately, they came under enemy fire again and, defenseless save for a single revolver, had to crawl away on their bellies through the scrub and rocks before finding shelter in the house of a sheikh. They eventually made their way back to safety via Cape Spartel, where they stayed with an old Scottish lighthouse keeper till the situation in Tangier defused somewhat. Once home, Pum was taken to task for being absent without trace and brought before the governor of Gibraltar, General Sir Frederick (Hookey) Forestier-Walker, who was apparently much amused and let him off with a scolding.

In 1907, shortly after this escapade, Pum was given his first posting to Egypt, which had been under British rule since 1882. He was seconded to the Egyptian Army as *bimbashi* (major) and was as pleased as

Punch, the Egyptian Army being a most sought-after appointment at the time. He went straight to the famous Shepheard's Hotel in Cairo and booked himself in with two newly acquired bulldogs, Fez and Fagan; he didn't much like to be alone.

6
Africa

Cairo had been a city of men's excess for centuries: at the end of the eighteenth century, the scholars and scientists—the "savants"—who went with Napoleon to Egypt and produced the *Description de l'Égypte* (a series published between 1809–29), estimated that two-thirds of Cairo's artisan class regularly indulged in opium and honeyed hashish balls. "The abundance and low price of bread, the existence of concerts and entertainments within and outside the city, and the easy fulfilment of desires: he does as he pleases, dancing in the markets, going about naked, and getting drunk on hashish."

In this extraordinary city at last, Pum decided to try the Indian hemp that held the country's "poorer classes" in its grip. He thought of it as a lighthearted piece of self-experiment, just as many of the medical profession had before him—they had recorded their drug experiences as case histories and valid scientific knowledge. This didn't stop most of them judging the "luxurious" drug use of the "lower classes" as indulgent and evil, though Pum was more liberally minded when it came to sex and drugs, knowing that he was not above judgment himself.

So it was that on a pleasantly warm evening after dinner in his hotel, Pum, having obtained a small quantity of hashish, some charcoal, and a pair of tweezers, put on his pajamas, retired early, and primed his ordinary tobacco pipe with the drug as he had often seen it done. Reclining on the sofa, he took the pipe between his teeth, applied a glowing piece of charcoal, and gave a few tentative and timorous sucks, not into his chest but only into his mouth. All he experienced was rather a disagreeable taste. So, growing bolder, he took a couple of quick, deep inhalations right into his lungs. "The effect was immediate!" he wrote. "The room swam round and I nearly lost consciousness; I experienced a sudden, intense feeling of fear mixed, oddly enough, with a mild exaltation and an insistent curiosity, or rather an overpowering urge to go on—a sort of devilish influence quite outside myself forced me to drink in another deep chestful." After that he had only a hazy and frightened recollection of horror and depression amounting to a despair that roared straight at him like an express train through a tunnel. He found himself at the window of his room and could see himself tearing at the stout wooden shutters, trying with all his might to force them open and throw himself into the courtyard three stories below. His brain seemed acutely aware, and the fear, horror, and rebellion, as well as an overwhelming desire to kill himself, increased, but the shutters held and no other means of suicide occurred to him—he was thankful he didn't have his automatic with him. Gradually he noticed a murmuring in his mind, a voice other than his own—or perhaps one of his own—urging him away from death, and there followed a terrible struggle between two powerful selves contending for his being, a nightmare wrestling match on the edge of a precipice. Very slowly, it seemed to him, "sanity gained an upper grip and with almost unbearable pain and strain it forced its terrible opponent over on to his back—suddenly the struggle was won and the 'horror' tumbled into the abyss."

Eventually he staggered back to his sofa where the hotel *marasla* (servant) found him the next morning. He had brought tea, removed the makeshift charcoal burner without any expression of surprise, and tidied up, merely saying, "Nahark said, Effendim" ("Good morning, sir"), and opening up the shutters to let in the bright sunlight. Disappointingly, there had been "no trance, no paradise, no visions of lovely naked houris [virgins of the Qu'ranic paradise], no delicious orgiastic sensations!" But Pum felt the supreme happiness of the convalescent, in spite of a racking headache, and the whole world seemed to be singing a song of thanksgiving.

His findings mirrored other clinical accounts that were dotted through the pages of the *Lancet* and the *British Medical Journal*. In the future, he decided, he would try and dissuade others from trying that or any other drug, or at least not to do it alone in an upstairs room. Nevertheless, he later used hashish or crude opium quite often; he found them pleasant stimulants for physical or mental effort, leaving only a light craving that he considered easy to resist. In this, he reflected the thinking of many long-term colonial doctors, who had almost always been at odds with the turning tide of European opinion on unorthodox drug use. Still, Pum thought that race had a determining effect on vulnerability to different drugs, and he considered that the Arabs who used hashish, as Pum and his friends used alcohol, were probably addicted to it—a marker of weakness and degeneration. He nonetheless held a liberal view toward his Egyptian servant's daily half grain of opium and "the Chinaman's addiction to that drug." When he was a child in America, he had been taken to an opium den in San Francisco's Chinatown and was told that the acrid smell and "yellow, drowsy reclining figures" were depraved and evil, and he had often wondered since then why tobacco and alcohol should be regarded as quite so respectable, given that all these drugs were bad if used unwisely or excessively.

Prejudice, poverty, disease, misery, cruelty, and human ingenuity were all familiar to Pum by now, even though he was still a young man. Arriving in Cairo had set him wondering anew about the trials of humanity and the relationships between psychology, sensibilities, and brutish nature. This was one side of the city that he wanted to explore; the other was the gay life at the height of the season.

All the young British officers were making the most of the city in this first decade of the twentieth century. They were in and out of the clubs, they played tennis and golf, and Pum even bought himself two ponies to play polo, that "best of all games." Soon he moved into the Egyptian Army Officer's Mess in Abdin Square, close to the royal palace—a comfortable if ramshackle building, alive with bugs—and began working as a surgeon at the hospital at Abbasiya. He got himself a uniform and tarboosh, a complete *bimbashi*'s rig, at a very good price from the Clothing Department; it had had one previous owner, an officer killed in Sudan.

Pum's lifelong affair with Egypt, its culture, and its people had begun. Reveling in the sights and smells of Egyptian life as he explored the "slummy" Islamic quarters of the city, he found it all so intoxicating that he was taken aback by the realization that he was an exception to the rule. Many of his fellow British officers couldn't speak Arabic and didn't bother to learn, despite a requirement that a British *bimbashi* must have a passable knowledge of the language within six months of arriving. Pum set about teaching himself the language and customs, unsatisfied with the military and utilitarian phrases used by his peers; even those were badly spoken, and many men were "barely able to talk with their servants or their women!"

As soon as his Arabic was passable, Pum began to mix with Egyptians and sought out Luxor antique dealers so that he could begin collecting beauty again. He became the customer and good friend of Sheikh Mansur, Girgis Gabrial and his two sons, Mishriki and Tadros Effendi, of Gabrial's brother Sheikh Swaris, the handsome Yusef Hassan, the half-blind Abd al-Rahim, and Sayed Moluttam, to whom he became very close. Pum also made a point of getting to know the octogenarian Hagg Mohamed Mohasib, a well-known dealer, who bought his pieces from tomb robbers and sold to the likes of General Herbert Kitchener, himself a keen collector, and to many of the "celebrities" who came to make the newly fashionable tour of Egypt. They had met at Luxor— "What it is about Luxor that makes it the most erotic of places I know not!"—while Pum was traveling to Khartoum to stand in for the local surgeon, who had been taken ill, and Pum bought his first beautiful little bronze Horus from this wealthy dealer. He later learned to be more cautious and to buy only from "less known and less-knowing" merchants, ignorant men without much expertise who charged a pittance for objects of great rarity and value.

Desperate to see the ancient sites as well as the artifacts, Pum went from Luxor upstream through Aswan, "a quiet winter resort" where he later briefly owned a tiny island in the Nile, and on to Shellal, where Fez and Fagan and his soldier-servant Ibrahim were waiting for him on board the post boat. Here he first saw the island of Philae, with its perfect, exquisite, small Ptolemaic temple. It was later submerged when the Aswan Low Dam, built by the British, was heightened for the first time. When Pum visited, the temple, one of the burying-places of Osiris known as "Pharaoh's Bed," was like a jewel, its palm-leaf, lotus, and papyrus-plant capitals quite undamaged, its coral and amber-colored external walls and interior still glowing with the original blues, yellows, and greens on the inscriptions and reliefs, all as bright in places as when first painted 2,500 years earlier. Especially bright were the azure blue ceilings with their yellow stars. All that had quite gone, swamped by the water, by the time Pum wrote his memoir in the 1940s, and the few ancient stones still exposed were covered in a layer of grey, dried slime. In the 1960s, UNESCO removed the temple complex to save it from its successive inundations and rebuilt it on the nearby island of Agilkia.

In the early 1930s, when Pum was a senior inspector in the Ministry of the Interior, he was sent off on a government steamer to examine the results of the second heightening of the Aswan Low Dam. He was charged with reporting on the impact of the works on the living conditions of the local people so that estimates for their compensation could be made. Traveling between Shellal and Halfa, through the Nubian country, he found a strange state of affairs. The fertile strips of land had all been drowned, with just the tops of palm trees poking up above the water. For the second time in a generation, the people had been forced to move their homes high up to the crags that now bordered the dam basin. The Nubians built their homes square and true and were not "mud-daubers" like their neighbors; their huts were pylon-like with vaulted mud roofs, strongly resembling the buildings of the ancient Egyptians. The main apartment, around which the others clustered, was half open to the sky, with the floor of the covered portion raised up a foot, and around the walls ran mud and brick divans handsomely covered with colored rugs and blankets. The old men, women, and children remained there, all dependent on their able-bodied men away working in Egypt or Sudan. These were peaceable, hard-working people, but virtually all their young men had left Nubia to become cooks, body-servants, waiters, or *syces* (grooms). Pum recorded their exile, but didn't really commiserate; after all, they made the best servants in Egypt. He described them as handsome and "coffee-colored," their children being "especially attractive," and in comparison to the Egyptians and the Sudanese, he regarded them as being far more civilized.

But back in 1907, in Khartoum, Pum discovered a pleasant, sociable place where, before motorcars, everyone went about on smartly groomed donkeys, each with a little "donkey-boy" to match. The boys ran alongside, all dressed up in white shirts, shorts, and turbans, holding on to a stirrup or the beast's tail. It was an incongruous sight to see a long-legged British officer in full white Review order, with sword, spurs, helmet, medals, and gold lace, astride his diminutive donkey, with his feet nearly touching the ground like Don Quixote. Pum relished the life there and the camaraderie that existed between the British of all ranks and services in Sudan. Everyone worked conscientiously and enjoyed their leisure to the full, and he was most reminded of the best of British public school life where, he wrote, youth, vigor, and kindly feeling combined in an efficient and cheerful atmosphere.

There he was introduced to the *sirdar*, Sir Reginald Wingate Pasha, a short, thickset, white-haired chap with warm eyes and waxed moustaches. He was *sirdar* (commander-in-chief) of the Egyptian Army and governor-general of Sudan, thus he controlled the entire military and civil life of an immense country. Pum considered him to be the "Father of the modern Sudan," for with his final battle in 1899 at Umm Dabriket on Abba Island, he had killed the khalifa and "ended Mahdiism once and for all." The Mahdi is the prophesied redeemer of Islam, and in the late nineteenth century a colonial war was fought between the Mahdist Sudanese, led by a man claiming to be the redeemer, who resented colonial rule and heavy taxes, and the Egyptian and later British forces. General Charles Gordon and his troops had been slaughtered in this war in 1885, and Winston Churchill had fought in its later stages, recounting his experiences in *The River War: An Historical Account of the Reconquest of the Soudan* (1899). Churchill had taken part in the cavalry charge at the Battle of Omdurman in 1898, the decisive battle in which Anglo-Egyptian forces under General Kitchener had defeated the Mahdist army of Mohamed Ahmed ibn 'Abd Allah and won back the Sudanese territory that he had held since 1881.

Wingate Pasha "reigned as uncrowned King" at Khartoum until 1916, when he became high commissioner of Egypt. Pum considered him to be the embodiment of "kindliness, efficiency, justice, and good sense that endeared him to the British, Egyptians and Sudanese alike." Perhaps even more endearing to the British establishment was Slatin Pasha, or Major General Baron Sir Rudolph Carl von Slatin. Here was a true romantic figure of the East, who looked as if he had stepped out of a Vienna State Opera performance of *Die Fledermaus*. A jovial and attractive Austrian, a frequent visitor to Queen Victoria, and a great friend of Lord Baden-Powell's, he wore rows of medals on his chest and had a booming Germanic voice and turned-up mustaches. As a protégé of Gordon's and a political officer in Darfur, he had been captured by the Mahdists, who used him as a pawn to try and persuade Gordon to surrender. Slatin was kept in chains, and when Gordon was killed and Sudan fell to the Mahdi, they brought the general's head to show him. He spent the next thirteen years as a slave before he finally escaped, took part in the reconquest of Sudan, and later became inspector general and a brigadier-general in the British Army. He wrote up his extraordinary tale in a best-selling book, *Fire and Sword in the Sudan: A Personal Narrative of Fighting and Serving the Dervishes, 1879–1895* (1896).

Along with everyone else, the young and impressionable Pum had heard many astonishing rumors about Slatin—not least of his circumcision, which, though he had converted to Islam, he had tried but failed to avoid (male infibulation fascinated Pum, and he kept a volume on this subject in his library in Cairo). In Kordofan, Pum had been present at a circumcision, an operation that in Europe took half an hour, many stitches, and much after-treatment, but which in the East was "over in a few seconds, required no anaesthetic, local or general (so rapid is the incision) and gives as good or better results than with us." Slatin later reversed his conversion and received absolution for it from the Pope.

Pum also spent many hours talking with General Gordon's old arch-enemy, al-Zubayr Rahma Mansur, the "Black Pasha" and the "Napoleon of the Sudan." Dealing with fanaticism and abolition, Gordon fought against this "fierce and unprincipled" slave and ivory trader whose life is recorded in his memoir, *Black Ivory and White! Or, The Story of El Zubeir Pasha, Slaver and Sultan, as Told By Himself* (1913). Al-Zubayr was in his eighties when Pum first met him at Omdurman, where he lived as a political prisoner, albeit with his women, female slaves, and servants. And he spoke well of Gordon, respectfully describing his death on the palace stairs at Khartoum, even though the general had once ridden into al-Zubayr's camp and carried off his eldest son to be executed for the many wrongs he was accused of. Al-Zubayr appeared, politically, to admire what he called this act of "justice and courage," seeming not to bear any ill will. Clad only in a voluminous nether garment, he displayed his old wounds to Pum, telling how each had been sustained. There were ninety-nine, "one for each of the attributes of Allah the Merciful, the Compassionate who has preserved me; the hundredth will be the last." Coincidentally, ninety-nine was also the magical number of children he claimed to have fathered, although as Pum looked at his shrunken old frame, he couldn't but think that he had probably been helped out a little in reaching that score. Al-Zubayr had a much-lined face, "like that of some ancient but ingratiating snake," and attributed his strength and longevity to a diet of milk, eggs, and coffee, to never smoking or drinking, and to having a daily full-body massage with *fitna*, a sickly smelling scent used by Sudanese women. Throughout his adult life, too, he made a point of always sleeping with a young girl at his side, "a good custom to which he still adhered."

Harems were often talked about among the British officers. Before the Great War, the sultan of Darfur (who sided with the Germans and was eventually flushed out by an Anglo-Egyptian detachment) was said by some to have kept "a magnificent hareem, an extraordinary and heterogeneous corps de ballet of slave-girls, women of all ages, babies, children and concubines of both sexes, all under the charge of a chief eunuch with the manner of a hen chiding her chicks." His palace was rumored to be guarded by cheetahs, each kept on a chain by a slave boy on either side of the doors that opened on to the audience chamber. The old sultans of Darfur and Kordofan "used to have their pet enemies, their best friends maybe!—especially those who had 'answered them back"—flayed, their lips sewn up and the complete pelt used as a girba, a water-skin, that was suspended on a tripod in the royal presence and from these the thirsty were invited to drink and to praise Allah."

These disturbing and surreal stories and experiences were interspersed with times of deep tranquility for Pum. Sent out from Khartoum to check on and deal with the general health of the people in an enormous area of Egypt and Sudan, he took the opportunity to explore further into the country. Trekking with the dignified, nomadic, cattle-owning Bagara people, he slept on cushions and rugs atop a cattle-born bed arched over by a wooden-ribbed shelter, lulled by the slow swaying of the bull's gait, its occasional lowing, and its heavy scent. There they all slept, much like Europeans did in express sleeping cars which bore them thundering across the continent. In these lilting shelters, Pum reflected, many of the Bagara were conceived and born, and the children were "lovely, especially their little virgins dressed only in the rabat (a short kilt of thin leather thongs dyed a red-purple)." The adults had a handsome, sleek, well-covered look common to milk-fed peoples. Their hair was worn long, thickly greased, and scented, and all their domestic articles were well designed and handmade. Pum felt a deep awe, as they seemed to travel as though part of some immutable process of nature, like a river or a glacier, rather than merely as people making their way from place to place on human business. At other times and to others he felt less generous, and when passing another caravan he described it as bearing "not bales and baggage, but 'baggages', the hareem of a Sudanese Battalion, some two or three hundred women . . . accompanied by female sergeants maintaining little semblance of order."

On a visit to Kordofan to treat the sick governor, Pum was again accompanied by his soldier-servant Ibrahim and his dogs Fez and Fagan, but this time the dogs had their own servant, a "little angel-faced café-au-lait" boy called Antar. Pum never tired of looking at the boy, so "sweet and pensive" did he find his expression. The dogs rode in soft baskets hung on either side of a lolloping camel, while the "lovely child" rode high between them. The boy's beauty made a stirring contrast, he felt, to the snub ugliness of the bulldogs, and it gave at least some visual relief from the agonies of the damned they were suffering, perched for nine days of desert trekking atop the wrong sort of camel. The group had been provided with baggage camels, *hamala*, rather than trotting ones, *hageen*, and the plodding gait of the *hamala* became very rough if you managed to get them to shift at a decent pace.

When they finally arrived in Kordofan, they found the chief medical officer, an Irishman named Stanley, waiting anxiously for them: the governor was in a critical state. It was twilight when they reached his fine old house, which had once belonged to the Mahdi and still smelled strongly of *fitna*. Inside, Pum found O'Connell, an unshaven skeleton propped on the vast, many-cushioned bed which he had had specially designed to hold three people comfortably. Now it held only one wasted man. His eyes burned from dark caverns in his grayish-yellow blotched face, his mouth grinned open, his lips were shriveled and hard. A woman crouched by him, mechanically swatting away the flies that buzzed around him. Two or three others were bundled in the semi-darkness upon the floor, and a little naked boy of seven or eight ran from one to the other, unheeded. Somewhere in a distant part of the house a shrill voice was wailing. Suspended above the sick man as he raved incoherently in his thick Irish brogue was an oil lamp, and from that hung a black, silken cord with a perch attached, on which, it was explained, there clung—although invisible to everyone but the sick man—a little hobgoblin. This was O'Connell's familiar: a friendly, intimate sort of leprechaun called Mickie, who kept just out of reach, but was cajoled and berated constantly by O'Connell in Irish and Arabic.

Cairo, 1912.

Thomas Grenville Gayer-Anderson (twin brother, born 1881), Reginald D'Arcy Anderson (1880–1917), and Robert Grenville Gayer-Anderson (1881–1945).

Henry Anderson (father, died 1927).

Mary Anderson (mother, died 1937).

Violet Mary Anderson
(sister, 1878–1910).

Tom, Pum and his son John, and mother Mary, Lavenham, Suffolk.

Recruiting sergeant, 1912.

Seconded to the Egyptian army, medical core, al-Obeid, Sudan, 1906, with dogs Fez and Fagan.

Evelyn Wynn (mother to John Gayer-Anderson).

At home in his Cairo apartment, 1920s.

A spot of restoration on the balcony, Heliopolis, Cairo, 1912.

Some of his collection on display at his Cairo apartment, 1920s.

Driving the three-wheeled Singer, nicknamed the 'Scarab,' with his twin brother Thomas and dogs Tim and Cuthbert, 1912.

As oriental secretary, 1922.

Pum diagnosed a liver abscess and operated on the governor as soon as he could at the inadequate and ill-equipped station hospital. O'Connell recovered well and was soon sent home again to great 'lu-luings' from his harem, though Mickie was never seen or heard from again. When he was almost fully well, the governor cleared out his house, let fresh air blow away the stifling smell of *fitna*, and pensioned off his wives. Within three weeks, invalided out of the service, he had severed all ties with his African home and made plans to return to Ireland and a minor role in the Home Guard. Once there, though, he only gave orders in Turkish and Arabic and acted as though he was on the parade ground at Omdurman. He was very soon a retired officer.

In Kordofan, Pum also supervised death. As ex-officio governor of the prison in al-Obeid he oversaw the public hangings of seven murderers, calculating the drop that was necessary to do the job, hearing their last words, and, finally, certifying their deaths. He admired their calm fatalism; they neither lamented nor struggled, only saying *bi-izn illah* (God willing). But he did protest that an unpremeditated murder was a crime of passion and should not be punishable with death, especially in such "an excitable people." They could be hanged for one moment of "unbalanced passion," and this seemed to Pum an excessively unfair punishment—perhaps the argument of one who knew about the fallibility of men in extreme situations. With a more objective eye, he believed that although these doomed men kicked their legs after the drop and their pulses continued to beat for up to ten minutes, conscious life was extinguished as soon as the rope tightened around their necks.

Violence in many forms was part of the culture, not just the preserve of the colonial authorities. Flogging was ritualized in Egypt and Sudan as a "barbaric and vile" means of showing off the fortitude and manliness of teenage boys, a sort of Eastern version of Henry's Spartanism. The *kurbash*, a long whip made of hippopotamus hide carried by all "Soudanese bloods," was the favored tool and could mean death for the weaker and more sensitive victims. Pum once witnessed an *akhu banat* ceremony ("the brothers of the girls"), where sixteen- to eighteen-year-old boys demonstrated their masculinity to the whole village, but especially to the girls. He thought it an extraordinary and savage sight to see the boys march around in a circle, each following the other about a yard apart, naked to the waist and chanting. In one hand each waved a *kurbash* aloft and then brought it down with full force across the back of the youth in front of him, who did the same to the one in front of him. The boys smiled, he wrote, as the blows fell and the weals appeared across their backs. Around and around they went.

7
Desert Fever

With a district as large as France to cover, Pum, like other members of the camel corps, soon organized his own trotting beasts: surefooted, comfortable to ride, and able to cover the ground at a steady eight to ten miles an hour. The animals drank only once every four to five days, and trekking like this was a fine art. On his camel, Pum carried a rifle, ammunition, a large water bottle, a few books, and enough emergency food to make him independent for a day or so, if need be. His orderly led another camel carrying more water and kitchen and camping equipment. Pum was of the "soft trekkers" school rather than Pasha Slatin's "hard-arse" school, and inclined to as much comfort as could possibly be had. Following Omar Khayyam's dictum of "The book of verse, a flask of wine and thou," Pum took good food, books, a gramophone and records, china, glass, and cutlery, and sometimes even a "thou" riding up among the master's luxuries and other paraphernalia. The "thous" who accompanied a "hard-arse" were so bundled up and bumped about as to have all the romance shaken out of them, which in Pum's opinion defeated the object of taking them along. Some trekkers he knew wouldn't go without cut glass and Georgian silver, and one friend, Stanley C. Dunn, once took along his dulcitone piano. Never did music sound more ravishing to Pum than in the incongruous setting of the immense and echoless desert, and often there was a beautiful boy's voice, too, with the yearning notes of a flute and graceful dancing figures in the firelight.

This fever for the desert was a thing to be learned. What was at first a bitter and strenuous experience could acquire, Pum thought, the same harsh allure that the sea offered to the sailor: it was something treacherous, fantastic, and terrible to be subdued and conquered. The more he trekked, the more Pum appreciated the Arab's grim regard and sardonic outlook on his environment. "God made the Sudan and then he laughed," is an Arab epigram, though Pum sometimes thought that perhaps the devil had made it.

The desert played fiendish tricks with mirage and distorted the effects of distance, disturbances of atmosphere, and electric storms. There were whirling dust devils known as *shitan*, or *haboob*, a glorious word meaning a great advancing wall of midday darkness made of electrically activated dust that could quickly shut a caravan into a weird night, with temperatures that alternately burned or froze. The unreality of the landscape obsessed those it embraced until they became devoutly or hellishly confused. In Kordofan, the billiard-table-flat deserts gave the impression that a traveler was always in the center of everything—it stuck to one and couldn't be shaken off. This unsettling sensation, the dry harsh air, the whistle and hiss of blown sand, were the stings that whipped a man into himself so that, if there was any small rift in his defenses, if he were rundown or overwrought, he succumbed to "Sudanese irritability," losing all control, humor, and proportion. Ants became elephants, and men appeared as trees walking; their jokes were all insults, and overheard words were steeped in innuendo. When he felt like this, even a mislaid collar stud in the morning could make Pum knock down his soldier-servant, abuse his cook, thrash his boy, jump on his hat, hurl the looking-glass to the ground, and generally behave as Henry used to do in one of his furies. There was only one remedy when it got like this: to get out of the desert and to stay away until he had recovered.

And the rain! The thunder and lightning, great greased forks of cold, consuming fire racing jaggedly over the flooded ground like huge, questing viper's tongues, killing whoever was unlucky enough to get in the way, melting their metal buttons into their skin. Hyenas howled in the night. One morning, when one of Pum's "camel-men" didn't get up, they discovered that a particularly brazen beast had slunk into camp and bitten a jaw-full out of the back of his skull, as one would scoop the top off a boiled egg. Some of the Fur people, the original inhabitants of Darfur, believed in a form of werewolf myth, that some men had the power to turn themselves into hyenas at night, returning to human form at dawn. Those who shot at hyenas often found their servants with bullet wounds the next day.

In southern Kordofan the desert gave way to wooded, hilly country intersected by the shallow beds of broad rivers. These rivers appeared and disappeared into the broken ground and when they dried up, the fish burrowed into the mud and sat tight. To find them, the people thumped the ground with the butts of their spears, listening for a hollow sound and then digging them out with the broad-ended blade. Pum tried it with his friend Reg Wilson, sub-governor of Kordofan, who was an excellent wet-fisherman but, as it turned out, a useless dry one. He wandered through this landscape along narrow paths, the grass high above his head, with a boy, Mukhtar, a small-bore rifle, and a scatter gun—bird-watching, examining the habits of insects, and getting lost.

Getting really lost was among Pum's most terrifying experiences in that implacable landscape, and he dealt with his fear by splitting his mind into two selves: one strong and cool, the other frightened and hysterical. The stronger would take hold of the weaker and steady him, but if either gave way, then both were truly lost: all sense of direction disappeared, neither the sun nor the stars could tell them anything. When this happened, then the thing to do was to stay put, light a bonfire, and wait for rescue, and when it came, Pum's shame was quite neutralized by his relief. Once, utterly lost and mad with thirst, he was eventually found naked and delirious. He learned to guard against sunstroke by wearing complicated headgear, though some madmen went without hats as a way of "hardening themselves up." The Sudanese were more likely than the teetotal Egyptian fellaheen to succumb to the heat when they drank *marissa*, their home-brewed buttermilk-flavored beer, but heatstroke hit everybody. Once, when the noon train arrived in Aswan in temperatures of 132 degrees Fahrenheit, there were six dead in the third-class carriages.

Pum was mesmerized by Southern Kordofan, a beautiful country whose great fortress-like mountains rose out of the land like wooded islands out of a clear vast sea. Each mountain seemed a sudden, colossal pile of granite boulders that Pum found inexplicably frightening at close quarters. Within these geological jumbles were endless intricacies of space, underground chambers, and tunnels leading away in all directions, familiar to the local people who would disappear into them and reappear further down the valley. In peacetime this was interesting, if disconcerting, but later, in the punitive expeditions Pum was on, it made it easy for the local people to hide and ambush the troops. Pum noted that they rarely came down onto the plains because the Arabs living below might carry off the women and children into slavery. He thought them astute, these Arab traders in gum, ivory, ostrich feathers, and human beings, and too well armed for the Nuba, who only had their stone hammers, flint knives, and maces.

In peacetime, as a senior medical officer, Pum had climbed one of these island mountains to meet its king and his *kagour* (wise man), and he found that many sick people had come with them, having heard that Pum was a healer. To his horror he saw that they were suffering from leprosy, and though he knew there was little he could do, he felt he needed to make some show, and make it a spectacular one. In front of the crowd he took out a brass washbasin, filled it with clear water, and dropped into it a few crystals of potassium permanganate. As he slowly stirred, great streaks and whorls of crimson dramatically manifested themselves until the liquid was a deep and impressive wine color, and the awestruck sick lined up to be anointed. Between the Nuba above and the Arabs below, there lived the Mowalid, a group that Pum described as being a "degenerate crossbreed race." They, too, were stricken with leprosy, and Pum later returned as a member of a leprosy commission to segregate the sufferers and try to bring them some relief.

The people had not been completely isolated, though, and British officers approaching Tagoi, one of the island hills, were greeted by "completely naked stone-age savages" repeatedly chanting, "Me Wild West Show, gib him mercy!" With the aid of an interpreter the officers discovered that the elder warrior was describing himself as a man of the world and calling for mercy for his followers. As a ten-year-old boy he had been in a group of women and children carried off by Arab slave traders. When, after a long and arduous journey, they reached Constantinople, he was sold into slavery to a Turkish household. Two years later he escaped and ran away with a traveling American Wild West show. Off they went to Vienna and then on a European tour until, when he had grown into a man, the show arrived in Cairo. He abandoned the troupe there and made his way back to Sudan, to Tagoi and his people.

During Pum's two years in Sudan, he was sent out on a punitive expedition intended to quell an uprising on three Nuban hills: Mandal, Sabai, and Tagoi. He left Khartoum with two Sudanese infantry battalions—one commanded by a character aptly named "Beery" Hutchinson—and they were to be met by a detachment of cavalry, artillery units, and the Camel Corps, all to march on together under the command of the adjutant-general of the Egyptian Army, El Lewa Asser Pasha. Beery was, Pum soon discovered, a sham and a blusterer with an unaccountable reputation as a military genius and daredevil. He drank *marissa* from morning to night, by which time he was more or less inanimate. His men followed both his example and the women who brewed the beer, and without them they proved useless and pitiable, suffering from sore feet, irritability, sunstroke, senile decay, and incipient delirium tremens. In this state they all boarded a steamer and chugged slowly upriver, Beery holding forth on his escapades while clutching a volume of Sophocles in Greek that he pretended to read, as the bank slid past and empty beer bottles bobbed away in their wake.

The first battle for Tagoi was carefully planned but poorly executed, as Beery's troops failed to turn up on time and the Nuba slipped through the net, going underground into the cave system to bide their time. Every village on the mountainside was deserted, even of livestock, and the "romantic" little huts fashioned of mud and straw and perched on boulders, or set between them with neat, green lawns, were bare of all pots, pans, and bedding. There was nothing to loot. Beneath their feet, though, the soldiers could hear the cattle lowing, babies crying, and women talking. The Nuba men were silent, but the soldiers knew they were there, too. Going from cave to cave, the interpreter called down to the people to come out, they would be well treated, and when a woman called back to send someone down to talk, Pum and his friend De Lancy Forth were eager to get down there and see what it was like. The commanding officer forbade it and instead sent down the interpreter, who was immediately and horribly killed. The troops then tried to smoke and starve the people out, but the caves had plentiful supplies of water and grain as well as ventilation shafts and alternative exits. In the end the troops picketed all the main entrances, and after carefully establishing some confidence with the Nuba, they persuaded them out: naked women, children, youths, and maidens, with their medleys of pots, pans, goats, chickens, beds, and bedding, came streaming out of the holes in the hills. The fine heads of cattle had to be pulled out by the horns with block and tackle. The women and children were sent back to their villages, but the "fine big boys and young men" were held captive, to be drafted eventually into drunken Sudanese battalions such as that commanded by the scurrilous Beery.

Pum thought the Nuba outstandingly handsome people, "splendid specimens," powerful and sleek with shapely legs. The less generous Rudyard Kipling had immortalized them in his poem "Fuzzy-Wuzzy" (1892). One particularly fine youth fought his captors "like a fiend" until he was overcome and shackled by six or eight Sudanese, while his "sweet little brother or son" looked on, disconsolately running to him when he was finally subdued. A *shaba* was placed on each man before he was marched away. This was a cruel contraption made from the forked branch of a tree some six feet long, of medium thickness, with the fork secured by a cord around the prisoner's neck so that the five or so feet of stem that projected behind completely hampered any untoward movement. On the move, in single file, the end of each *shaba* was held by the man following, thus forming a dejected crocodile.

The capture of the second mountain fortress did go to plan, but even though, according to Pum, the soldiers did all they could to limit the suffering and casualties among "the enemy," he found it a flagrantly distasteful one-sided fight. On Sabai, in the "rough and tumble," three Nuba were killed.

Pum had been asked to obtain as many Nuba skulls as he could for the collection of the Wellcome Historical Medical Museum in London, and he knew that this could be his chance to collect at least these few. He set about boiling down the heads of the dead men. Assisted by De Lancy Forth, he arranged three large clay pots and built and tended fires beneath them for a day and a night to free the bones from the flesh. This ghoulish activity took place in the "most lovely setting imaginable, on a flower-carpeted sward among cool green trees and great rocks," and as he bent over the pots, stirring the boiling broth from time to time with a long stick, the violence of the contrast between the place and the deed gave him a feeling of complete unreality. It seemed like a mad dream. Pum recorded that he had felt no disgust or horror at the time—neither had his friend—and soon after this incident, when he found several other bodies buried nearby, he did it again and dispatched these skulls to Sir Grafton Elliot Smith, anatomist and Egyptologist, at the Cairo School of Medicine. Pum understood that these bones eventually ended up in the Museum of the Royal College of Surgeons, London.

On the trek to Sabai, Pum had been taking grains of crude opium, which may go some way to explain the dream-like quality and his detached reaction to boiling dead men's heads in sylvan surroundings. He took the opium, he said, to boost his staying power and sustain himself on the dry trek—his lips were so dry that smiling was quite impossible. The lack of water in the desert has to be experienced to be understood, and Pum had many stories of the tragedies that extreme thirst caused, sometimes made crueler by the irony of the disaster. One such was of a caravan traveling from the Red Sea to Khartoum that never arrived. Search parties found the whole group, men and beasts dead, scattered by a sandstorm. Among the dozens of cases that lay with the dead camels was a large consignment of Schweppes soda water.

During his time in Sudan, Pum was sent into almost unknown country, among cannibalistic "wild tribes" hostile to civilization and he, at least, was excited and raring to go. As a member of the Sudan Sleeping Sickness Commission, he was charged with investigating the prevalence of the disease *(Trypanosoma gambiense)* and the distribution of the tsetse fly *(Glossina palpalis)* that carries it, and with establishing controls, including isolation camps, to try and alleviate the suffering of populations decimated by the disease in the first decade of the twentieth century. The risks of such an adventurous undertaking appealed to Pum no end.

For the journey into the "dark and little known area of The Bog" which lay between the equator and seventh parallel north, Pum collected the scientific and medical equipment he needed, plus stationery, books, clothing, supplies, and trade goods such as beads, brass and copper wire, packs of matches, and solid cones of sugar and salt, all to be used for barter. His armory, which he overestimated, was a shotgun, a double-barreled Rigby .450 (an elephant gun), a Rose Ely .303, a Mannlicher .280, a service revolver, and a small automatic. All this was carried on the backs of twenty donkeys, which were considered less likely than camels to fall prey to Negma, the tsetse-borne animal disease, but even so, their chances of survival were slight and none of them lived longer than a few months after reaching The Bog.

Along with Pum went his body-servant Abdul, "a kindly and faithful youth of eighteen," his indifferent cook, Amina, and three "donkey-boys." Everything was loaded onto an antiquated Nile steamer—the "Metemma," a flat-bottomed craft with a revolving gun turret—and the party began its trip to the impenetrable forests beyond the deserts north of Khartoum. They chugged along at four knots, passing mud banks heaving with crocodiles asleep in the sun, "their revolting pink-lined mouths wide-open." From the upper deck Pum would take aim and fire at these peaceful beasts—he called them "monsters"—with his small-bore rifle. When he hit one, it would appear to give a terrific yawn, then its mouth would snap shut as it slid rapidly into the water followed by its immediate neighbors. Pum felt no repugnance at what he did; he regarded it as a useful act, as well as good sport. He did not consider the animals sacred, as the local people did. He'd had an unholy near miss once when jumping a stream, landing with both feet on what he thought was a stone, but which turned out to be a croc-odile's head. Luckily it threw him high into the air and away from danger, but he never forgot his panic. And he recalled the time when Tom had shot and killed an enormous crocodile on the Pibor River in Abyssinia—a creature eighteen-feet long with a girth like a large ox—and had found in its belly a woman's brass bangles and other ornaments. Crocodiles were killers.

The Metemma made its slow way through the Sudd, a vast swamp-like wetland formed by the White Nile. It was tortuous to navigate, with its islands of floating, rank vegetation, mainly papyrus that grew high above the steamer. Their course would sweep in from the haunt-ing monotony of the Sudd's green "mid-ocean" to the forested edges where solid ground began again, and where they could tie up. As they took one of these bends, Pum was standing by the rail with an Ameri-can missionary and his wife whom he had taken on board, and they found themselves almost able to reach out a hand and touch a giant Shulluk youth of magnificent proportions who was standing on one leg with his other foot on his knee. Next to him was a little woman, wizened but still young. Both were quite naked. The shock of this sudden close contact with the "primeaval" startled them all, but after a short pause, the missionary recovered, turned to his wife, and thought-fully remarked in his strong Southern drawl, "Well, Sadie, after that I hope you're as proud of your sex as I am of mine."

Pum, not usually attracted to mature men, was proud. He had come across a great deal of nakedness in Africa and considered that beauty was "abundantly revealed to be very much in favour of the male." Among the "fine Nilotic tribes, Shulluks, Dinkas, Gours, etc.," he wrote, "the males are magnificent, and they know it."

But in his collection of poetry, "Obsessions," he gives another view of these magnificent men:

"Beau Savage"
To see his body nobly wrought
You'd say this savage was a God
Fashioned of bronze or ebony.
But when you view his hideous face
In all its ape-like ugliness
You'd guess the devil his sire and he
Half brother to a chimpanzee.

This poem reveals how brutality and sentimentality were irrevocably linked in some colonial attitudes, and Pum was a man of his time and place. There is a footnote, written later by Tom, which startlingly illustrates these prejudices: "The author is known to have had a strong antipathy to negroes, as well as to Jews, whom he termed 'intellectual niggers.'" This "repulsion," according to Tom, "was based on the terrible evidence of the ape in the black people; lips, teeth, nostrils, slouching shoulders, their gorilla stance, their loud voices and inane laughter . . . their sense of rhythm (which is the first human faculty a monkey acquires)."

After three weeks' slow chugging up the Nile, the party arrived at last at a post called Gigging and thankfully disembarked, but after weeks of rain it was like stepping out of a river onto a lake with a few islands dotted about. Nothing but small clumps of trees and groups of conical anthills greeted them, as far as the eye could see. The local police officer, the *ma'mour*, turned up, a kind Egyptian man who took Pum to stay in his comfortable thatched house till the flood subsided. At his door appeared "two plump little Dinka boy-girls, quite naked, and a dear little girl-boy brother ten or twelve-years-old, clad in a pair of khaki shorts which gave him an unusual, attractive, almost indecent appearance in this land of complete nakedness."

The *ma'mour* gave Pum four "nium-nium" dogs—named after the sound of lips smacking in anticipation of their delicious flavor when roasted—bred, kept, and fattened entirely for the dinner table. Indigenous to Central Africa, a region where no other domestic animals existed apart from fowl, these dogs were about the size and build of a small smooth-haired fox terrier, mousy in appearance and sharp snouted. They were unaffectionate and unsociable little beasts with vindictive pig eyes, prick ears, and very rounded rumps finished off with slightly twisted porcine tails. They never barked and seldom whined; they were independent and impudent. Pum liked them immensely, though not for dinner, and he took them with him when the party set off again on Christmas Day.

Leaving was a mistake. Adrift in a flood of biblical proportions, they were soon dripping and depressed. They waded on, often up to their knees in mud and with no sign of dry land on which to rest and put down their packs. Fed up and desperate, Pum decided to make for a group of anthills poking up above the water in the distance. Levelling the tops of the mounds as best they could, they built a platform of branches covered by a tarpaulin roof, and on this wretched homemade island they huddled with the snappy and morose nium-niums, while the miserable donkeys stood belly-deep in the lake, their heads drooping. Feeling he had to hide his feelings, being British and the "only Christian present," Pum attempted to put on a seasonal cheeriness and ordered his cook to prepare a Christmas dinner. Eventually, he got an abominable smoked and lukewarm soup disguised with Worcester sauce, cold bully beef with tepid, boiled tinned potatoes, followed by the traditional pièce de résistance, a tinned plum pudding (also tepid). He washed it down with several stiff whiskeys and made as good a show of it as he could—all eyes were upon him. But how he wished he had stayed in the *ma'mour*'s house with "those dear little savages."

Never before or after did Pum reach such depths of misery and discomfort. He was undecided whether his "inexplicable error of judgement" was the product of an exaggerated sense of duty, or the curious and almost irresistible urge that had at times obsessed him to do exactly the opposite of what he really wished or knew he should do. Perhaps it was a form of personal self-discipline, a punishment that he had to inflict in his father's absence.

Despite the terrible privations he endured to reach his destination, Pum lived what he called "The Marvellous Life" for the next two years. He was young, fit, and vigorous, plunging into the very heart of deep, unexplored forests, doctoring and doing good each day, every moment alive with interest and excitement. Traversing Sudan, he mapped out fly-infected areas, supervised working parties to cut river-clearings, and examined each village he came across for sleeping sickness. He measured yet more heads, recorded tribal customs, carefully dissected and preserved the poison fangs and pouches of snakes, and recorded and collected anthropological specimens for the Wellcome Research Laboratories. He was blissfully occupied every minute of every day for month after month.

Always on the move, Pum now led a group of some fifty carriers (most of the donkeys having died), a local police escort, and his two servants. The men carried up to forty-pound loads on their heads and walked about fifteen miles a day. And each day Pum shot game and fed them well. They looked well, too, handsome and louche. They hung strips of hippo blubber around their necks so that the oil melted by the sun oozed and slid down over their magnificent bodies. Rubbing the oil into their skin so that it gleamed and shone was an outward sign of wellbeing and contentment, and it was always accompanied by singing and joking.

Before dusk every evening they stopped to strike camp, cutting a clearing in the bush with billhooks. A hefty barrier of thorn branches, a *zeriba*, was quickly constructed, and they made them especially strong in lion or leopard country—Pum had lost one of his nium-niums to a hungry leopard. Within the *zeriba*, fires were lit to keep away insects and frighten off wild animals. Pum's bed was always beside a bonfire in the center, with the servants and policemen at a discreet distance. Nearer the perimeter, the naked carriers lay in pairs, and from time to time one would wake and replenish the fires that burned between them. At dawn Pum awoke and lay listening to the bush, planning his day. A golden glow spread almost imperceptibly in all directions, and the night sounds, the distinct, lonely roars and sudden shrieks of pain or terror, and the heavy thud of falling fruit gave way to the gregarious, busy sounds of the day—hungry twitterings of birds, gruff sleepy voices, fires crackling up, and the snorts and hysterical bray of Pum's one remaining donkey. There was the smell of smoke, of rousing men, and his morning tea.

At each village the day was spent making rounds, visiting the neat grass-woven huts that were perhaps ten feet across and raised on piles five feet or more off the ground, the open space beneath being used for cooking or lazing in the shade. He was struck by the general order and cleanliness, the excellence of the furniture and utensils the villagers made for themselves. The women displayed good sense and diligence, he wrote, while the men "also served" by lazily standing and waiting. Sometimes there were dances in which the whole village took part, ritual dances with a "sexual rhythm and significance."

Pum's job was to take their blood, something greeted with great suspicion by the people; they had a mystic and occult attitude to blood, but then so did many Europeans at this time. Blood-brotherhood was rife here, and the casting of spells was part of everyday existence. He was always treated well, though, greeted by the chief of each tribe surrounded by his hundreds of women and children, and his medicine man. Close by the chief's dwelling was always a carefully tended, leafy, sacred plant for the use of the chief and his medicine man alone. Under the influence of this plant they were seized with a "devil of divination and prophecy." It was *Cannabis sativa*, but how it had arrived there, no one knew.

Moving further south, in village after village, they found people ravaged by sleeping sickness. Some places were completely deserted, others had only the dead and dying left behind with a gourd of water and another of dough at their sides. The sick passed through a period of agitated delirium before entering a final and prolonged stage of emaciated but merciful coma. Besides these sleeping sufferers were madmen whose raving and screaming increased the horror and rang around the abandoned villages. Sometimes these poor wretches were left free to crawl about, but often they were confined behind a barred *zeriba*, either tethered to a post or with the cruel *shaba* around their necks. Pum's findings were eventually published in a government report, and his anthropological observations in "Some Tribal Customs in Relation to Medicine and Morals of the Nyam-Nyam and Gour Peoples."

At first, Pum's experiences in Africa had confirmed his belief that East and West, black and white, were worlds apart. Africa had seemed to him to be more like a different planet than a different continent. With his Victorian sensibilities, he had seen the people as "essentially different creatures whose cruelty, bestiality, ritual-murder, voodoo, mutilation, witchcraft and superstition, to us so dark and appalling, cannot be judged by civilised standards." But being there, working and living among them, he changed his mind. They were not "savages" at all but were usually "gentle, primitive, childish creatures"—unless and until what he considered the spiritual fourth dimension of incredible cruelty and superstition called voodoo infected them. The cannibals were, he wrote in his paternal manner, good-natured types who followed definite rules of etiquette: they might eat their enemies— roasted, boiled, or sun-dried—but they would never consume their own tribesmen, family, or friends. These they handed over to another cannibal people, who would return the favor, showing a delicacy of feeling toward their dead. Pum saw them as being just like any civilized men with a secret vice or kink. Although "savages" looked askance at the cannibals' peculiarities, they saw nothing unpleasant about their perverse propensity, very much, he mused, as the homoerotic sees nothing blameworthy in his.

Removed from European cultural influences, Pum was able to bask freely in his own feelings and ideas, stretching his preconceptions. His almost complete separation from white men also induced in him an intimate and comforting "thraldom." He wasn't lonely because he didn't want anyone. With a small-bore rifle and a scattergun, Pum wandered out examining and noting everything. He would pause under great trees on the banks of streams, closely watching insects or observing birds, listening to the jungle sounds of live creatures, following narrow paths through grass so tall that it met far above his head. He explored bowers and tunnels of woven branches so thickly interlaced that they completely cut out the light of the sun; he traced the courses of crystal-clear streams or the tracks of some little animal, the waft of some flower's scent—and all so intently that he was apt to lose count of time and direction.

Such was his mental and physical isolation from his "own kind" that, when he one day encountered a lone, "pink-faced European wearing a pith helmet" in this huge wilderness, his first instinct was to pass him by without exchanging a word. After a short but tough struggle with himself, he did manage to greet the man with just sufficient civility. The young man gave Pum a cheery response, so he was forced to stop and talk. This encounter was the start of the lifelong friendship between Pum and Stanley C. Dunn, the Sudan government geologist, the man who traveled with his dulcitone, though this time he was traveling light.

But Pum did occasionally meet other men who were as happy as he to be cut off from the outside world, one of whom was a man he referred to only as Walsh, an inspector of roads and transport and a captain in a line regiment, "a delightful young man who showed no signs of ever growing up." This Peter Pan figure was engaged to a girl at home and exchanged cables with her once a month, his only contact with the outside world. Walsh and Pum, Lost Boys both, formed a permanent camp for themselves away from the villages, and on two donkeys that had survived Negma they rode about exploring, trotting along with a guide running next to each of them. It was, thought Pum, complete paradise.

The land was thickly wooded, riven by streams with clear pools and cool waterfalls, and Pum and Walsh felt "like schoolboys," throwing spears, shooting with bows and arrows, fishing and canoeing. This was elephant country, too. Neither of them had exercised their game licenses, which allowed them to shoot two bulls a year—cows being strictly preserved—and to return to Khartoum without having "bagged their quota" would have been to lose face, and a lot of money. Raw ivory was then fetching twelve shillings a pound at Omdurman, and a pair of tusks seldom weighed less than one hundred twenty pounds; many officials stationed out there added between £150 and £800 a year to their income in this way. For the cool and experienced shot, it was a sure and easy sport. The governor of Mongalla Province, a strange and lonely Welshman called Owen Pasha (Lieutenant Colonel Roger Owen), who treated his servants and his flower garden with equal tenderness, usually killed his two elephants from his bungalow verandah, standing in his pajamas taking his morning cup of tea. Pum and Walsh, though, were less insouciant.

Having decided that "the time was ripe for the slaughter of [their] first elephants," they sent out trackers to locate a herd and set off at dawn a week later, each armed with one heavy and one light rifle. Downwind of the elephants, they carefully watched and crept from place to place, looking for the bulls with the best tusks. The air was full of the pungent smell of the huge beasts; their great droppings lay steaming all around. Pum picked his bull and decided on taking him with a "heart-shot"—an easier kill because the fatal area is three times the size of that of the "head-shot," which meant aiming at a small, deep, cup-like depression between the earhole and eye. He "drew a bead" on the bull, supporting his heavy rifle with an arm against the branch of a tree, and squeezed the trigger. "That great living creature, without a move, without a sound just collapsed—dropped down on to his hunkers where he stood and after a few tremors lay dead!" To be sure of his kill, Pum shot him again and then quickly squatted down behind the tree. His brief, puffed-up sense of exaltation at his kill was just that, and it evaporated in a second. He was swamped with guilt and horror at what he had so easily, so simply and brutally, done.

The licensing rules, the monetary gain, the raw excitement of the hunt, all belied the actual killing and the awesome panic of trumpeting, screaming, and squealing that he had unleashed with his shots. From a peaceful quiet the whole forest had broken into violent, excited life. Elephants crashed madly around in all directions, branches cracked, and almost immediately there came three more reports in rapid succession: "Walsh had engaged!" As the tumult died away, Walsh rushed over to him, hot and distressed, crying, "I've done a terrible thing! I've shot a lady and what's more I believe she is far gone in the family way!"

Unprepared, Walsh had heard Pum's shot and, seeing the herd breaking up, had fired at the biggest head he could see—and it had ended in a catastrophe. Pum couldn't say anything, there was nothing to be said. Walsh had done the unthinkable. Pum was full of pity, for the elephants and for his friend who would have to confront his shame and inform the Game Preservation Authorities. Stunned by their behavior, they stood and watched as two great frightened cows came up to the inert bull and, standing pathetically over his corpse, pushed and pulled him with their trunks as if trying to wake him. Finally, shaking their heads, they turned and wandered away.

From all around, naked men appeared, shouting and exulting. Taking no notice of Pum and Walsh, they swarmed like ants over the vast carcass and, apparently without method or direction, commenced work as if to an intuitive system, opening the great body with sharp, huge-bladed spears, pulling out the still motile viscera, cutting off huge chunks of skin and meat with their knives, and chopping away with small hatchets to free the tusks. The ivory they had bagged weighed a good one hundred forty pounds. Pum was elated once more, the horror receded, but Walsh remained deeply depressed. They parted regretfully and never saw nor heard from each other again.

Although Pum had enjoyed his friend's charming, boyish, adventurous ways, the elephant shoot had produced in him a "rather superior and patronising sympathy." He began to feel that his success "was the simplest and paying form of murder: you just pulled a trigger and received a dividend of of seventy pounds," and it highlighted Walsh's abject failure. This pomposity and emotional detachment was soon reversed once more, though, when his second hunt went badly wrong and he needed many shots to kill his next elephant, which died slowly and in heart-rending distress. Not only this, but jungle fires and broken country soon had Pum lost on his way back to camp, his carriers deserted him, and he was forced to leave his haul of ivory behind, keeping only a few toenails that he could carry.

When he finally reached help, more dead than alive, at Shambe, he was met and cared for by the British inspector, Captain Percy Matthew

Dove, and lived with him for three weeks while he recovered. Dove was a keen naturalist and a lover of strange and beautiful things, and their time and walks together weaned Pum back from his silent ways and solitary habits. The members of Dove's household were all chosen for their beauty, among them his *suffragi*, a "handsome, light-colored Berberi lad" named Ibrahim, and a small, very "lovely and amusing houseboy." But chief among his staff, "so fair to look upon was a buxom local wench whom Dove called his 'Housekeeper,' a delightful mis-nomer the incongruity of which pleased us both." This girl, owned in all ways by the British officer, was followed about by a "sweet little copper-colored cupid of two who wore a shirt so short that it scarce concealed his navel." Dove wasn't quite so sanguine about owning the child, however. "She says it's mine," he said, "but I strongly suspect that damned suffragi. Now, perhaps you as a Doctor . . . ?" Pum picked up the little boy and looking into his eyes proclaimed, "They are the eyes of a Dove." The officers, at least, were pleased with the situation.

Pum continued to risk his life hunting elephants, their screams of fury sounding like some terrible brass instrument or a "taxicab skid-ding in a London street" as they bore down on him. In one incident, he barely escaped by hiding in a termite hill, but in his fear and delirium he again got lost in a thunderous storm that followed the hunt, and was only rescued when his hunter-guide and two servants returned for him. They made camp, and he spent days in a high fever, unable even to read the labels on his medicine bottles, so he couldn't treat himself, which was perhaps, he thought afterwards, no bad thing.

As thin as a death's head, with shrunken eyes and a thick, red, untidy beard, he had lost his apparatus, books, and records, his clothes had decayed, he had only one nium-nium left, and all his ivory had been stolen. He found himself in the company of two Spaniards on a shoot-ing trip and "Karamojo" Bell, the most celebrated of all ivory hunters. Walter D.M. Bell (1880–1954) was a Scottish adventurer. Orphaned as a small boy, he had run away to sea when he was thirteen, panned for gold in the Yukon, and then joined the Canadian Mounted Rifles during the Boer War. He took to hunting big game and running safaris in the wilderness of Karamojo, North Eastern Uganda, and was reported to have killed over 1,500 elephants during his "career," making himself a huge fortune. Eventually, having retired to Scotland, he wrote several autobiographical books about his bloody exploits. Pum knew him as a reserved and silent man, "most attractive . . . with a pair of amazingly light blue eyes." He seemed like some Elizabethan humanist, combining tenderness and delicacy with cruelty and violence. He was practical and romantic, with an uncanny feeling for the country and acute skill in marksmanship. But however much Pum admired Bell, he had been on his last elephant hunt. Things had turned out so badly that he made up his mind never to visit the heart of Africa again and, especially, never to fire another shot in sport or in vain.

After his two years' service in the wilds of Sudan he was very glad indeed to get back to Khartoum, to the comforts of brick walls, stout doors, and electric lamps. He was due for a leave of absence to England and thereafter a change of station, leaving behind him a mess full of friends, "a few ladies of my acquaintance, sorrowing but perhaps soon to be consoled," and all his animals. The night before his departure, he was returning on the crowded ferry from the mess at Omdurman under a full moon, with the Nile boiling and swirling at its height, when a shocking event shook any dwindling sense of complacency he may have retained. An Egyptian officer hurrying on board at the last minute and watched by all on deck lost his footing and fell into the river. He immediately disappeared. There was a gasp and some giggles from the onlookers—it was, as he later recalled in his memoir, so "like one of those joke-mishaps one saw at the cinema"—the man would surely bob back up to the surface in a moment or two, looking ridiculous and everyone would laugh. But he didn't. There was something particularly appalling to Pum in this abrupt annihilation, the irrevocability of the accident. "A man was there, of this world, one second and was gone the next, completely gone, leaving no trace, no ripple on the River's surface." On the battlefield such sudden dismissals had not rocked Pum, but here, with the moon, the gaiety, and no tangible proof of the man remaining, it seemed arbitrary and desperately frightening.

Perhaps a crocodile had come down on the flood or, more likely, a Nile turtle, a huge beast that would grab and hang on to anything that touched it, not out of malice but from fear.

Pum's journey home to England in 1909 took him from Cairo to Alexandria, Athens, and then by train across Europe. He went straight to see his mother at Blackheath, London, near to D'Arcy and Tom, who were stationed at Woolwich.

On the first mile of his journey he was accompanied by friends—Europeans, Egyptians, and Sudanese, half the garrison and civil service were there. There were Greek merchants on donkeys, Arab sheikhs on camels, grateful patients, and two or three "young-bloods"—dervishes dressed to the nines—all of them turned out to see him off. Now that he was leaving Egypt, Pum realized how much he had changed, how he had lost his innocence and the first fine raptures that had brought him. He knew that these last two years had been the most extraordinary of his life so far. The lasting effect of it reinforced in him an intense love of solitude, of getting away from his own kind and retreating into himself: he believed this to be essential to his future wellbeing.

His experiences had wrought an indelible effect on his psyche and had thrust him into maturity, whether he liked it or not. But this did not mean that he was now emotionally free: he considered that he had retained his "emotional paralysis" in his public dealings, but had successfully built himself a private, surreal inner life. These were now his markers of manhood, inculcated in him since childhood.

8
"Psychic Tomb-Robbing"

I solation and adventure had changed Pum to such an extent that medicine no longer interested him. Cairo and its pleasures did, though, and he felt a powerful urge to get back there. In late 1909 he landed himself a new position as inspector of recruiting for the Sa'id, the seven provinces of Upper Egypt, and from his base in Cairo he journeyed out and about on long tours.

Pum's pleasure and enthusiasm were matched by the reluctance of the young fellaheen to be recruited by him. Egyptian soldiery was disgracefully paid and treated, and casualties were high from neglect, disease, and active service in Sudan. Unsurprisingly, some Egyptian mothers went to terrible extremes to have their sons exempted: little boys were purposely blinded in one eye by pricking with a red-hot needle, while wealthier parents relied on bribery and trickery. Should their sons be taken, mothers would set up great wails of lamentation, or "lu-luings" as Pum called them, as if their boys were already dead, their faces "hideous with exaggerated expressions of grief . . . they rent their dirty black gowns and threw handfuls of dust on their heads." Recruitment being considered the equivalent of a death sentence, and sons being vital to a family's economic survival, it seems harsh to accuse them of exaggeration.

The young fellaheen were called up twice a year to be medically examined, and from those passed as fit, a small number were chosen by ballot, the rest placed "under call" to be held in reserve. Each of Pum's tours lasted a month or so, during which he visited each town, staying in government rest houses along with his small staff. After an early breakfast he would ride out on a horse, escorted by mounted police, kicking up clouds of dust along the roads and canal banks and through villages, with much officious shouting to clear the way. Merkaz was a typical town, big enough to warrant a police post, prison cells, a law court, and a dense crowd that would gather, excitedly shouting and crying. The prospective conscripts squatted fatalistically in the deep dust surrounded by family and friends. Inside the local hall, the recruiting commission seated themselves behind tables, scales, and measuring apparatus, and the naked youths were led in. All those shorter than 167 centimeters were considered below standard and released permanently without further examination. The taller ones were passed on to Pum, who inspected them thoroughly and detained them if he thought them fit, "much to their chagrin and alarm." The rejected youths rushed joyously from the hall, still naked, into the arms of their rapturous families, who embraced and kissed them wildly and bore them away. The unlucky ones were greeted with wailings of "ya akhhi, ya akhhi!" ("my brother, my brother!"). The crowd, partly celebrating, partly grieving hysterically, swallowed up the naked boys and swayed to and fro in a confusion only increased by the police cordon making a great show of mercilessly beating them with whips, though taking care to land the resounding whacks only on the gowns of the men. Pum attributed the displays of emotion as "just the dramatic and excited sham so dear to the Egyptian"; the presence of vendors crying out to sell breads, sweetmeats, sweet drinks, and sherbets, flashing and clashing their brightly polished brass drinking bowls added to the "typical Eastern din."

Much as Pum objectified the Egyptian people, their culture fascinated him. He liked to watch the *huwa*, the snake charmers, turbaned men of the Rifai order, each with a globular basket writhing with deadly serpents. Among them there would be a few toothless, veteran cobras for fooling the crowds, but much of the action was genuine. Snakes infested Egypt, and each year about twenty were cleared from the army stores. The charmer who got this job had to strip naked apart from a single outer garment, to make sure he didn't steal anything while he was in there, before he entered the store with his basket and long stick, weaving his way through the interminable galleries piled high with clothes and equipment. Chanting a slow, rhythmic dirge as he progressed, every so often he poked a pile of overcoats and out popped a snake and came wriggling toward him. Usually they were harmless, but sometimes there were horned vipers, adders, and occasionally a cobra. These were treated with the greatest respect: the charmer might take up to fifteen minutes to maneuver it into position, then feint with his hand before gripping it just behind the head and plunging it into his basket. Pum was entranced by the whole performance, likening it to bullfighting. The *huwa* were said to eat snakes' livers to protect them from the poison, but they nearly all came to the same end: bitten and killed. One charmer he knew, Moussa, had died within ten minutes of a cobra bite, just as his father and grandfather had before him, and as his son, a "bright handsome boy of thirteen," would surely one day, too.

Cairo was an extravagant and gay place in the Season, full of the "smart set" and American and English tourists wanting to immerse themselves in the fad for Egyptology. The work of Flinders Petrie, archaeologist and first chair of Egyptology in England, who had surveyed the Pyramids in 1880, had ignited this burgeoning interest. Many rich, eligible young women arrived in the city, and Pum noted that toward the end of their Egyptian service, many penniless *bimbashi*s contrived to get themselves engaged to one of these just before they had to relinquish their freedoms to settle down into a "greyer, more reasonable existence"—something he himself was to narrowly avoid. His friend, Captain Malcolm Leckie, an easy-going chap devoted to what Pum coyly called the "cult of Venus," led such a carefree life and one that, like "British supremacy," was still largely unchallenged. Leckie and another British officer had a mutually satisfactory polyandrous ménage: they "kept and shared a charming French lady and her baby girl." The two "husbands" arranged matters so that they never chanced to meet on the stairs, each keeping strictly to his allotted days.

The French "wife" told Pum that Leckie had "les yeux spermatiques," but Pum thought him "myopic and unable to play ball games," hence his concentration on women. Leckie kept Egyptian girlfriends, too, and had a notebook of useful phrases that included "ya bint" ("Oh, girl"), "ya bekr" ("Oh, virgin"), and "wa tithak leh lamma ana adrab tiz-ak?" ("And why do you laugh when I smack your backside?"). He indulged in good works, too, chiefly in the Society for the Redemption of Fallen Girls, and any ill-treatment of animals made him quite furious.

In 1912, Pum used his growing influence to arrange for Tom to be seconded into the Egyptian Army as well, and soon Pum, Tom, Leckie (who was inspector of recruiting for the Nile Delta as Pum was for the Sa'id), and a terrier named Zwintz were sharing an apartment on the road to Heliopolis. Pum accumulated many animals in his Cairo homes—he had variously kept a pet hyena that eventually escaped, two cheetahs that he reared on lentil soup, a gazelle, and a wild cat whose eye teeth he tried to extract under chloroform, though at the first whiff of the drug it died, "much to my surprise and sorrow." There was a chameleon that expired during a thunderstorm trying to keep up with the colors, a tortoise, a lame wild duck, a shoebill stork, a monkey that took to drink, and, of course, the bulldogs, Fez and Fagan.

This parody of a family that Pum constructed lived in Beit al-Madara (the house of the telescope), which had been built as an observatory by Khedive Ismail Pasha. It was a substantial stone house set in a large garden and surrounded by a high wall. Their flat had six large rooms, a roof garden where a miniature donkey called Butn lived in a tiny horsebox, and the unused observatory that towered over them all. They kept a tandem dogcart and drove out regularly through the already difficult and badly regulated Cairo traffic, to play polo on two light grey Arab ponies at the famous Ghezireh Sporting Club. Later, they bought a small three-wheeled Singer "autocar," one of the very earliest motor-driven vehicles in the city; black and low, it was nicknamed "The Scarab." It constantly broke down, and when one night it was mysteriously destroyed by fire outside Shepheard's Hotel, Pum was quite put off and vowed never to own another car.

In November 1912, with the five-day feast of Eid al-Adha approaching, Pum, Tom, Leckie, and Zwintz boarded a government steamer and set off on a jaunt to Esna, visiting the temple complex. They arrived on November 22 and, after a late breakfast, set out on foot with a soldier-servant to see the town. Strolling along the foreshore, they passed through the lowest quarter, full of brothels and cheap bars crowded with the drunk and drugged, celebrating the festival. The British occupation was not terribly popular at the time, as Pum put it, and the place was simmering with resentment as they threaded their way past the numerous feluccas moored on the Nile's mud banks. Some local boys began shouting and making lewd gestures, and Pum's servant rushed at them with his stick, catching one boy a blow that sent him crashing into the water and hitting his head on the rudder of a boat on his way down. They quickly pulled him out and Pum examined him, finding "nothing more amiss than a slight cut on the forehead from which blood oozed." But it looked bad enough to the gathering crowd, and the local revelers were soon on their feet crying, "The Affrangis [Europeans] have killed Ahmed!" and "The English have murdered the son of Abdullah the sailor!"

A dangerous crowd swarmed down to the scene, gesticulating and crying for revenge. Pum tried to quell them by shouting out in Arabic that they were British inspectors in the Egyptian government, but his voice was drowned out just as he felt the first crack of someone's stick on his shoulder. The three men and the dog (their servant had disappeared) managed to keep together and fight off the mob as they struggled back toward the safety of the steamer, a good half a mile away. Their unorganized assailants didn't try to cut them off, but as they made the last three hundred yards along a narrow path they found it flanked by a high wall and the crowd above pelted them with bricks. Fortunately, these were only the softer, sunbaked variety and the men were wearing their helmets, but Tom was hit on the forehead and fell to the ground, stunned. He begged them to go on and leave him, but they all believed this would mean his certain death and managed to get him up, wipe the blood from his eyes—he thought he had gone blind—and stagger on beneath the fury of the enraged locals. At the last moment one of the town's notables, a Coptic Christian named Mustafa Hetta, intervened and held the mob back until the three could make the landing stage and board the steamer.

With most of the steamer crew on shore somewhere, the small, exhausted group lined up on deck armed with revolvers and shotguns. This checked things a little, long enough for Leckie to cut the mooring ropes and set the boat adrift. A swift Nile current dragged them away and there arose a "terrible animal roar of baffled fury" accompanied by an ineffective volley of missiles aimed in their retreating direction. And, as usual in Egypt, Pum wrote dismissively, the police turned up just as the trouble was over. With great pleasure they watched them lay into the people and arrest a good few of the ones they didn't like. It was a frighteningly close shave, but after the first few seconds of fear it had become an impersonal and rarefied affair "made tense by a grim concentration and haunted by sub-human fiendish faces, each intent on murder." Zwintz the terrier had enjoyed it enormously, barking and snapping as he appeared and disappeared between the legs of the mob. The vanished servant later returned and told them that he had been captured and kept prisoner until the affair was over, and Pum felt sure this story was true because he knew the man to be "brave and devoted." He stitched up the gash on his brother's head and treated all their abrasions and bruises. They were so stiff after the brawl that they could hardly move for two days, while the dog ran from man to man, puzzled at their indolence.

Upwards of fifty local men were arrested during the fracas, though apart from ten or so ringleaders it was impossible to point the finger of guilt except to say that it was certain the rest had been among the "hundreds of evil, excited and bloodthirsty faces imprinted on [their] minds." Forty were detained for trial. The incident caused quite a stir in Cairo, and Pum was summoned to explain the matter to Kitchener, a man whom Kipling had called "a fatted Pharaoh in spurs," and whom T.E. Lawrence thought, according to Pum, to be "a great man, if clay-footed, wooden and normally dull." Kitchener was upset at the incident having arisen at that critical time, but not to the degree that he forgot to ask if Pum had found any antiques worth having while he was there. The three "had their tails twisted," were officially interrogated, and an enquiry was opened. The upshot was a return to Esna and a trial lasting just one day, which "was most expeditiously run by an Egyptian judge." All the suspects were found guilty and sentenced to various overlong terms of imprisonment or floggings; the town was put under curfew and its tourist trade restricted for a considerable time. All this, Pum wrote later, revealed the unreasoning and inhuman ways of the time, yet it had filled them all with a sense of vengeful justice done. They followed up with a holiday in Luxor.

Leckie, a year younger than Pum and a student at Guy's Hospital at the same time as he, was killed in the Great War less than two years later. His obituary appeared in the *Guy's Hospital Gazette* on January 2, 1915, written by Arthur Conan Doyle, whose second wife, Jean, was Leckie's sister. The brothers-in-law had become great friends despite an age gap of some twenty years, so much so that Leckie had given Conan Doyle the guinea he had been paid for his first fee as a doctor, and the author wore it always on his watch chain. When Lily Loder-Symonds, a close friend of Jean's and bridesmaid at her wedding, claimed to have received a message from Leckie after his death, in the form of automatic writing, Conan Doyle was immediately keen to know more. She gave him details of a private conversation about the guinea between the two men, information that the writer had thought was known only to himself and the dead man. This apparent psychic revelation convinced him of the truth of Spiritualism, a belief that brought him great comfort, as he had lost seven members of his family between 1906 and the end of the Great War. He became a member of the Ghost Club, a group that at different times counted among its members Charles Dickens, W.B. Yeats, Siegfried Sassoon, and Julian Huxley. They met to discuss different forms of psychic phenomena, including second sight and Egyptian magic.

Conan Doyle's relation to Leckie and his interest in Spiritualism and antiquities meant that he and Pum got on well, and he asked Pum for help with his own collecting. Writing from Shepheard's Hotel, he asked,

If you have an Isis carrying Horus among your "spares" I should be glad to have it if it is within my means. I have some thoughts (if I have any spare cash) of making a little Cabinet museum of Comparative Religions—are there not some old Egyptian figurines of a man-God put to death between two malefactors. I seem to have read of it. A figurine of an old Egyptian priest showing where our vestments and tonsure came from, would also be the sort of thing. Have you any pieces which bear upon this—or are they attainable? Expect you at 8 tomorrow—if you can come a little earlier do.

In the years up to 1914, Pum had done an extraordinary amount of dealing and collecting. As a recruiting officer, traveling the length of the Nile several times a year, he got to know local traders who would dash up to him wherever his boat docked to show him their finds. Small objects fascinated him and were easily portable: scarabs, figurines, jewelry, glassware, seals, crystal, and ostraca; a favorite piece was a tiny phallic emblem of Ptah (who he said was the god of learning and lechery), which he wore continuously until he died. He also collected the occasional piece of furniture, carpets, paintings, silks and embroidered Arab costumes, relief fragments, coffins, and such like. He didn't rule out relatively modern objects either, and later acquired pieces from Turkey, Persia, Syria, and India where Tom was stationed in the 1920s. Any object, even the most prosaic, might catch his eye and strike him with its particular beauty.

In late 1913, on a visit to Constantinople to see the bazaars of the city, he found many strange and beautiful pieces, everything was "gayer and more European than the antiquities of Cairo." There were clocks and watches of every kind, date, and design, including early English lantern clocks, London-made in Oliver Cromwell's time. There were music boxes and mechanical singing birds, carved gilt boxes, mirrors, miniatures, and manuscripts. He bought a lot. On his way back he stopped at Smyrna, acting as British consul, and met with a Dutch-English settler, Alfred Oscar van Lennep, an antique dealer who had a great many Tanagra figurines—"Greek colored terracottas of some beauty"—wrought with laughter and vulgarity, grotesque and pornographic. Pum would make a "striking" collection of Roman obscenities, most of them "redeemed by a droll humour and delightfully free technique," which he presented to the Wellcome Museum in 1943. In Smyrna, too, he bought a large, wrought-iron coffer or ship's safe for £3, beautifully ornamented externally but locked and without a key. He had a lot of trouble getting it through customs—they were looking for hashish—but with generous baksheesh he got it home. A Greek mechanic at the military hospital in Abbasiya agreed to unpick the lock, and with an electro-magnet plus heating, hammering, oiling, and probing, he finally opened it. The lock took up the whole of the inside of the lid, about three and a half feet by two, and it had sixteen large bolts fitting into all four sides which, as they turned, set off alarm bells that rang in rapid repetition as the bolts were shot or withdrawn. It was dated 1634. Within the safe was a little "Holy of Holies" with a lid of similar design and six bolts. Pum sold it, eventually and satisfyingly, to the Benaki Museum in Athens for "a very considerable sum."

Collecting and dealing became a serious occupation from this time on, compelling and instinctive. So compelling, in fact, that it became the main business of his life, to the detriment of his service ambitions. Egypt was the cradle and storehouse of civilizations, and Cairo was a natural center for all Middle and Far Eastern art, tapping Persia, India, and China. He was tempted by beauty and ridiculously low prices, and although at first he tried to be selective, he soon found himself incapable of limitations and gathered up anything that he fancied. The Greek shopkeepers he often went to in the "historical Eden" of Fayoum had, he thought, no idea of the rarity and value of the objects they sold him. This was the "most exciting and fascinating place I know from an historical and antique-collecting point of view. Nowhere in the world can one see history and pre-history more abundantly and consecutively written." Searching through their trays and drawers of common stuff, he could take away magnificent man-made objects covering a period of twenty thousand years for very little money indeed. His haul might include a beautifully flaked flint knife, a pre-dynastic ornamented pot, a fragment of an early dynasty stone-relief, a pharaonic Eighteenth Dynasty sculptor's model in limestone, a Saitic bronze figurine, a hand from a Ptolemaic wooden statue, a Greek terracotta head, an iridescent Roman glass bottle, or a Coptic stone relief. The findings were endless, almost hallucinatory.

There were mistakes made, though. Pum and Tom got quite carried away once, and bought up many wooden figures which all turned out to be *khazooks* (fakes) and which later fed a sacrificial bonfire. But in the main he was adept at selecting pieces and soon considered himself expert at cleaning, repairing, and restoring them, enhancing their beauty and raising their value up to a hundredfold. The bronzes were often "so encrusted with salts, strongly incorporated chemically and mechanically with sand and other extraneous matter," that they required careful flaking and expert chipping to expose the original surface. Pum quite quickly found that he became a recognized authority on Egyptian antiques and was frequently consulted by others in cases of doubt. He soon learned to spot a *khazook* (a delightful word, he thought, which could be applied to sham persons as well as the objects commonly on display in many important museums, especially in America).

It was his mania for collecting that had brought Pum to his first meeting with Kitchener, a "keen and rather indiscriminate" collector. The versatile Ronald Storrs was Kitchener's Oriental secretary and asked Pum to come over and check out his boss's collection, especially his bronzes. Pum found talking with Kitchener a little unnerving because he seemed to look sideways over his head, due to a cast in one eye. His ruthless acquisitiveness was well known in Cairo. Once, when he was being taken around the government offices in Dongola Province, he spied a locked door and demanded to know what was behind it. The governor told him it was full of antiques that had been found and brought in and that they sent it all off to the museum in

Khartoum once a year. "'Don't do that,' said 'K' sternly. 'Send it to me at the Residency.'" And they did. Pum believed Kitchener to be, if not overtly unscrupulous, then at the very least coercive in obtaining what he wanted, and decided he would never let him near his own collection.

Pum felt that his intensely intuitive psychic experiences gave him an edge in his collecting. His knowledge, he thought, was more profound and true than that delivered by the recognized senses, and he believed that many of his better finds were guided by this receptivity. From his early days as a collector, Pum had experienced a "meant feeling" about certain objects, one of inevitability and wonder, accompanied by unusual happiness. He believed that on these occasions a telepathic bond was set up between himself and the particular antique concerned, whereby a "Beauty in Distress" called to him—distress due to neglect, or lack of appreciation, danger, or destruction. These sensations seemed to him to be far more than merely odd coincidences; they were psychic influences at work, and he felt a certain paranormal quality of "apprehension" when touching an object.

The first of his "Psychic Adventures" with antiques happened in Cairo, just before the Great War, when he bought the upper part of a rare bronze statuette of Toth, the ibis-headed god. It had "silver-inlet" eyes and was of very high quality craftsmanship; it had been cleanly but jaggedly broken at the waist. A year later and a thousand miles away in Luxor, he called on an Egyptian friend, neither dealer nor serious collector, and on his writing desk spotted the lower part of such a statuette. Now Pum often collected the fragments of such statuettes, which often broke at the narrow waist, so that he could—legitimately, he thought—complete them. He picked up this one, handling it as he talked, and was overcome with a feeling of pleasure much greater than he usually experienced when touching beautiful things. "Take it as an Abbassiah," said his friend. "It is only the wrong half of a god." Back in Cairo, the two halves of Toth interlocked perfectly, and Pum was struck with extreme happiness and a sense of inevitability.

He began to feel, or hear, that psychic call more often. Searching for furniture for the observatory flat, he went to the European second-hand bazaars to look for a bed—something he would not ordinarily have done for fear of bringing bugs into the house. On a very hot day he took off for the small shops run by Greeks, where he knew no one, and went into the first that took his fancy—all very out of character. In the back of a dirty, disordered junk-room he saw something that made him gasp. Propped against the wall with its legs turned outwards was what looked like an ordinary couch, an *angareeb*, but he recognized it as an extremely ancient Egyptian bed. He was staggered and struggled to hide it, and, though he was in a "dream-state from excitement . . . full of supreme exaltation," and despite the fact that, ordinarily, he would have balked at the possibility of buying bedbugs, he felt compelled to have the piece.

As casually as he could, he asked to look at it, and it was pulled out with its new plush and gaudy mattress attached. It was shorter and broader than beds he had seen in the museum, only about five feet long, and had finely carved bulls' feet at the end of each leg, whereas there were usually two bulls' feet and two lions', or all four were lions'. It was in fine condition, hard and sound. The new mattress sat on a cheap modern frame, but he could see a deep groove beneath in the *sunt* (acacia wood) still holding fragments of the original palm-fiber cording that had once crisscrossed the bed. The "little Greek storekeeper-dealer" dismissed it as an ordinary Sudanese *angareeb* and said he would take 100 piastres (about £1 then) for it and not a penny less, implying that the bargaining could now begin. Pum was in such a state of excitement that he paid him his money straight away without even worrying that this was unprecedented in such transactions. The man was delighted but suspicious, which threw Pum into a panic of discovery, and he immediately called for a hammer, took off the mattress and the new boarding, and carried the bed out to a waiting cab. "But you are forgetting the mattress, Effendi!" called the shopkeeper, and when Pum said he could keep it as baksheesh, he cried pityingly, "God keep you, Effendi, but it is worth far more than the bed." Pum drove off in ecstatic triumph with his prize.

The bed caused a great stir among fellow Egyptologists, for they hadn't seen anything like it before. Gaston Maspero, then director of antiquities to the Egyptian government, came to view it and declared it pre- or proto-Dynastic, dating from about four thousand years BCE. He noted that people of that time slept, and were buried, on their sides with their knees drawn up, so that their beds, including their funerary beds, were short and broad. The bed eventually went to the Egyptian Museum of Stockholm for a considerable sum.

Most of these pieces had been "raped," Pum wrote, from ancient tombs, for he was collecting in a "portion of the globe more calculated to entice and satisfy" than any other, the "cradle and storehouse" for all Middle and Far Eastern art. His language didn't mean that he was averse to this sort of violation himself: for example, he had taken the mummy cartonnage known as the "Little Black Princess," which ended up in his Cairo house, from its tomb at Thebes when he was there with his friends Arthur Boland and Mrs. Warren Low. He had pilfered it at dusk in a sand cart and got it on board a chartered boat to Luxor. The reluctant boatmen took it across to the Bella Donna House (made famous in Robert Hichens's novel *Bella Donna*, published in 1909), where Pum's friend Owen Pasha was living. Pum and Boland carried it up from the landing stage, deposited it in Owen's shed, and the next day sent it to Cairo by train in a box marked "Fruit—with care." It was, Pum thought, a form of "Psychic Tomb-Robbing."

There is always this disturbing mix, in Pum's recollections, of the mystic and the pragmatic, but though the former often seduced him, he was never completely beguiled. Time and time again Pum was faced with the ethical problem of dealing in the objects that so entranced him. He could not escape the idea that the professional Egyptologist was no more than a tomb robber and body snatcher: though "the grave he desecrates be five thousand years old and the religion he profanes long dead, he cares nothing for the individual to whom the tomb belonged and will dig him up and cast him aside without a thought— and no one thinks any the worse of him."

Much digging was done in the "sacred name of scientific research," whereas, Pum thought, if the same people had plundered a European church or graveyard and dug up some long-dead old lady to secure her locket and rings, no punishment would be too great for so vile and wanton an act. Less scientific tomb robbers had been working all over Egypt since the earliest of times, scouring the higher uncultivated rocky ground, mostly by night, where the desert cliff joins the sown[1] and most of the ancient burials are sited. They took, and were still taking in Pum's time, any loose objects they unearthed, but they also defaced reliefs and inscriptions by chiseling out fragments to bring back for sale. The traffic was highly illegal and the looters liable to imprisonment, yet the shop owners and other middlemen were allowed to buy the plunder and, until the 1970s, obtain a license permitting them to resell the objects. The pieces went to other small dealers, on to larger ones in Luxor, Cairo, and Alexandria, and then to wealthier clients in London, Paris, and New York, the prices mounting in leaps and bounds throughout the process. The whole system and the regulations governing it were, Pum thought, ill-conceived and ineffective in the extreme, doing little but encouraging the destruction and scattering of antiques and the defacement of tombs and temples.

But the regulations were also convenient to anyone who knew the true value of an object. They enabled Pum to short circuit the larger dealers by going directly to the small fry and getting first choice of the prizes. He bought from the shopkeepers or from the original finders, the *sebakheen*, who had an ancient and legal right dating from the days of the Turkish suzerainty to sift the *sebakh*, the dust and debris from a site. And from these families he got the rarest pieces for a tiny fraction

---

1 Here, 'sown' comes from a translation of one of the Rubaiyyat of Omar Khayyam. These were much loved in Pum's days—and still are—especially from the translations of Edward FitzGerald. The following translation of his explains the juncture of desert and agricultural land:

"With me along the strip of herbage strown
That just divides the desert from the sown,
Where name of Slave and Sultan is forgot—
And pity Sultan Mahmud on his throne."

Also, see Gertrude Bell's *The Desert and the Sown* (1907).

of their final value. In this way he amassed large collections of all sorts. He sold some of them, making himself good money, but he also bought for many of the larger museums in the United Kingdom, Sweden, and America, and intended to leave his own personal collections to them after his death. These pieces, he wrote, were his children.

9
Crippled in Love

Now in his early thirties, Pum was recognized as an authority on ancient Egyptian and Saracenic antiquities. His increasing introspection had allowed him to become ever more absorbed by his passionate collecting. As he gathered objects of beauty around him and spent many hours alone working on them, he accumulated insights into his personality and behavior that quickened the pace and depth of his discovery, as he described it, of his real self.

He knew he was not an "ordinary young Britisher" in Cairo and that what he most wanted in life was to be allowed to be himself, to do what he wanted and not what others required of him. He wanted to live "à la mode orientale," to wear whatever he wanted, and to see as little as possible of everybody except those he really liked. He decided to give up sport and take only as much exercise as he needed to keep himself fit. His shooting days had ended with the horror of the elephant kill, and now he found all sports and games, indoor and outdoor, quite pointless and a complete bore. Parties, dances, and the like were also a tiresome waste of time and energy, and he was repulsed by the idea of having to "cut a figure" among his peers. He promised himself that, public and professional occasions aside, he would live his life on his own terms, even if that made him appear antisocial or self-centered. Pretty much abandoning all his doctoring, except when an Egyptian friend needed help, he began to dress carelessly, as he put it, in brightly colored shirts and ties and sometimes, in the privacy of his flat, in Arab finery and exotic jewelry. He was especially fond of wearing rings, which held a special mystic symbolism for him. People were welcome to think that he had been crossed in love, or lost money and gone mad, or, worse, "gone native." Never mind, let them. The solitary life was immensely pleasurable to him, and he decided he had become "ego-centric," selfish, and self-sufficient. The affection he felt for some of his European friends was not enough to disturb him, and he ceased to feel any intimacy, unless for those of a similar "lonely type." He simply would not care for convention in his private life any longer.

As his circle of European friends diminished, so his Egyptian social circle increased. If possible, he loved Egypt—the people, climate, and culture—more and more. Cairo became his true home, and he had no desire to return to a cold, gray, stiff England. Making new friends seemed absurd, and it came as a revelation to him that, though he could tolerate people, he could no longer love them; any of them, that is, apart from his mother, for whom he continued to avow complete love. Something had been burned out of him, extinguished, and the over-whelming sensations that had been aroused by Kathleen Silver, and even by his twin, had all been cauterized. He was "crippled in love," especially when it came to women. His friends, Humphrey and Ste-phen Spender, "both sexually fluid, were perfectly aware," according to Humphrey, of Pum's (and Tom's) homosexuality; Humphrey "found it funny the way it was concealed behind this formal façade. But it was never discussed. He must occasionally have been expecting questions, but it didn't occur to people in those days to ask."

Pum's sexuality cannot, though, be pinned down to one category. The Greeks had a range of words for love—*agapē, erōs, philia,* and *storge*—roughly translated as affection, desire, companionship, and parental bonding, and Pum divvied up his desires and loves, too, com-partmentalized them, and rated some above others. The only true love Pum now felt capable of was the sensual kind, and he worried that this was a debility, a spiritual laziness or deficiency, and was ashamed of himself. He knew it was born of disillusionment with life in general and with his relations with men in particular; like everyone else, he had longed for a "real friend," but time and again he had been disappointed. One of his poems from this period includes the lines:

Give me a friend I need not tell my heart to,
Since he divines it better than I do.
A friend whose eyes I look into and see through,
His mind as mine, with no disguise at all,
His fellowship so fond and mutual.

Pum did have one final crack at getting engaged to a woman, in 1914, but it was a half-hearted and ill-considered affair made in the exhilarating months before the Great War began, and it came to nothing. He had been fond enough of the girl, he wrote, but never in love with her, although she was "a charming young girl (of considerable prospects), an only child of well-off parents who spent each winter at Aswan—she was fluffy, sweetly pretty and quite empty-headed." He seems to have become affianced through a duty and expectation to marry and beget—and there was the financial situation to think of—but he extricated himself at the very last minute. Tom proposed to a woman at the same time, and when his engagement was called off, too, the twins were greatly relieved. Pum and Tom developed an emphatic distaste for relations with females, to the extent that the idea of marriage and intimacy was "from early manhood to late middle-age the subject of a recurring nightmare." Pum pondered that there might possibly be some advantages to such an "arrangement," some solace from "the petty worries of life that unprofitably occupy a bachelor," but they seemed too nugatory. He was quite certain that it wouldn't suit him to put up with the "constant, inescapable presence, the possessiveness, the fussy intervention of any woman." In his poem "Mounted," Pum described how foolish it was to make the "two-backed beast" with a woman; "undignified, unseemly, and obscene . . . pricked on by Priapus, she wriggles, heaves and quakes / While like a jockey he jerks up and down . . . a buffoon, a clown."

Despite this distaste, what Pum really desired "with the strongest paternal, almost maternal, instinct, was to possess a child (a son) of my own." Possession seems to have been his paramount need, and possess a son he would, one day, but without marrying and with the least possible sexual contact. Admitting that he loved beautiful objects more than he loved his family and friends, he acknowledged that a boy would be one more beautiful object. The woman who later bore his son, Evelyn Wynn, with whom he had a very unconventional arrangement and spent just one night, thought that Pum and Tom "pitied the limitations of women, a pity mixed with contempt." All their lives the twins had "lusted to possess things—furniture, pictures, statues, antiques of all kinds" but never women, from whom they constantly and "incontinently fled." Nevertheless, Evelyn wrote that Pum had taught her "to think broadly of all kinds and degrees of love. There is nothing left undiscussed, or considered impossible. And [he] always preached the right of the individual to complete freedom in these matters." But he found the reality of loving women embarrassing and awkward, even vile, and very unlike the ideal "David and Jonathan union" of his dreams. In his poem "Our Ronnie," Pum revealed the double standard, made a list of derogatory names for sexually active women, and extolled the simpler, noble relations of men and boys:

Had Ronnie been a wench I'm sure
He'd have proved a paramour
Tart, trollop, toy, a kissing nan,
Slut, concubine, or courtesan,
A dame, a demi-monde, coquotte [sic],
A pet, a pander, a what-not,
A strumpet, quean, a blatant whore,
A demi-rep, a drab d'amour,
A doxie, darling, dollie nell,
A minion, painted Jezebel.
Indeed the whole gamut and more
Of harlots, counted by the score.

How well it is that rather than
A wench, our Ronald proved a man.

Heterosexual love was tarnished for Pum; it was a matter of base lust, and lust, to him, could never be innocent or beautiful. His poem "We are not born of love" is a lament:

We are not born of love, but out of lust
Conceived, that ruder, cruder, malier passion
Who come by lechery that knoweth not disgust
Nor all the niceties of lovers fashion.
Love is too finikin to father us
Far too effeminate, fastidious . . .

In another he writes:

In each of us, no matter who,
There are a few vile virile inches that must be
Always too manly to be gentlemanly.

*

Pum wrote his poetry secretly throughout his life, marking milestones and drawing on his emotions, visions, and premonitions. Several volumes of poetry, his "Obsessions," written between 1910 and 1935 and often illustrated by himself and Tom, were privately bound in Cairo. They were originally produced under the nom-de-plume "John Gayer," and there are some fifty-odd poems in each volume. According to notes that Tom later made on Pum's memoir, his twin was "addicted to the coining of words, in order to amplify, sometimes to disguise his meaning," words such as "ambesexterous," "hallic," "phalosophies," and he characterized his works as being either first, second, or third degree, "used in its police-court, inquisitorial sense—and applied according to the frightfulness or naughtiness of the verses concerned." Though Pum showed the poems to no one other than Tom during his lifetime, not "even to his intimates," he intended them to be his "literary remains," a "post-mortem display . . . carefully planned and outlined." Gentle and rough, sexual and fey, innocent and very worldly, they would post-humously and therefore safely "express and reveal facet by facet an intimate, introspective second-self that intrigued him and by which by its very wisdom-cum-wantonness, he hoped and believed might appeal to a limited number of enquiring minds akin to his own."

The poems were "introspective and metaphysical . . . of irreligious convictions, philosophic wonders and doubts, sex ethics, love abstractions, speculations on death, psychological surmise and the like." They were sometimes surreal—he admired Lewis Carroll and Edward Lear—they could be whimsical and philosophical, psychic or violent, and were occasionally racist and anti-Semitic. In the volume "Quaint Conceits" are several of Pum's "favourite secondary subjects, or shall we say his minor obsessions?" Tom wrote later. These included "mirrors and moons, shadows and reflections, sacraments [sic], second-selves and the like," harmless symbols of the spiritual sphere; but there were also "his pet aversions—Jews, Jehovah, niggers, duchesses, the Romish church, priests, parsons etc etc etc." Privately bound books could contain private prejudices.

Pum knew that his "OBSESSIONS, philosophies of QUAINT CONCEITS, the religious ethics of DEVIOUS DEVOTIONS, the sex suggestions of LOVE, EROTICS" were "hidden complexes"—this was the time of Freud, after all. He also thought that although everyone had such complexes, society considered those who were "richly and profitably" endowed to be thoroughly perverse. Accordingly, these "characteristics, thoughts and expressions must be hidden away and refused acknowledgment or recognition as though they were something unnatural, even criminal that both the law and decency forbid." Tom declared that his twin railed against these "exaggerated barriers of modesty, shame and the like" and that he wrote poetry for the "essential self-revelation he sought and required, and which he believed [his] books would bring others of like temperament, as a relief from those repressions and inhibitions that else would have made life a burden."

Pum's world was predominantly a masculine one, but it was not homogenous. Early Victorian men could be sentimental in their friendships, naturally linking arms and having romantic attachments with each other. This would change. In 1895, when Pum was fourteen, Oscar Wilde spoke at his first trial of "the great affection of an elder for a younger man . . . such as Plato made the very basis of his philosophy, and such as you find in the sonnets of Michelangelo and Shakespeare. It is that deep, spiritual affection that is as pure as it is perfect . . . it is in this century misunderstood." By the early twentieth century, manliness had come to mean virility and hardness, with an emphasis on games and quasi-militarization in schools. Colonial life, though, had allowed some conspicuously "inveterate bachelors" to flourish in this atmosphere, men such as Gordon, Kitchener, and T.E. Lawrence. As a fourteen-year-old, Gordon had wished to be a eunuch and, as an adult, was quite happy as long as he could give the occasional bath to a dirty urchin and talk to him of God. He adored his "Gravesend laddies." Kitchener's male friendships were sentimentally fervent; he had no use for married men on his staff, and only young officers were admitted to his house—he called them his "cubs" or "my happy family of boys." T.E. Lawrence had his "commune" in the Punjab, there were "Howe's boys" in Calcutta, Wolesley's "Staff Ring," Rhode's "lambs," Sir Robert Hart's "kindergarten" in Canton, and Lord Milner's in South Africa. During the Great War, Baden-Powell watched the soldiers "trooping in to be washed in nature's garb, with their strong well-built naked wonderfully made bodies." This was his "happy brave family laughing together."

Stephen Spender wrote about Pum's fondness for boys in his preface to the posthumously published volume of Pum's verse, *Christeros and Other Poems.* Spender himself had written in a letter to Christopher Isherwood in September 1934: "I find boys much more attractive, in fact I am rather more than usually susceptible, but actually I find the actual sexual act with women more satisfactory, more terrible, more disgusting, and, in fact, more everything." Describing Pum's own happy family of boys that he had gathered around him in Cairo, Spender wrote that, "He was devoted to children, and there were always two or three small boys (sons of servants or from outside) employed in his establishment in one minor capacity or another. Their real function was to add to the general atmosphere of the place that element of tenderness, immature human beauty and ingenuous humour that was essential to [his] wellbeing. They all attended every meal picturesquely dressed, and one of them 'on duty', accompanied by the dog, followed his master at all times to carry things or run errands. . . . The mealtimes were the happiest periods of relaxation in the day for him and his guests and doubtless the children too, for they all loved him and his teasings and jokings. They realized instinctively that he was, in a subtle way, one of themselves besides being their 'father and mother.' He tended their ailments, supervised their education, encouraged their hobbies, minded their savings and interested himself in each one of them until he was launched in life. For similar reasons [he] was fond of both dogs and cats."

Pum noted what he thought of as the "precociousness" of these boys, that they were "little men of the world," and he elaborated on his preference for their company, platonic or otherwise, in his poem "Boy-Wife":

> When you see one whose pretty young spouse is
> Clad as a lad in shirt coat and trowsies
> You may be sure
> He'd far rather she were.

After Sir Hector MacDonald, a hero at Omdurman and "given to quaint practices," got caught in a compromising position in a train carriage in Ceylon with four Sinhalese boys in 1903, he shot himself. In 1922, Lewis Harcourt, "Loulou," an ex-colonial secretary, made a pass at a teenage houseguest who complained to his mother. Loulou, too, killed himself. They were by no means alone. Humphrey Spender recalled that Pum told him a "strange story of a fellow medical officer who was the subject of an improvised court, where they asked him many questions until eventually extracting from him a confession of homosexuality. So they said 'We will give you a service revolver and leave you alone. The thing is entirely in your hands.' Dreadful, they expected him to shoot himself."

Before the mid-twentieth century, discretion seemed to be the accepted thing. In a very unpopular move in the early 1930s, General Montgomery cracked down on the flourishing "fleshpots" of Egypt. This was a man who denied himself sex, even during his ten-year marriage, despite or because of his tenderness for prepubertal boys, and these desires drove him to react against them in an exaggerated way. Many years later, in 1965, he attacked the Wolfenden proposals and even suggested the age of consent be set at eighty. As with Gordon, looking at naked boys seemed to be as far as he could or would let himself go.

All these "men's men" were being boys together, and it has been said that many of the great heroes of the British Empire were essentially boy-men enjoying escapades. Ronald Hyam, in his book *Empire and Sexuality: The British Experience*, has suggested that they were "not well-adjusted personalities . . . many members of the ruling elite seem to have suffered degrees of emotional retardation." But many were impoverished, even diminished, by the legal and moral codes of the day, in what Jeffrey Weeks calls the "construction of homosexuality." With male-oriented love and sex banished from "normal" life and experience, it came to be defined in a cultic, romantic way. Pum exhibited this, and a self-consciously ambivalent attitude to the sex he liked, in his writing—he was coy and, of course, cautious. He left florid descriptions of the beauty of boys and youths, and dotted about his references and allusions to love between men. This "most shocking" self-discovery, he confided, had thrown all his ideas about friendship and love between men and women into a confusion best avoided.

Sublimation, the repression of sexual instinct, is the psychoanalytic concept often proposed as an animating force behind empire-building: love's loss is empire's gain. Hyam quotes the historian Lawrence Stone as suggesting that sublimation probably accounted for the "extraordinary military aggressiveness, the thrift, the passion for hard work, and the entrepreneurial and intellectual atmosphere," but he himself argues for a more subtle understanding of the internal ordering of the mind and its relation to the external world. This is a reminder of how complex people can be that allows us to view historical figures with a more compassionate understanding. Pum came from—and read about—the idea of Western desire as biological instinct, that there is a "science of sexuality," and in the Middle East he came face to face with, rubbed up against, the alien eroticism of the Orient and an idea of sex that had emerged from a very different cultural background. He tried to fuse the two.

Freud had argued in *Three Essays on Sexuality* (1905) that apparently non-sexual activities, especially artistic creation and intellectual enquiry, could be an expression of sexual instinct by a deflection from sexuality. Pum and his friends, including the artist Eric Gill, thought similarly. Pum appears to have attempted this deflection (unlike Gill), or hoped for it, or at least pretended it. Perhaps his sexual interest in boys just ran parallel, was only partially repressed, and consciously or not he used his passion for beauty as a convenient blind.

As well as the volumes of poetry that reveal his obsessions, there are his folios of drawings and watercolors. Both he and Tom produced large, cloth-bound books with gold embossed titles on their covers, full of sketches showing delicately and lovingly drawn boys, with curly hair and glowing, pink, plump flesh. Some of the drawings are in the possession of the family and include intimate, often quite homely sketches such as Tom's "Ernest dressing by my study fire," a portrait of one of the World War II evacuees that came to live with them for the duration. Most of the folios, though, were bequeathed to the Bodleian Library, Oxford; the drawings are mostly of little boys, taking acrobatic poses, wrestling, fishing, ice-skating, playing cricket or rugby, but they are all naked. In *Vive Le Sport No.4*, a rugby scrum drawn from above has all the small boys wearing rugby shirts but no shorts. Some are injured and languish on the grass with tears on their cheeks; some are playing conkers and tiddly-winks, flying kites, shooting their bows and arrows, or boxing—naked. They are watched by amused chaps in dinner jackets, bow ties, and monocles. On a polo pony a "Young Raja" rides in just his shirt, another wears riding chaps and nothing else, showing his blushing bottom. Pum's and Tom's drawings emulate the early twentieth-century passion for decorative children's books that were also—possibly mainly—intended to fascinate adults. What is known as the Edwardian "Golden Age" of illustration peaked between 1905 and 1914 with popular illustrators such as Arthur Rackham, Edmund Dulac, and Mabel-Lucie Attwell. The last's impish and chubby, pink-cheeked toddlers are portrayed with adult sentimentality, and Pum's and Tom's work is very similar, but with a darker edge and an almost whimsical violence to it.

The folios entitled *Virginibus Puerisque* (1935–45) include more blatantly erotic drawings of boys kissing and wrapping themselves around each other, and boys in bondage suspended by their elbows tied behind their backs, or with a rope around a neck. Many of the sketches, especially the more surreal ones, were, wrote Pum, "full of veiled allusions to myself and my twin." There are poems, too, about the pornographic nature of the drawings, such as "Art and Sex":

Where can one draw the line in art
Between the belly and the heart?
Between the soul and sexual part?
*

I do not know, I cannot guess,
Although I've felt, I must confess
Some pictures strike below the belt
Through their sheer wantonness.

Humphrey, discussing Pum's love of boys, remembered "one naughty story which I oughtn't to tell you. He asked me once to drive him up to London. As we were going up the hill to Sudbury there was a small boy, about ten years old, and Gayer said, 'Ooh, look at that lovely little button bottom.' And I found that absolutely hilarious just coming out of nowhere, and I burst out laughing and he burst out laughing, and for ten minutes the whole thing broke down. I wished that, more often, I could have been with him on those relaxed terms. Otherwise, the language of sexuality and desire and eroticism was kept on very formal levels. I've no doubt that hidden away amongst the treasures there's a lot of erotica."

Pum's house in Suffolk, he recalled, "was swarming with little boys [who] would go, without mum or dad, and pose in the nude . . . if that was going on now the police would be there in a trice. But nobody bothered, nobody noticed." Tom in particular, did things

> which now simply couldn't be done . . . all the little boys in the
> village were asked to pose for drawings, he simply suggested
> that it would be nice if they took their clothes off and he'd like
> them to sit there and keep quite still and so on. Well, nowadays
> any mother of any of those children would have been immedi-
> ately suspicious and simply accused him of child abuse.

Humphrey thought that Tom "was simply very interested" in the boys and made incredible drawings of them, some of which were "very interesting semi-pornographic drawings . . . of little boys riding bicycles and quite often with physical erections and so on, and when he died he had asked me to be his artistic executor."

One drawing, of a naked turbaned boy, is tightly surrounded by typed script telling of how Pum had seen this child with his father in an Egyptian paddy field. The father is the color of the mud and dull like his oxen, but the boy is a "warm glowing loveliness of brown and marigold and purple and rose of ochered greens and gold. Pathetic and lovely in his nakedness, still lifeloving and almost gay in this light drudgery . . . slenderlimbed poised like the golden plaything of a god he plunged his way through the deep cool mud." But he will sink into the mud eventually like his father, and all his loveliness will be destroyed.

Childish Nudes Vol II has a drawing of a perfect naked child, surrounded by naked adults and lamenting, "I'm crying because one day I'll look like all of you!" The figure of Peter Pan, the boy who wouldn't grow up, constantly comes to mind, and it is not hard to see the innocent eternal boy in Pum's and Tom's "doodlings"—always there are boys and always boy-lovers, with only the occasional Wendy.

The eternal boy, the *puer aeturnus*, is a psychological archetype, identified by Jung, describing an older man who remains emotionally an adolescent, still dependent on his mother, incapable of "undergoing the pain of relinquishing [this] first love of his life." In "The Syzygy: Anima and Animus," Jung argues that our most intimate and significant relationship with the opposite sex is within ourselves, the inner, dual realities of psyche and spirit that must be put together to form an individual identity. It could be said that Pum never really managed to acquire an identity sufficiently free of his mother or his twin. The imagery of bondage is a common symptom of *puer* psychology, unconscious ties to the unfettered world of childhood. Pum always said that he and Tom "remained in a state of fundamental infantilism": they reacted as children do. They felt "intense, passionate and beautiful (though half-guilty) love for the immature being, more especially, as I have said, of one's own sex."

Tom mixed the eternal child with sexual indeterminacy, a quasi-mystical philosophy, and religion in his startlingly erotic and illustrated verse-monologue, "He/She: The World's Sweetheart" (1941), an unpublished volume he dedicated to P.U.M. It is the story of He/She, born with a female and a male body attached to one head, told in sixty thousand words and forty-seven illustrations. This ideal "alloy of the sexes" fascinated the twins as a harmonious, asexual compromise, and though they barely discussed their mutual desires together until late in their lives, their thoughts on androgyny are encapsulated in this book. Tom had begun work on it, clandestinely, during the Great War, drawing the children that he had always found, "be they boys or girls, dark or fair, naked or clothed, between the ages of about three and thirteen years, to be the most delectable, lovely, and humorously delightful to look upon of all God's creatures!" He had allowed Pum to see his other drawings, but he kept He/She to himself, "due to a sort of jealousy concerning the delectable double-sexed creature HESHE with whom I fell in love at first sight!"

Each chapter is devoted to a year of his (Tom always refers to He/She in the masculine) growing up, his sexual adventures, examinations by doctors, surgeons, biologists, and psychologists, and his increasing worldwide fame: He/Sheism eventually becomes a religion as he relates an "amazing number of sexual and emotional adventures . . . those happenings taking place wherever I showed myself in public . . . . There were men of all ages who loved me with a devouring mania for the beauty and implications of He's boyhood and boyishness!" At the age of nine, the hero tours the south of France where a "marquise was very attentive to me . . . and did a lot of unnecessary handling and kissing of me but I enjoyed it in spite of that for it was fun to be naked amongst all those lovely little naked bodies and to find what intense excitement their owners got from examining and touching me."

In the late nineteenth century, when Pum and Tom were children, boyhood was seen intrinsically as a time and a state of innocence. The turning point in this understanding came later, in the 1920s. The Uranian writer Ralph Chubb was obsessed with pederasty, and his *Water-Cherubs* (1937) is very similar to Tom's He/She, raising the adoration to the realms of religious experience. "I choose the Boyish Body," wrote Chubb,

> because it is the divine image and better than anything else expresses the whole mystery of life. . . . Love never harms, it blesses body & soul . . . everything in life without a single exception—from the Buttercup to the Sun, from the comma or tadpole or human babe to the unfolding World—is a sexual symbol of a Spiritual Fact. Everything in life therefore is clean & pure & holy & divine . . . the nudity of Art is for ventilation and purification. I REDEEM.

Attitudes to relationships between men and boys were much more ambiguous before the Great War; most of the anxieties about the sexual corruption of innocence had historically been concentrated on girls. But by the 1920s, the focus was shifting to include "problem" boys whose relationships with men were classified as "indecent assaults," "molestation," and "corruption," even when they seemed to have entered willingly; the historian Matt Houlbrook argues that the consent of youth was now assumed absent, a boy was always a victim. These relationships, brief or not, began to be spoken of and in terms of "sexual danger" wrapped up in the anxieties surrounding the condition of Britain, its declining imperial status and the disruption of long-held notions of Britishness. Ronald Hyam debates the meaning of "perversion" at this time, arguing that human sexual behavior lies in variation rather than deviation, that intention, attitude, and consent are the important elements. A "loving relationship between a man and a consenting boy, usually at or past the age of puberty—and such alone was the classical Greek version—might become for later generations incomprehensible, misguided, or illegal, but it is not from a theoretical point of view a perversion."

The modern, Western, highly problematic idea of boy-lovers is far removed from the Greek ideal, but the real changes began a hundred years ago, when Pum was a young man. His poetry idealized the beauty and love of boys, reflecting the Uranian poetry popular at the time. This form emerged from classical study and Hellenism as a justification for "heavenly" love between males, the *paiderastia* of ancient Greece, describing it as a noble and intellectual love, not frightening, disgusting, or immoral. Uranian verse embodied the longing for an attachment to a boy, usually a lower-class boy, and it has been suggested that this sort of relationship relieved the older man of the rigors and responsibilities of a love affair with an intellectual equal, or that the boys were sexually uninhibited at a time when women were more restrained or had too much to lose. It had a central role in upper-class homosexual subculture and included the poets John Addington Symonds, Lord Alfred Douglas, and the Rev. E.E. Bradford, among others. In July 1914, the Uranians founded an official organization, the British Society for the Study of Sex Psychology, ostensibly to delve into all forms of sexual pathology and psychology, but it concentrated itself on pederasty, considering it superior to the "animal sexuality" between men and women. This stance was openly and disastrously mocked as "the higher sodomy." Hostility to this love continued to grow over the twentieth century.

10
"Weep, Weep!"—The Great War

For the first decade of the new century Pum existed in state of "supreme happiness," wonderfully ignorant that the world was, as he later wrote, "on the brink of a volcano . . . Bolshevism and Communism, Nazi-ism and Fascism were as yet undreamed of."

Just a week before the British declaration of war on August 4, 1914, Pum and Tom had arrived at their parents' home in Blackheath on leave. They were ordered to re-embark on a cargo steamer, the "Mooltan," and sail straight back to Egypt (Archduke Franz Ferdinand of Austria had been assassinated in Sarajevo by the Black Hand on June 28). Pum's main concern at this moment was his collection of antiques, packed up and shipped to England; relieved, he saw it arrive safely days before he sailed off to war.

The Egyptian War Office wanted all British officers to go to their original posts, but there were arrangements that allowed them to be "loaned" to whichever theater of operations needed them most. It seemed like a workable system, but it faltered. British units were soon refusing to send any of the very valuable experienced officers back to the Egyptian army, which found itself operating with the bare minimum of those who had stayed. These men remained for the duration, made good careers for themselves, and had a much better chance of survival than those sent to the European front. Pum's friend Leckie, a captain, had been "loaned" to the Northumberland Fusiliers and was sent to the front with the Expeditionary Force. He died there, at Mons, on August 28, not two weeks after he arrived.

Tom was sent to Khartoum and Pum to Cairo again, where he was promoted to the rank of *miralay* (full colonel); this meant an increase in pay and a return to living at the observatory. He carried on in recruitment, and though not much seemed to have changed outwardly, there was a blighted, silent fear that permeated life. He was alone: even Butn had found a new home, Zwintz the terrier had gone back to England and promptly got run over, and Zwintz's unworthy son Cuthbert had been pinched. Occasionally, Pum went to the Turf Club, but it was disconcertingly filled with new faces as troops poured into Egypt from all directions.

Within six months he was on the books of the newly formed Arab Bureau of the Intelligence Department, and told he would be succeeding Ronald Storrs as political officer of the Red Sea Patrol. Storrs was, according to T.E. Lawrence, the most brilliant Englishman in the Near East, and subtly efficient, despite his habit of diverting his energies into music, letters, sculpture, painting, and whatever else he found "beautiful in the world's fruit." Storrs and Pum were of a kind.

Now responsible for supervising the littoral on both sides of the Red Sea, Pum was in charge of an area that stretched as far south as Jeddah and Suakin, beyond which it came under Indian government control. With his "faithful Saifi" (soldier-servant), necessary kit, coins (Turkish, Egyptian, and English) for gifts and bribes, propaganda tracts, maps, instructions, and intelligence reports, he set out aboard the Indian Navy ship, HMS Dufferin. It was mostly simple work and pleasant, a bit like an armed and edgy picnic, slowly patrolling the coast by day and anchoring offshore at night. Pum went ashore daily with an escort of six British marines and rowed by a dozen lascars to distribute tea, coffee, tobacco, and propaganda while sowing as much distrust and dislike as he could of the Turks, allies of Germany. Between-times he walked and collected shells and artifacts lying in the sands and bathed in the coral pools, though beset by spiny urchins and a fear of sharks, noting that "one always feels so completely defenceless when naked!"

Pum's anthropological curiosity was aroused: he described the indigenous inhabitants of the Arabian littoral as subhuman, primitive, barbaric, half-naked troglodytes, without religion or ethics, homes or villages. They lived mainly, he noted, on seaweed and shellfish and what little they caught in their inadequate nets. None he met admitted to being able to read or write and he assumed "they had no idea of what civilisation meant, much less war." Their language seemed unrelated to Arabic and consisted of a series of grunts, clicks, and whistles, similar to what he had heard among the "savages and pygmies" of Central Africa, and usually incomprehensible to his interpreter. Based on his lack of understanding, he imagined their mental development as equivalent to that of Neanderthals. There were Bedouin there, too, "some of whom were honest and likeable," but many he disparaged as "cunning treacherous folk."

Contact was made with various secret service agents, from Syrian soap vendors to Belgian Catholic missionaries. Pum thought them strange and perturbing types, largely frauds and ne'er-do-wells, as ready to deal with one side as the other and capable of romancing their information without, ironically, any real knowledge of the facts. HMS Dufferin gave the sea towns and ports a wide berth as these were mainly occupied by the Turkish army. Turks, according to Pum, had a potential for intense cruelty, although other than that, they resembled the average Britisher, being lazy, conservative, fond of sport and children, and somewhat dense.

On the beach of Sanafir Island (which lies in the Straits of Tiran between the Sinai and Arabian Peninsulas, separating the Gulf of Aqaba from the Red Sea), Pum and his men found four huge marine mines, probably left by the Turks under German supervision with a view to mining the Gulf of Aqaba. Despite having only a cursory knowledge of these things, Pum decided to dismantle them; it was unnecessary, but he needed something exciting to do. It took him two days to finish what was a reckless, delicate, and extremely dangerous job. Within the great spherical bodies were the central cylinders containing detonating mechanisms that had to be painstakingly removed before the mines could be emptied of explosives. As they were taking apart the third mine, things went disastrously wrong: the detonator exploded and two of the lascars were badly injured; Pum suffered a nasty leg wound. He blew up the fourth mine by shooting at it with a rifle. There was no hero's welcome when he returned to ship: he had been gone too long, they had heard the explosions, and men had been hurt. Pum and the captain quarreled, though when he telegraphed his adventure to Cairo he was congratulated and told to carry on.

After a disappointing search for more mines, Pum made his way back around Sinai and on to Cairo to see General Gilbert Clayton, director of the Arab Bureau of the Intelligence Department. Clayton's office was in a suite at the Savoy Hotel, once one of the most exclusive and luxurious in the city, and here he introduced Pum to a new arrival, "one Lawrence, a young archeologist," who would provide him with maps for his next venture. T.E. Lawrence was, wrote Pum, "an attractive young man below middle height, with a large head and an extremely open and boyish expression of face." Pum was much taken by his boyishness, his eagerness, and his pleasant, almost ingratiating, manner. He was just the sort of young man Pum was attracted to, and he immediately bore him off to lunch at the Turf Club. This was Pum's first meeting with Lawrence of Arabia, whose "meteoric progress was just about to start." Lawrence, "consciously or not," exerted a "feminine attraction" over Europeans and Arabs, and it seemed plain to Pum that this was the reason for the young man's subsequent success. It also, he wrote, explained the "strange interlude darkly alluded to in *Seven Pillars of Wisdom*, for among Arabs love between men is openly accepted."

When the two met again, nearly a year later, Lawrence was a famous man. Instead of his army uniform, he now wore a silk robe with a gold filet wound around a white and gold scarf on his head, and this time it was he who invited Pum to lunch, at the Continental. Pum was not in the least attracted to him now: Lawrence had lost his charming boyishness, his face had matured and seemed longer and harder, his manner was no longer diffident, but dry and cynical. They met several more times, but only on official occasions or on duties connected to the Arab Bureau, and it seemed to Pum that Lawrence had a devious genius for keeping aloof while manipulating affairs behind the scenes. Had he been trammeled by military rank and discipline, Pum thought that Lawrence could never have done what he did, and that he knew this of himself and made sure to remain free, "dancing like some all-pervading Puck before the narrow eyes and above the hard heads of his senior military colleagues." Some senior officers, Clayton included, recognized Lawrence's wayward intelligence and cooperated with him, though it brought them little credit. Lawrence himself described Clayton as "the perfect leader for such a band of wild men as we were," a man who worked by influence and was "like water, or permeating oil, creeping silently and insistently through everything." Lawrence despised and distrusted his seniors, often with justification, and they returned the sentiment, though they still "danced to his tune or jerked to his string-pulling." This "strange and complex personality" was not understood by his critics or his admirers, but Pum felt he knew him well.

Back on the Red Sea again, Pum steamed across to Jeddah, a mysterious and beautiful city with narrow streets, overhanging windows, and deeply shadowed doorways. Dhow traffic still sailed across to the African coast, once an active slave route between Abyssinia, Central Africa, and Sudan on the one hand, and Egypt and Turkey via the Arabian Peninsula on the other. Part of Pum's business was to stop and search the dhows, heavily laden with merchandise and with a few passengers squatting on top, some of whom, women and children usually, he suspected of being slaves, and then he would direct the vessel back to port or have it trailed by the nearest destroyer.

It was all fairly leisurely, with only the odd serious scrape, one of which happened at Mowila on the main Arabian coast, due east of the tip of the Sinai Peninsula. Pum's agents had reported that the Turks had withdrawn, so he slipped ashore to explore and give out propaganda. They had to moor two miles out due to shallow waters, and a contingent of six marines, twelve lascars, a lieutenant corsair, Pum, and his *saifi*, rowed in on a longboat. As they started shoreward between the coral reefs, Pum experienced such a deep feeling of dread and foreboding that he suggested turning back, but Corsair didn't take him seriously. They could see palm trees edging a narrow navigable channel, certainly a good place for ambush, and as the boat beached and Pum and his *saifi* jumped out, a volley of rifle fire lashed them. The soldier-servant fell forward into the water. Pum's fears came sickeningly true as the volleys became rapid continuous fire. One of the lascars jumped out to help, and between them they made a supreme effort to push off the boat and turn her around to face the sea, while the marines returned fire. When they were well afloat, Pum had to be dragged back into the boat over the stern, his backside a most conspicuous target. The Turks had run forward by now and were firing from the dunes, killing two lascars and wounding the others, who were prone in the bilge. The marines made a barricade of biscuit tins and retaliated over that while Pum and two others rowed hell-for-leather for the ship, bullets ripping into and through the little boat. One "fine corporal" was hit in the chest, and Corsair caught a bullet that shattered his jaw. Pum tried to persuade him to hand over the tiller but he wouldn't until another shot opened his right arm. Suddenly, unseen field guns added to the Turks' bombardment, but they were terrible shots and the shrapnel burst over the heads of Pum's group. All this could be seen from the Dufferin, but no help was given until they were already out of firing range. When they came alongside, their splintered boat was half-full of water, two men were dead, and fourteen were wounded. Pum had been lucky: a bullet had torn his shirtsleeve but not his flesh.

From the Red Sea, Pum was sent to northeastern Egypt, to Ismail-iya, "The City of Beauty and Enchantment," where he was political officer on the Suez Canal. Here he dealt with Arab-speaking Syrians who, much against their will, had been swallowed up into the Turkish troops, and he was also charged with organizing the Medical Services, which turned out to be completely unprepared for the numbers of wounded from both sides.

In the summer of 1915, Pum was posted to Gallipoli, traveling on a small troop transport so packed with men of a Lancashire regiment that there was no room to sit down except for those who dangled their legs over the sides. They landed at Suvla Bay one gray dawn and were confronted by a low, inhospitable beach hedged with sparse scrub and evergreen oak. Beyond that was a vast circle of shell-pitted trench-defenses filled with the living, the injured, and the dead. Pum was attached to a field ambulance here in "the hell of war."

The Allied attack on the Gallipoli Peninsula was, according to the historian Peter Hart, "a lunacy that never could have succeeded, an idiocy generated by muddled thinking." The war had stalled on the Western Front, and the attack was intended to knock Turkey out, weaken Germany, and gain control of the Dardanelles straits that separated Asia and Europe; the Balkan states might then be pressured into joining the Allies. It was an epically terrible mistake that diverted men and arms away from the main battles and resulted in dreadful slaughter. Winston Churchill, first lord of the Admiralty, was vilified, while Mustafa Kemal, then a Turkish Army officer, went on to lead his country as Kemal Ataturk.

From April 1915 to January 1916, nearly half a million Allied soldiers landed on the peninsula and clung to it: British, French, Australian, New Zealand, and Indian troops fought there, and of these the British Empire alone lost 205,000, killed, wounded, missing, or evacuated sick. They lacked military technology, logistics, weaponry, and tactics; they had no chance against the Turks, who were well dug in and well-armed. The campaign was, writes Hart, flawed by arrogance, self-delusion, incompetence, inexperience, and the fatal assumption of racial superiority.

A month into the campaign, after a German U-boat had torpedoed the HMS Triumph, all support ships were withdrawn and the soldiers were left alone. As spring gave way to a blistering summer followed by a freezing, wet winter, conditions markedly deteriorated. Misery, desperation, and disease were rife, the rotting corpses of soldiers lay everywhere, and day after day attacks and counter-attacks continued. At Anzac Cove, named for the landing place of ANZAC troops (Australian and New Zealand Army Corps) on April 25, 1915, their commanding officer wrote, "The beautiful battalions of April 25th are wasted skeletons." Pum was working less than a dozen yards from the Turkish trenches and close enough to hear their conversations. *The Gallipoli Diary* of Major John Gillam vividly describes the noise of battle:

hearing the heavens being torn asunder by an unseen hand—the noise of the tearing developing into a mighty hiss and shriek, ending in a great explosion which shakes the earth under your feet and echoes far away into the distance, followed by the whine of flying pieces of hot metal, sometimes very near your head. . . . It is like the rending of linen. . . . This gets louder and louder, and then, as the projectile nears the end of its journey, one hears a whine, half whistle, half scream, and then the explosion . . . there is an acrid smell in the air. One's feelings are difficult to describe . . . you feel absolutely helpless.

The ping-ping of bullets went on incessantly while life continued around the dugout tables, the men smoking and chatting as if enjoying after-dinner coffee and cigars at a dinner party when the ladies had gone to the drawing room; the conversation held no mention of war. But outside, the stifling heat was laced with the sickly smells of the dead and chloride of lime. Pum lived and worked in a dense cloud of flies in his badly made dugout on a conspicuous hillock above Suvla Bay. With the field ambulance and in dressing stations up and down the endless labyrinth of trenches, he was constantly exposed to enemy strafing, hand grenades, and snipers hiding among the rocks and stunted trees as he attempted to treat and stretcher out mortally wounded men. As well as their injuries, they suffered from dysentery, paratyphoid, malaria, jaundice, severe frostbite in the hard winter, and the ever-present lice. The medical officer in charge of one of the advanced dressing stations at Suvla, Lieutenant Norman King-Wilson, wrote of the injured and sick queuing up for treatment: "They looked so ill, poor devils, that it required a heart of stone to send the lighter cases, say of simple diarrhoea, back to duty. However, one had to remember the military exigencies, and my heart used to bleed as I watched some poor, diarrhoea-stricken, emaciated skeleton, with sunken lack-lustre eyes and unsteady gait, accept without murmur my decisions that he must return to duty, pick up his kit and slowly return to the stinking, pestilence-stricken, ill-constructed trenches."

Yet occasionally, and with immense contradiction, Pum felt his spirits lift when he heard nightingales singing in the early morning, or watched the fine, tough, young Antipodean troops. They seemed, he thought, different creatures to the dejected "raw" Irish and North Country men, and to have come to Gallipoli as much for the sport and adventure of it all as for any other reason. When they arrived, they were tanned, strong, and loose-limbed, and cavalier about discipline, a quality that enraged some British officers. But not Pum; he was full of admiration for them. Scores of these young men stripped naked and sunned themselves or played about in the breakers beneath the cliffs that sloped down from the battlefront. The Turks knew this was their habit and occasionally lobbed over a shell or two, but the New Zealand and Australian "boys were adept at anticipating and dodging the fire and, though there were a few casualties, they refused to give up their games."

Tom was also somewhere on the peninsula, having arrived soon after the first landing as a brigade major of the 29th Infantry Brigade, and eventually he and Pum found each other. They were both "dead-beat and dispirited." Huddled amid this misery in a shallow and cramped dugout, they struggled to find any cheer in each other's company. They were scared about their immediate situation but also about their future intimacy, and struggled to find any vital element of their former close filial relationship. When, many years later, Pum thought back to this time, he was overcome with remorse at their mutual estrangement.

The twins got out of Gallipoli before the evacuation, Tom to Salonica and Pum back to Cairo, where he wrote a poem, "Weep, Weep!," about the appalling "loss of young life, of youth, almost boy-hood, for many young soldiers were still in their teens":

Weep, weep, the unborn for the unborn,
And generations not to be for generations dead,
The ungot yield of many a youthful loin
The seed unscattered and unharvested.

11
"Salaam aleyk"

On the night he got back to Cairo from Gallipoli, Pum had a vivid dream about a seventeenth-century Spanish oil painting of the Madonna and Child. He had spotted it just before the war, in a dealer's shop opposite Shepheard's Hotel. It was encased in a contemporary carved wood frame and was absurdly cheap, but someone else had already bought it. Now he dreamed that the painting was back in the shop and it filled him with unspeakable joy. Waking in the morning he dismissed it, only to have the very same dream the next night, too. His psychic antique adventures had not deserted him. He left his desk the next morning, unable to wait any longer, and rushed off to the shop. Great feelings of elation and hope and a terrible fear of disappointment assailed him, as though he were hoping to meet a lover, but unsure if they would turn up or not. Coolly pretending he was just passing by, he was invited into the dealer's back room for coffee and on the way he saw the Madonna hanging on the wall again, just as it had been in his dreams. As casually as he could, he mentioned it and discovered that the previous buyer had returned it because the varnish was badly stuck to the glass. The dealer eyed him up, tried to read his thoughts, and then suggested he might like it at a price almost half the original. Pum said he would take it on spec, just to see if it could be fixed, and when it was agreed he had to sit and sip his coffee without

149

betraying his fervent pleasure and excitement. He hung the painting in his office before shipping it to England where Tom repaired it by heating it in front of the fire until the varnish melted, and the picture could be peeled away from the glass and scraped clean with a dinner knife.

In 1916 he managed to get up to Alexandria for a brief meeting with Henry and D'Arcy, who had arrived on the hospital ship, the Asturias, and were now at the Casino Hotel. Henry was an acting Red Cross searcher in the Mediterranean—these were honorary duties to try and trace the missing and unidentified—and D'Arcy was now seriously ill with tremors and palsy in his limbs. He was no longer fit for duty and was convalescing, but had permission to travel with his father so that both still felt part of the war effort. The meeting cheered Pum, but on returning to Cairo he began to feel his preferred solitary joy again, a state of happiness made possible by a "constant telepathic interchange of loving thought between my Mother and myself." He resumed his recruiting duties around the country, living "among the fruits and streams of Fayoum" and visiting Luxor, "that seventh heaven of my fancy," where he bought antiques at rock-bottom prices because no one else was buying during wartime.

Too soon, Pum was off on his next appointment as political officer to a desert patrol, on a mission to extirpate the Senussi sect of Islam, which had succeeded in thoroughly scaring the European powers. The sect was a "puritanical revival of Mohammedanism," akin to the more recent and "virile" Wahhabi movement, which had swept away the ancient Hashemite dynasty and placed its own leader, Sheikh Ibn Saud, on the throne of Arabia. Its founder, the Grand Senussi, born in the early nineteenth century in North Africa, believed that Islam had become decadent, devoted himself to reforming the faith, and gathered about him a large following. They were said to have peopled the whole of North Africa, establishing monasteries from which to proselytize the Middle and Far East. European anxieties had reached their peak shortly before the start of the war, just when the sect itself was declining. Their holy city, Jaghbub, which Pum referred to at the time as "Jarabub," was on the border of Egypt and Libya, and throughout the war the Senussis were a thorn in the side of the Italians, who eventually asked their allies to "settle the matter . . . and sort out the demarcation of Egypto-Tripolitanian border." Pum and his party set off to tackle the job, into the uncharted, monotonous western desert in six semi-armored Ford vans, but the operation effectively ended his war.

Jaghbub was isolated and mysterious, built on a small oasis, and it took many days of tiring travel to reach it. The tiny vans got repeatedly stuck in the sand or bogged down in shallow floods. On a cold March morning they finally arrived at the forbidden city and, because they were Christians, camped outside it. As the sun rose and drove away the mist, the pure white, "Moorish" walled city assembled itself in front of them. Massive and ethereal in the pale early light, the great square palace appeared, then the college and the impressive mosque with its single dome, under which rested the remains of the Grand Senussi. This was the hub of the Senussi faith, a center which had once attracted youths from all over the East to study "in medieval fashion" the tenets of Islamic life and learning.

It appeared deserted: there were a guard, a few loiterers at the gate, and just the occasional student passing by, clad completely in white. A herd of goats and a ragged boy drifted out through the gate to pasture beyond the walls, as a string of laden camels shambled lugubriously in from the desert. A non-commissioned officer had been sent ahead to warn Sheikh Safi al-Din of their arrival, and the small party stood, stamping their feet in the cold, waiting for a response. The sheikh himself appeared, followed by a throng of councilors, retainers, relations, and soldiery, and seemed delighted, greeting them with all the effusive love and courteous manners of an "Oriental" friend and gentleman. To their enormous surprise they were invited inside the city walls, even as the sheikh admitted that it was against the principles of the sect and had never been allowed before. "Things have changed," the sheikh said, politically. "And after all, you are our best friends."

Entering on foot, they were taken first to the mosque to be presented at the tomb of the Grand Senussi. The palace opened up from the mosque and, guided upstairs, they were allowed to perform their ablutions and take a breakfast brought on brass trays while they squatted in groups on rugs on the floor. After eating, they washed again and, forming a wide circle, began their conference. The party were told that the Italians were persecuting the people and that they lived in dread of being overrun—they wanted Jaghbub to be included within the Egyptian borders, otherwise they would be forced to abandon their city and establish themselves in Siwa or Kufra Oasis (which they later did). The British made no promises—this was only a tentative mission—but they bestowed their sympathy and promised to do their best.

After the conference, the men stayed to sit and lazily smoke together, drinking sweet coffee and even sweeter mint tea. As they talked, they learned that the sheikh's daughter was ill and there was no doctor to help her. Pum, of course, immediately offered his skills and was led quickly away, up a flight of stairs and along a corridor to the women's quarters. There, "a great eunuch" stepped forward to open the door and preceded them into the vestibule, clapping his hands as he entered to warn "all the bright young things" to hide themselves from view. Through one room, full of children and "stout old black slave women" wearing robes like print nightdresses and with pattens on their feet, they passed into another chamber where more slaves stood around a mattress on the floor. Here lay the sheikh's daughter, "a pretty little girl of nine or ten, pale and emaciated."

After a little persuasion by her father, the girl allowed Pum to examine her. Diagnosing dysentery, he sent out to the car for his medicine box, and while they waited he became aware of the women whispering and glancing at him. Soon, one approached and spoke into the sheikh's ear asking if Pum would also see "the slave-woman Zainab." He thought it impossible for the British doctor to bother with servants, but Pum agreed to see anyone who needed his help, and in a minute or two a flood of patients began pouring into the room. Some were reluctant and needed a shove forward, but soon, he wrote, their readiness was almost embarrassing. Zainab came first, then "several black children and a couple of little Arab girls." There were great comings and goings, door-openings and shuttings, whisperings, callings, and beckonings—word spread fast through the palace. The sheikh wrote down the prescriptions for each patient by name so that there would be no confusion after Pum had left. Most of them were suffering from dysentery or malaria, and soon his stocks of ipecacuanha and quinine had run out; he later sent a package of drugs from Cairo. Toward the end of his surgery, a fair-skinned young woman, completely muffled from view, was escorted in by four slaves. She was one of Safi al-Din's wives, and was so shy that she would only speak to him in a whisper and could not even be persuaded to present her hand to Pum. In the end, they resorted to holding up a sheet between the woman and the doctor, held up by two of her slaves while the others retired behind it with the patient. A small hole was slit in the middle of the cloth and through this her hand was thrust so that he could take her pulse. He asked to look at her tongue and this she stuck through the hole so that he could slip a thermometer under it. Pum described the scene as amusing—the "caryatid figures with black faces wearing extremely solemn expressions, the white expanse of sheet with its tiny proscenium, the series of peep-shows with the accompaniment of shuffling and giggling from the other side. It had much the air of a Punch and Judy show." So Pum spent his morning in the Grand Senussi's harem—the only male Christian to have done so, as far as he knew. "Such," he wrote, "is one of the privileges of being a doctor!"

Returning to a sweltering Cairo, Pum came down with dysentery himself and then caught diphtheria, too, from his servant boy, Awad. He was so sick that, despite having self-diagnosed by pressing a teaspoon on his tongue, he couldn't get to the infectious-fever hospital until he was rushed there by an alarmed friend. They gave him an injection of "serum," but it did no good, he was too ill, and it even made things worse by giving him an agonizing "serum-rash." Desperately ill and scarcely alive, he was unable to do anything to help himself. Einstein's words echoed around his mind, "We have free will but we only do as we must." Awad came each day to the window with flowers and would sit outside on the grass bank watching over his master. At first he just sat and wept, but as Pum began to recover Awad brought books, letters, and Pum's dachshund, Fadl Effendi ("Make yourself at home, Sir"). The boy entertained Pum through the open window, laughing, chattering, and telling him stories and gossip. He trained the dog to do tricks for him and to say "salaam aleyk" ("peace be upon you") in a series of staccato sneezes. His faithful boy, wrote Pum, kept him sane.

When he recovered sufficiently to go back home to the observatory, he slipped into a sorry depression and couldn't be roused even by Tom, who had arrived to nurse him. It was decided that he should sail for England to be treated at Somerville College, Oxford, now converted into an officers' hospital. Here, Mary and Henry visited daily and took him out in a bath chair. While love and sympathy radiated from his mother, his father's awkward affection, "his typical, grudging, slightly apologetic smile," evoked only remorse and sadness in the son.

They took him home with them to Marston, outside Oxford, and he undertook a few light duties at the hospital to keep himself occupied. He joined the Oxford Country Club and met interesting, like-minded men, dined at college high tables, and became acquainted with the papyrologist Professor Alan Gardiner and Professor Griffiths, the eminent Egyptologist. They were very involved with that part of Pum's collection that he was loaning to the Ashmolean Museum, especially the *heb sed* festival stela (now in the Fitzwilliam Museum, Cambridge) commemorating the jubilee of Akhenaten. It tells of the enigmatic "heretic King" of the Eighteenth Dynasty who reigned over Egypt some fifteen centuries before Christ, and whom Professor James Breasted called "the first individual in history."

It was summer 1917. Tom came home on leave, and D'Arcy arrived too, with his wife Nora and small son John. It was the last time the brothers were all together. D'Arcy was dying; once the most capable of the three boys, he had become a tragic man in Pum's estimation because "he was one of those who ought to have done exceptionally well, yet in his short life he never succeeded as the world counts success. He once said to Mother in his characteristic spirit of self-criticism, 'I am an anxious-minded beggar,' and indeed he was, but whether that predisposed him to worldly failure it is hard to say." D'Arcy died of his mysterious malady three weeks later in the Arabian Gulf and was buried at sea. Pum had seen his brother's death clearly laid out in a premonition—a vision of his body tumbling into the sea.

Pum's own eventual recovery astonished him, so ill and so low had he been. Now he was ready to have another go at life. When fit enough for work, Pum was sent to London as military secretary and assistant to the director general of medical services at the War Office, at De Kayser's Hotel close by Blackfriars Bridge. It turned out that his job was mainly to protect his boss from the "clutches of Society women, cranks, self-seekers and well-wishers," and the unpalatable work made him unpunctual, slack, and dissipated. It was anathema to him: too much time pointlessly spent "in social functions and with the fair sex."

He took lodgings at the Gate House, Cliffords Inn, a tiny, three-hundred-year-old dwelling tucked away in the maze of courts and alleys in the City of London. It was a few minutes' walk from the Royal Courts of Justice and not far from Dr. Johnson's house. Every day Pum walked down Fetter Lane, where the Great Fire of London in 1666 was finally arrested, toward the river and on into Fleet Street, where he would lunch at the Cheshire Cheese, or Ye Olde Cock Tavern across the way. All the shopping was done in Fetter Lane, which then had an oil shop, a grocer, baker, and milkman, as though it were a tiny village.

There was enormous pleasure to be had in furnishing this tiny house, and he went off looking for pieces whenever he could. On one memorable furniture-buying trip to an emporium off Oxford Street he was shown to a large attic to look around by himself. He walked into a long, dark room stacked floor to ceiling with treasures and junk; at the far end was a large leather armchair, and seated comfortably in it was an old man in contemporary dress, bending slightly forward. As Pum gazed at him he stood up and took a few steps toward him before rising off the floor to float up into the deeper dusk of the roof and vanish. Pum felt no fear, but neither did he ask the proprietor any questions. Pum had explored the idea of a pristine intuition, that child-like innocence and power which decays in adolescence. He thought of poltergeist activity, which he knew attached to young people and children, especially to girls just reaching the age of puberty, and he was deeply irritated, sometimes to the point of hatred, when others exhibited this sense after he himself felt he had lost it, destroyed it with his experience and expertise.

Walking home through Sergeant's Inn one day, he stopped to watch a group of men at work. They were demolishing an old brick wall, and Pum noticed three large pieces of a colored and glazed terracotta relief in the rubble, obviously bits of a Della Robbia plaque that had been built into the wall. The pieces formed a semi-circular plaque about two feet in diameter, a relief of a girl kneeling in prayer against a blue background with a garland in yellow and green swung behind her, probably the top portion of a large religious piece. The workmen let him have it for the price of a drink, ten shillings (50 pence). He carried it triumphantly back to the Gate House, eventually finding a home for it in his Lavenham house in Suffolk.

The Gate House was wholly his own, furnished with antiques and items from his collection. Mrs. Winder, the wife of a "beery-faced cockney porter," came in and did for him as best she could: the place was only "partly modernized," the sanitation was primitive. There was an air of ancient, ornate shabbiness, and the rooms held the imprint of lives now long gone. Pum adored the place—it was so quaintly contained, "like a child's doll's house," and like all his favorite possessions, he had found it by chance. He lived in the Gate House for the last eighteen months of the Great War and kept it on as his town house until 1935.

12
Revolution

Pum was on a slow, wood-burning troop train from a dreary Paris when peace broke out, declared by the stationmaster at Ventimiglia. All the fine young officers celebrated in the carriages, drinking great bottles of strong, sweet peasant red wine and dining on bully beef and grapes. He was thirty-seven, alive, buoyant, strong, and on his way to the East again. From his War Office job in London, he was moving into the dangerous intrigue that was Egyptian politics.

Unrest, rioting, and murder had sporadically plagued Egypt under martial law since 1914, and now it was on the brink of the most serious conflagration since the British occupation had begun. During the war, the British had conscripted young Egyptian men into laboring for the military in the Levant and had requisitioned crops and animals for supplies. The people were hungry and fearful, and becoming increasingly hostile to a colonial elite that seemed greedy and dismissive. Resentment and nationalist agitation grew and rallied behind Saad Zaghloul and his party, the Wafd, especially when they were excluded from the Paris Peace Conference in early 1919. The opposition was ignited, insurrection and independence were in the air, riots erupted, murders were committed, property was destroyed, and all the main road, rail, and telegraph communications throughout the country were cut. In the spring and summer of that year some seventy-five Britons were killed or

157

injured, but at least a thousand Egyptians also died as the British troops tried to contain the uprising. Demobilization had been a slow process, and there were still about 130,000 soldiers in Egypt in June that year.

The revolution would continue until the unilateral declaration of Egypt's independence in February 1922 and the implementation of the new constitution a year later. Even after the British Protectorate ceased and the sultan became king, British authority remained undiminished: the British commissioner still advised King Fouad I; each department of state had a British adviser to the minister; British judges sat in the courts along with Egyptian judges; and the occupying army remained and refused to withdraw from the Suez Canal zone. An Edinburgh doctor living and working in Cairo described the British officials as "a splendid body of men, not particularly brainy but scrupulously honest and just."

When the "whole country burst into flames" in 1919, Pum believed it was a carefully planned and executed coup carried out by Bolshevik agents exploiting anti-British feeling. The revolutionaries declared that the British government had cheated and deceived Egypt throughout the last war and were now evading their responsibilities, withholding any prospect of independence. Mayhem filled the Cairo streets, Europeans were stoned on sight, and in spite of the protestations of loyalty from his friends and neighbors, Pum rarely ventured out from his flat in the "native" quarter, so far from European protection.

Amid the hostilities, Pum was caught up in Egyptian politics: he was now second political officer in Upper Egypt and was sent to defend the large besieged British and American contingent in Asyut, the region's capital. He and his commanding officer, A.W. Hazel, senior inspector in the Ministry of the Interior, were each given a fully armed steamboat from Cook's Nile fleet. Tourist cruises along the Nile had been popular since the middle of the nineteenth century, when travelers sailed in *dahabiyas* (large houseboats with cross-sails), but after 1870 Thomas Cook Ltd brought in its luxurious and fast Scottish-built steamers, turning a three-month cruise into a twenty-day sight-seeing trip. By 1900 it was said that there were two empires on the Nile: Britain's military occupation and Cook's Egyptian travel.

Pum and Hazel set out on a cold March day, supported by an armored troop train with a hundred British soldiers on board that ran parallel to the river on the west bank, though it was constantly hampered by damage to the tracks and culverts, points, and signals. They traveled for nearly a week with little sign of trouble; the country seemed deserted, the fields empty and the waterwheels idle. But where they passed a town, crowds gathered to shout and throw stones, and occasionally fire a shot at them. At Minya, it suddenly got worse: Hazel was shot in the head and died there and then. Pum gave the order to attack the "rabble" on the bank as they ran helter-skelter across the mud of the irrigated fields, dropping their weapons as they went. Hazel was buried the following day at Asyut, and three hundred or so beleaguered Europeans, mostly women and children, were taken on board the steamers. They had been subject to violent attacks by angry mobs from surrounding "brigand towns," though most of these men were poorly armed with sickles, pikes, staves, and the odd shotgun. A company of Sikhs had got off a passing troop train to help and had killed or wounded many, others had jumped into the Nile, some were drowned, and dozens of vulture-picked bodies were still strewn around when Pum and his party arrived. The Sikhs had been on a night train from Luxor to Cairo—the same one that had been the scene of the infamous Deirut train murders, when six British officers and NCOs were brutally killed further down the line on March 18, 1919.

Pum was now directed to investigate this incident and prepare the ground for the trial of the murderers. He recounted the story as he found it, and it was covered by newspapers across the world, from the *Times* in London to the *Dominion* in New Zealand. The six officers had been on leave in Luxor when the revolution began and had received orders to get back to Cairo as soon as possible. They jumped on the night express, along with some two hundred Sikhs. At Asyut the train was held up, and the Sikhs got off to aid the British and American civilians who were being attacked. That left the British officers to go on alone, now vulnerable and "easy prey." They moved from the second to the first-class carriage, and the conductor stayed behind to deny that they were on board. All doors and windows were firmly closed. Inexplicably, not one of the British was armed. Further up the track, at Deirut, other "militants" were waiting for them and began battering the carriage, armed with knives, hoes, stones, and heavy sticks. They broke in on the men, who tried to fight them off with their fists, kit-bags, and even the seat cushions. The "cowardly" local police arrived late, according to Pum, even though they had been warned of trouble, but they apparently made little effort to intervene. The engine driver stayed for fifteen minutes at Deirut, out of fear or collusion, and three of the British were beaten and killed in their carriage. According to a newspaper correspondent in Cairo, the soldiers were "battered, jumped on until their bodies were beyond recognition, every conceivable brutality was committed on them and it is stated that one had his leg cut off and that some assailants in their frenzy drank his blood, another was hung up, [they] were spat on and had filth thrown on them," as stated by an article published in the *Marlborough Express* in New Zealand. By the time the train arrived at the next stop, Deir Mowas, an even larger crowd, "a fanatic mob howling with excitement," as Pum described it, had surrounded the station. The three surviving soldiers tried to make a run for it. One, Pope Bey, managed to get out onto the opposite line but was caught, stunned, stripped, "insulted," and flung for dead into a goods van. Meanwhile, the other two terrified men nevertheless managed to reach and uncouple the engine. One was killed there, the other boarded the engine and got it moving, but not fast enough, and, as Pum wrote, "an orgy of blood-lust ensued." Five of the bodies were dragged onto the platform, all were stripped and "insulted," and their teeth were knocked out while the women in the mob loudly ululated and danced over the naked, bloody corpses. Eventually the engine was recoupled, the bodies thrown back on board, and the train made off for the next station, Mallawi.

When they arrived, the goods van was opened and the sixth soldier, still just about alive, "naked and blood-bespattered, a terrible figure," staggered out into the arms of another mob. He, too, was swiftly overwhelmed and "murdered." The six bodies were laid out on the platform on their backs as the local band turned up to play, lustily.

There was a babel of shouts and wild screaming, loud reports of shot-guns and pistols fired into the air, as the "loose ladies of Mallawi did a loathsome dance over the British dead." According to Pum, all the singers, dancers, and conjurors of the town had gathered to take part in the bloody entertainment. Among them a "troupe of ladies of spe-cially ponderous proportions but of very light virtue had assembled, and were about to start a sort of hippopotamus dance of death over the victims when their sheikha [leader], Sitt Hanim, rushed onto the platform, burst into tears and forbade her 'girls' to join the orgy." She pushed them back, haranguing the crowd furiously, calling them sons of dogs for killing "such fine men" and swearing that she would inform on all of them personally—which she later did, to Pum, who made sure she was awarded the sum of £300 in her chosen form of gold anklets. Sitt Hanim told the crowd to get out quick before retribution arrived, and they soon did just that, heaving the bodies back onto the train, deserting the station, and leaving the "gallant courtesan and her troupe of hippo-whores" to go back to their quarters unmolested. Another witness, "a very strange creature, by no means so fine and feminine as the Sitt Hanim," also came to Pum. She was a woman, he decided, but went under the name of Hamid Effendi (Mr. Hamid) and "dressed and acted as a man and looked like a little hard-bitten bank-clerk." Pum discovered that she was "married" to another woman, and as man and wife they ran a corn-merchant's business. She claimed to have knelt beside each of the six victims, to have given them water to drink and heard their last words, and she wanted to be hired as a secret agent. He kept her in suspense, even though he knew her story was a complete fabrication, not because he thought she might be useful but because he wanted "to see more of this strange alloy of the sexes, which is by no means so usual in Egypt as the girl-ish boy, the womanly man type."

Because the trains had stopped running, Pum set out to investigate the murders on a stately and magnificent Nile *gyassa*, one hundred feet long, shallow and slender with a peaked bow turned up like a slipper and an enormous triangular sail. He was heading for Minya, where the six mutilated bodies had been secretly buried and the bloodied railway carriages preserved, left untouched as an exhibit. But it was the trip that moved him most. He had a camp bed under an awning on top of the load of firewood that the *gyassa* was carrying, open to the breezes fore and aft and commanding a magnificent view. He was well away from the captain and crew and was accompanied by his boy, Abd al-Wahid, who cooked for him on a charcoal stove. Abd al-Wahid (whose name Pum translates as meaning "slave of the one and only [God]") was just sixteen years old, a "sad, gentle grey-eyed lad with a quiet voice and a slow smile . . . good-looking in an effeminate way," who liked to wear women's undergarments and jewels.

Pum "thoroughly enjoyed" the trip; it restored him as he read, ate, slept, and scanned the shore through field glasses or listened to his servant's stories. Sanitary arrangements were somewhat difficult, he recorded, and perilous, for he had to balance himself on the rudder that protruded astern for some ten feet—a risky performance, particularly when the vessel was in rapid motion. On reaching Minya, Pum boarded an armored train complete with twenty British "Tommies" and a NCO, with whom Abd al-Wahid made firm friends.

The town and province had declared itself "Soviet," as had many of the bigger towns in Upper Egypt—"all things were for all men in common"—and the trains that ran between them were quite free and covered to the roofs with cheering crowds of ecstatic people. Pum immediately called on the Soviet-styled commissar and sub-commissar (a lawyer and a doctor, respectively) and had them arrested and dispatched to Cairo. With military force he clamped down on the uprising and maintained a degree of calm until an adequate force of civil police arrived. This he managed with the help of his good friend Mahmud Shaheen Bey MC DSO, a "fanatically pro-British" Egyptian cavalry officer whom Pum had known since his forays into the Nuba mountains. Shaheen was feared and fearless, a fine polo player and trick rider. Unpopular with his countrymen, this wizened, middle-aged man had a puckered yellow face, "Mongolian" eyes, and a cold, terrifying smile. He was "unbelievably cruel" in subduing his own people, and was "invaluable" to Pum.

When his train arrived at Mallawi, Pum met a wall of almost total silence. The local officials tried to suppress informers, but a few Copts agreed to speak; one or two of these were later murdered for their trouble. Moving on to Asyut, Pum ensconced himself on a beautiful houseboat, the Antar, built by and for George Somers Clarke, one-time architect of St. Paul's Cathedral, as Pum noted with pleasure. For three months he lived and worked on the boat, taking evidence, interviewing witnesses, and receiving reports—much of which, "as usually happens in the East," was false or given under intimidation, through personal enmity, bribery, and corruption. On the canal bank outside Pum's window, the witnesses and accused were lined up so that he could have a good look at them without being seen himself: "they were an unpleasant-looking lot." One of Pum's most assiduous helpers was a police officer, Abd al-Salaam Fahmy, a "dark-skinned, flabby, underhand fellow" who professed undying loyalty but who turned out to be one of the ringleaders of the revolt. Pum had him arrested and imprisoned, but, oddly, the charges were later dropped at Pum's say-so, though he doesn't explain why. The man was released and became his "best friend for life and a staunch adherent of the right cause ever after."

As conductor of the prosecution, Pum amassed sufficient material to put a hundred of the "most flagrant perpetrators of the crime" on trial, thirty-seven of whom were publicly executed at the towns involved in the massacre. Pum pitied the sorry-looking militants at their trial, yet alongside this emotion and because of his deep involvement with the crime, he again experienced "that horrible lust" for revenge. He felt that the Counsel for the Prosecution, all friends of his, were less than thorough, and that the defense, also his friends, were almost bitter enemies using underhanded tricks and evasion to get the accused off the hook. He realized he had become vindictive and completely preju-diced, but still "would like to have seen the whole lot condemned and led off to the scaffold." The work had seemed a "charnel-house" to him; he was sickened by it all and refused the invitation to stay and watch the hangings, filled as he was with the conflicting emotions of shame and triumph. Instead, he went off to Luxor for a rest and to avoid the anonymous death threats and a threatening "breakdown."

Despite the nature of his task and the dangers and injustices it involved, he still found time to do a little antique collecting. He was staying at Chicago House with the American archaeologist Ambrose Lansing, then working on excavations at Thebes for the New York Metropolitan Museum of Art's Egyptian Expedition. In Luxor, Pum had visited the Tombs of the Nobles at Gourna and the Eighteenth Dynasty tomb of (Rahmes) Ramesses, and so enamored was he that he spent two days casting the reliefs cut into the exquisite fine-grained limestone. His method of casting was to dust the relief with a camel-hair brush, then to lay over the whole a single leaf of fine silver paper, brushing it in with a stiff brush so it "took." Next, he pressed plasticine an inch thick, piece by piece, onto the surface, pressing it down with a section of flat plyboard bristling with half-driven tacks. When he removed it, it brought with it a negative of the relief. He made nine of these beautiful pieces and then destroyed his molds. They are now built into a wall at Beit al-Kretliya. Satisfying and painstaking it may well have been, but it was, Pum acknowledged, "extremely irregular, in fact quite illegal"—but as chief political officer of Upper Egypt, who was going to stop him?

Cairo apartment, 1920s.

On acquiring Beit al-Kretliya, 1935.

Sightseeing with his son John, Philae, 1931.

Beit al-Kretliya, after Comité restoration, 1935.

Beit al-Kretliya and Mosque of Ibn Tulun, aerial view, after Comité restoration, 1935.

Beit al-Kretliya, interior courtyard, 1935.

Beit al-Kretliya, fountain room, 1935.

Beit al-Kretliya, a fraction of Pum's collection, mid 1930s.

Beit al-Kretliya, Pum and brother Thomas, staff, and dog 'Fedel Effendi,' 1940s.

Pum and Thomas aboard a Nile steamboat, late 1930s or early 1940s.

Pum and cat, Lavenham, Suffolk, 1940s.

Pum and Thomas in front of the Horus statue at Edfu Temple, c.1935.

Pum in 'Arab dress,' Beit al-Kretliya, 1930s.

Pum in 'Arab dress' on the roof of Beit al-Kretliya, 1930s.

Gravestone for Pum, carved by Eric Gill, with a dedication by King Farouk.

13
Murder and Mayhem

Back in Cairo, despite his lack of passion for medicine, Pum was attached to the Citadel Hospital and lodged in al-Gawhara Palace, now a museum. Also known as the Bijou Palace, it was commissioned in 1814 by Mohamed Ali Pasha, an Albanian commander in the Ottoman army who became *wali* and khedive of Egypt and Sudan in the early nineteenth century. His palace was part of an ancient, impregnable stronghold looking out over and commanding the whole city. From here, Pum explored the Citadel to the north, its walls, towers, turrets, gates, and bastions; the roofless Mosque of al-Nasir Mohamed, the early Turkish Mosque of Sidi Siriyya, the humble tomb of Sheikh Kikhya, patron saint of water carriers; and the thirteenth-century Joseph's Well, a square shaft over three hundred feet deep. From the mouth of the well ran a wall where spies and traitors were shot during the war, a place the locals avoided at night.

The Bijou Palace had a large marble fountain, columned terraces and porticoes, and a menagerie that had been home to a lion, two tigers, and an elephant, a gift from the British. A high-walled garden of flowerbeds and orange groves hid the harem; there were vast painted halls and stairways, and a huge subterranean water-storage cistern cut out of the rock where Pum went rowing in the dark in a small boat. In the harem was a great Italian marble bathroom with a beautiful sunken alabaster bath where Mohamed Ali had once luxuriated and chatted with his bathmen. The myth also tells that from his bath he had ordered the massacre of five hundred Mamluks who had ruled Egypt for the previous six hundred years. The strain of that terrible act was said to have left Mohamed Ali with a nervous cough, and the same problem afflicted his great-grandson King Fouad I after an assassination attempt. Pum said he felt a peculiarly morbid pleasure when walking along the steep, rock-hewn road where those five hundred had been trapped and murdered. It was said that their blood flowed in a stream down the rock gutters, past the little "Mosque of Blood," which was never used again for worship after the bodies were collected there, and on through Bab al-Azab ("the Bachelor's Gate"), where there is a chair kept only for use of the righteous who have reached the age of a hundred years. Below this gate was Ramla Square, for centuries the scene of public torture and executions and where they held the Mulid al-Far ("Saint's Day of the Rat"), a carnival of "jovial obscenity" later banned by Khedive Ismail Pasha, apparently for fear of offending European decency. From here you could walk between the two great mosques of Sultan Hassan and al-Rifa'i, close by the most ancient mosque in Cairo, that of Ibn Tulun.

Over coffee and *shisha* in the evening, Pum watched the Bektashi Dervishes rolling over and over down the steep incline in front of their monastery beneath the Muqattam cliff to the south of the Citadel. The supplicants were mostly women wanting babies, with the odd penitent mixed in. He thought them "ridiculous" even as he reveled in the alien nature of the Arab world, but he would rather relax and watch them than go to the mess and spend time with the "sealed pattern" army types hanging out there. He did go to the Turf Club in the European part of Cairo to meet his friend Bill Truman, and eventually he moved into an annex on the roof of Truman's flat on Sharia Maghraby, close to the club, where he began taking all his meals.

He contrived to remain socially isolated, though, except when Tom visited from Constantinople, where he was on General George Milne's staff busy dismantling the Ottoman Empire. The British, French, and Italian occupation of Constantinople lasted from the end of the Great

War until 1923. Together, the twins tried to sleep through the sweltering nights on the roof of Pum's new flat, somewhat incommoded by a great ram being fattened up for Eid al-Adha by the landlord, Hagg Rashid, a "squint-eyed and cunning" builder. The ram had been living with the family and had become very affectionate; it kept them awake with its constant nuzzling. Pum and Tom traveled back to Constantinople and stayed in the GHQ mess, once the townhouse of the German arms magnate, Herr Krupp von Essen. It was, Pum wrote, an "atrociously vulgar," luxurious house with plate-glass windows overlooking the Bosphorus and rich silk brocades draped everywhere. In compensation, though, there was a very good wine cellar to plunder. They went sightseeing through the ruined city, where the people were "pinched, underfed and dressed in rags," but still retained what Pum called a "primarily Oriental characteristic, the potentiality of intense cruelty"—the Mamluk dynasty had been the "most fiendishly cruel class in the whole of the East."

Tom and Pum went about together, looked alike, even grew identical mustaches, but they still felt the estrangement that had begun in Gallipoli. The "fine rapture of mutual devotion and complete oneness, that boundless love and mutual appreciation which our natures longed for and longed to give" had faded. Returning to Cairo alone, Pum took the opportunity to stop off at Smyrna to enjoy, "shamelessly and blatantly," the pleasures to be had there now that he was "alone and free." He couldn't have done this with Tom, because even despite their present estrangement and intermittent intimacy, they had "always had a strong complex when together which made [them] shy and uncommunicative in all sex matters."

Back at his flat above Truman's, with no one but his closest friends knowing where he was, Pum felt like a hermit, an early Christian father, or a Theban troglodyte. He had just his boy, Abd al-Wahid, to cater to him. Truman was a bachelor, too, the chief inspector of arts and crafts in the Ministry of Education, and a gifted painter with an attractive husky voice. He and Pum liked and understood each other well, and got into the habit of going, once a week, to the *hammams*, which were not much used by the Europeans then, especially the "stiff and conventional Britisher who fears and mistrusts everything 'native.'" There were probably seventy or so *hammams* in Cairo, "good and bad." Some were for men only, but others catered for women by day and men by night and so needed two sets of staff: male and female pedicurists, masseurs, hairdressers, and "intimate attendants." Even the most respectable baths, according to Pum, lent themselves to "amorous intrigue," while the less salubrious offered "much sexual license." You made of them, he confided, whatever you liked. That natural and necessary virtue, discretion, which he had acquired early on in life, was vital to preserving his reputation.

Soon enough, Pum's eyrie on Truman's roof became more widely known about, and he decided to quit it. Hagg Rashid let him a new apartment in a "native block," where he removed all the modern doors and replaced them with ancient screens of *mashrabiya*-work, intricate paneling set at right-angles to the doorways which brought light and air to the rooms but prevented people outside from seeing in. The flat was next to the Citadel and behind al-Rifa'i Mosque, the dynastic burial palace of the Royal House of Egypt, and the air was full of the sounds of death rituals carried out on the appointed dates for each member of the royal family entombed there. This mainly involved the sacrifice and cooking of animals and the distribution of their flesh to the poor. Close by, too, was a convent of Sudanese "witch-women" who practiced divination using seashells and cards, as opposed to the *ramaal* or sand horoscope of the Egyptians, and who were devoted to the art of *zahr*, the propitiation or casting-out of evil spirits. And "what a racket they made," with their wailing, keening, and banging of drums (they also had a profitable sideline brewing and selling beer). The incessant, discordant noise kept Pum awake until he got Hagg Rashid to make them turn it down. He had never come across anything like them in Sudan and believed they were all for show, exploiting and pandering to the Egyptian taste for the superstitious. They had quite a hold on the local women, who wanted help with their hopes, fears, and ailments. Hagg Rashid's wife was chronically unwell and was completely in the hands of the "witch-women," whose demands, made through a presiding spirit, became steadily more exacting. One night, coming home late, Pum was met on the stone stairs by a group of fel-laheen pushing and pulling an indignant and protesting camel up to his landlord's flat. He had to wait a good fifteen minutes till they got it past his landing, while Hagg Rashid shouted down apologetically to him that the women required the camel to be sacrificed in his sitting room and its flesh distributed around the neighborhood. Pum listened from below while they did the deed, but didn't discover whether the sick wife improved at all. It wasn't just the camel that suffered in the flats, Pum very nearly suffocated when his charcoal burners were all lit and the doors were closed against the penetrating cold. Many Egyp-tians died like this every winter.

Abd al-Wahid was an excellent cook, so Pum only needed a small twelve-year-old Syrian boy, whom he called "Dovdah," which would be Arabic for "frog," to complete his household. Dovdah was a "dear little fellow, thin with harrassed eyes," who had no friends or family, was diligent and affectionate, and "made an excellent waiter at table." With good food, milk, and kindness, the boy plumped out, lost his dejected, hunted look, and became cheerful and happy like Abd al-Wahid. In the evenings the boys would sit by Pum's bed and tell stories slowly in Arabic while Pum wrote them down. Some he published, but many remain in manuscript, now in his grandson Theo's care. They are anything, wrote Pum, from "naively broad to downright pornographic, which is perhaps why I am fond of them . . . most of them are unpublishable without an expurgation which would quite alter and spoil them." But Pum's clan-destine idyll would not last. It would end in murder.

In 1920 Pum was, as he wished, seconded from the British army and attached for Oriental liaison to the British Residency. One of his first jobs was to accompany and entertain the "Sultan of Koweit [sic] (a small Sultanate in Southern Arabia)" and his *wazir* (prime minister), the *amir* Ahmed, and to show them the sights of the city. He quickly became intimate friends with this "delightfully naive and simple pair." They had no retainers with them, so they all put up at Shepheard's Hotel.

There was still so much disturbance that British officers were directed to wear uniform and carry firearms, but to dress like that when off duty would have spoiled all Pum's fun. In the evenings, then, he wore Arab clothes. By day they called on British and Egyptian officials—Pum in his smartest khaki—but at night he became as completely Arab as his guests, using some gear from his own wardrobe and borrowing other items from the sultan, who instructed him in how to dress properly. Standing in front of the long cheval glass in his bedroom, he discovered that once he had "darkened my face slightly with gipsy powder, I was transformed into a magnificent Arab somewhat more benign looking than Richard Burton in his make-up but quite as convincing—my large Anglo-Saxon head, like Lawrence's, being completely re-formed and remodelled by the scarf and cord." Into his broad silk belt, he stuck an Arab dagger in its silver-gilt sheath that the sultan had given him.

It quickly became obvious that the sultan and his *wazir* were not remotely interested in "European entertainments." "Why come to a place like this?" they cried. "We want to be amused and to laugh, don't we?" And so the three of them began to sneak out at night from the back entrance of the hotel gardens in search of adventure in the "best and gayest native resorts." They wanted the Arab music halls and cafés, so cheerful and dazzling compared to what they were used to in Kuwait. The sultan relished the

> antics and droll native wit of Kish Kash (Rihani), the voluptuous songs of Tawhiga at the 'Alfa Lehla Wa Lehl' (The Thousand Nights and a Night), the amorous miming, singing and danc- ing, the 'beauty of the many exquisite girls' which provoked in the audience a 'quite unabashed, frenzy of spontaneous rapture which, in spite of the [performers'] reputation for being out- wardly cold and unemotional, is peculiarly oriental.

Pum and the "two charming Orientals" visited many low haunts, but were never suspected of being anything other than well-to-do Arabs from the Ghezireh Palace Hotel, Zamalek.

About six months later, Pum was deputed to act as personal liai- son officer to Amir Abdullah of Transjordan, in Cairo as a guest of the British government, on his first visit there since the beginning of the Great War. He and his retinue put up at the Continental Hotel and Pum moved in there for two weeks, too. Again, it was a round of official and unofficial meetings, and again Pum found that, like the sultan of Kuwait, this visitor didn't care for the dull entertainments on offer, nor the military displays and inspections he had to attend. Pum discovered that their tastes were pleasingly similar to his own. What the *amir* enjoyed most turned out to be tea in his hotel suite followed by "an early retirement after dinner to his bedroom, surrounded by his familiars, peach-cheeked and gazelle-eyed youths, page boys of good family and doubtless chosen especially for their charm and good-looks." The boys "all wore long locks that almost dripped, so heavily oiled and scented were they, and fell down on either side beneath the thin brown cord framing their faces to the greatest advantage." In 1850, the French novelist Gustave Flaubert was in Cairo and had written to tell to a friend that sex with boys was "quite accepted. One admits one's sodomy, and it is spoken of at table in the hotel . . . we have considered it our duty to indulge in this form of ejaculation." Not much had changed; boy prostitution was common, and the pederast or scopophiliac could easily find his fulfillment.

The eldest of the *amir's* boys was perhaps sixteen: "a faint golden fluff fledged his chin and upper lip, giving him the appearance of a very young, budding Christ." The youngest, in Pum's estimation, was thirteen or fourteen and looked "extremely girlish, and was obviously the spoilt darling of the party, such as one so often meets in an Oriental establishment; with a gaiety and impudence about him that was quite irresistible." The *amir* would recline on his bed, propped up on pillows in one corner, while Pum sat at the foot enjoying the fun as the boys clambered around laughing and joking and showing little if any outward respect for their indulgent master. He treated them with "the easy freedom of a father who relies on affection rather than discipline." When the two weeks of pleasure were up, Pum was extremely sad to part with them all, and on the final day, the *amir* and he exchanged signed photographs and they all gave each other parting gifts. The youthful Jesus gave him a bag of Yemeni coffee, another boy gave a bundle of Arabian cigarettes, and the "little playboy, the wag, a look at parting which I cannot forget." The group was sadly, silently waiting for the Residency cars to take them to the station when the *amir* plunged his hand into his broad silk belt, brought out a magnificent gold watch on a delicate chain, and thrust it into Pum's hand without a word. Foolishly, Pum misread his intentions, admired the watch and passed it back to him, but again the *amir* thrust it at him. A whispered instruction came from behind him: "Take it, Bey, the watch alone costs fifty pounds!" Only then did he realize that this was another parting gift, and he was deeply moved.

Soon after this, Pum was offered the post of senior inspector in the Ministry of the Interior. The money was good, the work congenial and among friends, so he accepted immediately and resigned from the British army. With his friend John Young, the chief inspector, Pum set about reorganizing the Inspectorate (which oversaw law enforcement, public health, and public engineering) and in the process getting to know John better. They had much in common apart from their work: John was an accomplished painter, and they shared a catholic love of pictures, books, and beautiful objects. They both had a powerful sympathy for the East, for Islam, and the Egyptian people, and shared many friends, from fellah to pasha. Above all they both loved Cairo, its mosques and mausoleums, bazaars and caravansaries, ancient streets and squares. Eventually, John and his servant took the flat above Pum's and they shared the same roof terrace.

Fouad, sultan of Egypt and Sudan since 1917, took the title of king on Egyptian Independence in 1922 and undertook a "tour of ingratiation" in the provinces at the suggestion of the Residency. Public appearances made Fouad nervous, but he needed to increase his popularity, and it was Pum who accompanied him. They traveled to the six *mudiriyas*, or provinces, of the Nile Delta, and stood in big decorated marquees as the notables of the district filed past to shake hands with the uncomfortable king. At these ceremonies, a poet would declaim his work written especially for the occasion, and Fouad would wave his hand, mutter asides under his breath, and, at intervals, give a sudden barking cough that frightened those who were not familiar with it. A small Egyptian girl selected for the honor of presenting him with a bouquet panicked when she heard it, dropped her flowers and bolted for the daylight, down the red carpet, out of the tent and away. Knowing that another child would be attempting the same feat the next day at the next *mudiriya*, a dress rehearsal was hurriedly arranged and the poor child had to repeatedly approach the throne and be barked at by a stand-in until she was quite bark-proof. At the actual ceremony she stood her ground and presented her bouquet with complete sangfroid.

On March 13, 1922, Pum was appointed Oriental secretary to the high commissioner, a post once occupied by Ronald Storrs of the Arab Bureau of Intelligence. He was attached to the Foreign Office with the rank of first secretary (equivalent to the army rank of brigadier) and handsomely paid. Now Pum's chief was Field Marshall Viscount Allenby, in his opinion a "brilliant strategist and conquerer of Palestine." He was known in the British Army as "The Bull" because of his hot temper and harsh expression. Pum, worried about fitting in with a man apparently so alien to his own character, actually found him to be a kind, considerate, and courteous fellow with an equally pleasant wife. Pum got quite close to Mabel Allenby, sending her "charms" and other small gifts, and accepting invitations to suppers and parties. The Bull appeared to have a strange prescience and a useful capacity for getting at the essentials of any matter. On top of all this, Pum thought him intuitive, full of common sense, and one of the handsomest and most imposing men he had ever met. Tall and stately, he had fine regular features and "an aura of greatness about him." As if concerned that this sounded a little too much like an infatuation, Pum did mention that Allenby was not a ready speaker, preferring to sit and listen, and neither was he a particularly subtle diplomat. He found it hard to cope with the "sly Oriental" or the subterfuges and rivalries of his staff who, having been born and bred in the Foreign Office, resented his military personality and his direct, sometimes arbitrary ways. Lord Carnarvon, who financed Howard Carter's excavations in the Valley of the Kings and often had to rely on Allenby during his battles with the *Times*, described him as a weak man and a drinker, very straight, but slow and rather stupid. In his weekly roundtable conferences attended by the senior secretaries and ministerial advisers, Allenby would coolly lean back in his chair and say, "Now, you fellows with the brains, get on with it!"

To keep up with political opinion, Pum joined the select Mohamed Ali Club where the Egyptian and European social and political "lions" gathered, speaking only French and Arabic. It had the best chef and cellar in the land and made the Turf Club look like a pothouse: English-speaking and aimlessly good-natured, dedicated to swapping risqué stories and sporting anecdotes. Oddly, though, the Turf maintained a reputation among Egyptians for being the place where important decisions were made and where appointments and offices were bestowed.

Pum's flat was his private haven where he was mostly solitary, but where he occasionally invited his close friends. Entertained by a lute player or a reader of the Qu'ran, they would sit about drinking tea and smoking in the Oriental atmosphere he nurtured there. Abd al-Wahid also brought friends back, mostly Egyptian students, and was flattered to be allowed to have them there. Pum performed small favors for these young men, writing letters of recommendation and such, and in return they brought him gifts of flowers, sweetmeats, poems, and drawings. He sent Dovdah in to them with tea and cigarettes, and learned later that Abd al-Wahid had shown them through his private quarters while he was out, proudly and innocently showing them the master's treasures. Pum watched the students exercise in the garden below his window. Ahmed Effendi, a "young Hercules" stripped to the waist and lifting weights, and Mohamed Ibrahim Effendi engaging in staff-play. They formed a fitness club with Hagg Rashid's five sons, aged between eight and thirteen, and elected Pum as their patron. And then one day Dovdah disappeared. All that remained of him were his slippers, his best shorts, a cap pistol, and an empty purse. He was never seen again.

Now it was just Pum and Abd al-Wahid, but this boy's mother had chosen him a wife. He sold his bicycle, bought pots, pans, and presents, took all his savings and a gift from Pum, and set off for Fayoum for two weeks—somewhat sadly, thought Pum. In less than ten days he was back, looking a little sheepish and saying that though he liked his bride he liked Cairo even better, so he had left her with his mother. The city was still full of unrest; attempts on the lives of British officers continued, and there was gunfire in the streets at night. Pum was advised to arm himself, not to go out after dark, and never to isolated places. He was glad of the students and their fitness club, as they seemed to afford him some protection. They even said they didn't look upon him as an Englishman, a compliment he received with mixed emotions. But then, suddenly, Abd al-Wahid vanished too, just as Dovdah had done.

The police were called; they interviewed the mother and wife in Fayoum, but they hadn't seen Abd al-Wahid since his return to Cairo. Endless rumors about the boy began to circulate: that he had been seen at an evil haunt in the city; that he had been seen running for a train at Alexandria; on a *gyassa* at al-Wasta; in a crowd. . . . Pum and the police assumed he had gone off for a while and would eventually return. A replacement servant was found.

Life became more difficult, and anti-British feeling increased. The students no longer exercised outside Pum's flat, but they visited more frequently and attempted to make friends with the new servant. They began to ask, a tad too firmly for Pum's liking, for more favors and letters of introduction to Egyptian ministers.

One evening Pum missed the late train home from a friend's house in Maadi and, worried about the general situation, decided to stay over. This happened again a few days later, but this time he got a cab and arrived home in the early hours. Climbing the stairs, he was startled by one of the students emerging from the shadows; he said he had been visiting Hagg Rashid's sons. Pum noticed that he was clutching a short, thick stick with a leather-bound handle known as a "life-preserver," but then lots of people were carrying these weapons for protection, including Pum himself. The boy's manner was strange, though, as if he had been drinking, so Pum quickly said goodnight and unlocked his door, but found the light switch broken and had to grope his way to the next room to a lamp behind a large Arab screen. Before he could reach it, a heavy blow, doubtless aimed at his head, crashed down onto his shoulder. There were two assailants that he could make out, and more blows caught him in quick succession. He dodged about punching with his left hand while fumbling for his holster and the automatic with his right. He got it out, cocked it, and was just about to fire at where he thought his attackers were when he tripped and fell. He heard two more blows hit the wall behind him before the two jumped over him and ran out of the flat and away down the stairs.

Shaken, but not seriously injured, he stumbled into his servant's bedroom and found him apparently fast asleep—the fight had been grim but perhaps quite silent. The next day he called the secret police, and although they were busy with other similar cases of attacks on British officers, they gave him, as an important figure, their full attention. Several of the students were arrested, as well as two of Hagg Rashid's sons. The one Pum had met on the stairs quickly turned informer and revealed the whole conspiracy. The fitness club, it was discovered, was a branch of the "Egypt for the Egyptians Club." It was thought that they had murdered little Dovdah, either because he had discovered them or had refused to help them, and that they had then easily enrolled Abd al-Wahid into their group. Flattered by their apparent intellect and glamor, Abd al-Wahid had told them all about Pum's daily routine and shown them the flat, but when they revealed to the unworldly youth that with his help they intended to murder his master, he had wanted out immediately. Persuading him that it was a merely a ruse to test his loyalty and that there were no hard feelings, they invited him on one of their picnics to the Muqattam Hills, honeycombed with caves and passages, a lair for thugs and criminals. He never came home.

The plot to murder Pum was botched when he had stayed at Maadi on the first allotted night, and when they tried it again only two of the group actually turned up. They had chosen him because of his position—his murder would cause a great stir—and because of his involvement with the train massacre trials: relatives of the thirty-five executed men still wanted vengeance.

In 1959, *Mostly Murder*, a book about violent crime in Egypt, covered the discovery of a body in the Muqattam Hills. Sir Sydney Smith, professor of forensic medicine at Edinburgh University and former principal medico-legal expert to the Egyptian government, noted the "extraordinary amount of crime in Egypt, specially crimes of violence," and that "truthfulness was considered something of an idiosyncrasy." In the summer of 1922, he wrote, a desiccated body was found in a cave high up in the Hills, dressed in a sweater, vest, cotton drawers, and a pair of socks. The remains belonged to "an Egyptian with slight Negroid characteristics, male . . . strongly built, with dark, curly hair." He had been hit over the head, the first blow knocking him over and then others hitting him while he was down. His throat had been cut. Smith deduced that the victim was the domestic servant of a European and that his employer had been a British official named Gayer-Anderson. It sounds a little like a Conan Doyle puzzle, but the skeleton was wearing rather fine cashmere socks and sewn inside each was a small piece of tape bearing the name "Gayer-Anderson."

In March 1923, Pum gave evidence at a trial, the culprits were hanged, and the whole country punished with a fine of half a million pounds. From this money, Abd al-Wahid's mother was compensated for the loss of her son, and Pum made a life-long monthly allowance to the boy's wife. For his own safety, he had to leave his flat in the "native" part of the city and return to Sharia Maghraby in the European quarter—safer, but too civilized for Pum. It later became clear that the murders of Dovdah and Abd al-Wahid and the attempt on Pum's life were part of a larger plot, known as the "Conspiracy Case," which culminated in the assassination in 1924 of the *sirdar*, General Sir Lee Stack Pasha, governor-general of Sudan and commander-general of the Egyptian army. His fatal shooting as he drove through Cairo had terrible consequences for nationalism and made way for the autocratic powers of King Fouad I. Egypt's first democratically elected government, the Saad Zaghloul cabinet, known as "the People's Government," had fallen.

14
Negative Differences

P um worked hard throughout the 1920s, socialized when required, but often hid himself away to "commune with beauty." When he retired from the Egyptian government in 1923, at the age of forty-two, his pension allowed him even more time to work with his antiques and write his poems and articles "on artistic and archaeological subjects," including "How to Buy a Scarab" and "How to Care for your Oriental Carpet" for magazines such as the *Sphinx* and the *Egyptian Gazette*.

He kept around him a small group of male friends who met in the evenings at Pum's apartment at 27 Sharia Maghraby, once every two weeks. They called themselves the Shubbuk Society. Desultory in their loose, comfortable, "native" garb, the Shubbuk Society lay back upon cushions, talked literature, art, and religion, drank innumerable cups of coffee, and puffed on their *shubbuks*, traditional Turkish pipes. These pipes had a small, usually quite plain clay bowl at the end of a straight stem of cherry or jasmine wood, often about five or six feet long. Smokers sucked on large, detachable amber mouthpieces that were often highly ornamented, rimmed with gold and enamelwork in elaborate patterns and enriched with precious stones. Each pipe would have been very personal to the Turkish smoker of the wealthier classes, and a great deal of care and cost had been spent on the designs and choice.

The "cool and refreshing" smoke came streaming up the long stem "without the chesty effort that comes with smoking a shesha." They used uncut Syrian leaf tobacco, damped and coiled like a turban over the bowl. With a small pair of tongs, a boy, the "slave of the bowl," took pieces of glowing charcoal from a special brazier and placed them, one by one, on top of the primed pipe as the smoker drew in deeply. He kept vigil over the bowl, removing ash, adding freshly glowing charcoal, and replenishing his master's cup with powerful Turkish coffee. The coffee cups were small and delicate, made of porcelain, and rested on silver or gold holders, incised or chased with intricate designs, again in enamel or studded with gems.

The Shubbuk Society was a select affair. It included Pum's best friend Bill Truman, plus Hamza Carr, Abd al-Malek Hamza, and Ahmed Hassanein Pasha of Western Desert fame who became grand chamberlain to the king before being killed in a motor accident in Cairo. Hassanein had lived quite a life, and was educated at Balliol College, Oxford, before setting off to explore the South Western Desert in 1921. He was accompanied there by the English explorer and travel writer, Rosita Forbes, the first European woman to visit the area, which was largely closed to Westerners at that time. She wrote a book about it on her return, but was damned with faint praise by the male establishment, who considered it a very one-sided account of the journey; they really didn't care for her version of Hassanein's "capabilities."

The Shubbuk Society was even more critical: they considered Forbes a "bitch and a charlatan," prey to a raging feminine vanity, and believed she had tricked Hassanein into giving her an undertaking that he wouldn't write up their joint experiences for at least a year. In retaliation, and not wanting to be sidelined or outdone by a woman, Hassanein organized another trek into the desert starting from the point at which they had finished the first. His account of this longer journey won many accolades, including the Royal Society's gold medal (Forbes had only won the silver the previous year), and according to the resolutely male Shubbuk Society, undermined and reduced her account to a routine trek. Pum thought his friend Hassanein's trek completely topped Forbes's, and his own account of visiting the sacred and forbidden city of Jaghbub also apparently bettered hers by far. Whereas she claimed to have been the first Christian woman ever to spend a night in the harem there, Pum had been the only Christian *man* ever to have entered it.

The Shubbuk Society was arguably a substitute family for Pum in Cairo, along with his carefully chosen servants, including Debish [sic], "who overeats and just glows like a silk worm." He "superintendents the work of the others without doing a hand turn himself so you can see what a leisurely existence his is." In Cairo in 1927, they experienced "record heat this past 10 days . . . we hardly ventured out but spent the days indoors a state of extreme neglige, drinking long drinks and plunging into baths and under showers at intervals." The only one who enjoyed this temperature was Debish, "who flitted about in a gauzy shirt like a little puck among the flames, very merry in his silent manner carrying lemons and syphons which he loved to manipulate like a gruesome-ish fireman trying to extinguish our burning." All the "tourists have either been killed or driven out of the garden with flaming swords . . . and we who have eaten of the tree of knowledge lurk, knowing that May is the best of months." Tom was in Rome with Mary, at art school, and they would all meet and travel back to England together in June, "ansh allah!" or God willing, as he wrote.

Pum still felt an emotional estrangement from Tom, who was stationed in India during the 1920s, and a deep sense of regret and isolation. Their relationship was intense, close or not, and was a source of pleasure, pain, and great curiosity to them both. Pum had a well-thumbed copy of the Victorian eugenicist Francis Galton's *Inquiries into Human Faculty* (1883); it still sits on a shelf in his library in Beit al-Kretliya. The book explores the meaning of twinship, and Pum and Tom avidly and repeatedly read it, searching for a meaning to their often-difficult relationship.

Galton's *Inquiries* contains a "scientific" study of twins, with material that relates to thirty-five pairs of identical twins. This greatly stimulated Pum's curiosity and made him "realise more than ever how truly identical Tom and I are in almost every way." He and Tom included among their "likenesses of body, mind and character some of those differences which Galton refers to as 'mirror-image' or 'complimentary' and which, before I read him I had already recognised with Tom and myself, and christened 'negative differences' on account of the analogy between them and the negative and positive of a photograph." Pum says that Galton's conclusion in the matter of human development is that "Nature is stronger than Nurture," and he believed him without doubt to be right, that the majority of his and Tom's similarities and differences of all sorts were "basically genetic." There were particular external influences that came within Galton's specification of nurture: their different adult environments and professions (perhaps not so very different to an objective observer) and their father's "unfortunate tendency to be unfair to me in my childhood—and his drastic and unorthodox training methods." All these had affected the twins, "which of course varied according to our temperaments." On the whole, though, Pum considered that external influences had no very serious consequences upon either of them, that it was nature that was the dominant force in shaping them, and it had used the same mold.

The *Inquiries* argued that the likeness of twins was constantly changing, even to the extent of one or both of a pair becoming more like the other, rather than remaining as themselves, a sort of interchange of facial appearance and expression. "Our bones and limbs, our hands and feet, our heads, features, hair and coloring and all else physical about us," wrote Pum, "was exactly similar and has remained very much so ever since, partly by reason of such connivances by 'Nature' as our hair in each case starting to recede when we were about twenty-one and to do so and to turn grey, when the time came, to an exactly similar extent without producing marked baldness or whiteness; or to our both discovering a year or so later that we had very similar astigmatisms (each more marked in the left eye) which caused us to wear glasses for reading ever since (the glasses were interchangeable between us). . . . We have always been able to fit and wear each other's clothes, hats, boots, collars and gloves and have often done so." They would often as not dress alike, even when apart. Once, when Pum had just qualified as a doctor, he went to visit Tom at his army base, and when they met on the station platform at Newcastle-upon-Tyne they were both wearing bright yellow ties they had each bought for the occasion.

The twins were so close that they felt each other's illnesses and displayed the same symptoms, even when Pum was in Cairo and Tom was in Lavenham, Suffolk. Pum thought Galton quite right to suggest that identical twins might suffer the same illnesses, often at the same time, as though to prevent them losing their strong resemblance. Tom and he did seem to suffer alike throughout their lives: for their first forty years they were both "martyrs to severe quinseys," though neither of them had their tonsils out till middle age. Each of them nearly died of a throat complaint: Pum of diphtheria in Cairo in 1916, Tom of strep throat in India in 1927. Later, as a result of these illnesses, which in both cases were seriously mismanaged, they developed grave heart trouble that made them semi-invalids for many years, "and will probably cause our deaths." They had each suffered malaria and dysentery in the East, too (but then so had almost everyone else who was out there).

The twins were astonishingly alike; even their voices were indistinguishable. Pum and Tom were forever answering alike and beginning the same sentence at the same time, so much so that they often became silent in company because of embarrassment. During childhood and youth, he wrote, they were "always as likely as not to be mistaken for one another when together (at times even by the rest of the family) and after reaching manhood continued to be much mistaken when apart." In 1899, when Pum was a student at Guy's, Tom was lunching with him at the hospital, and a colleague of Pum's, Glenville, came over to their table to talk to him. He cast a quick glance at Pum and then began to talk to Tom, whom he had never seen nor met before. Tom was embarrassed. "My brother!" he said, and waved a hand across the table. Glenville took this as an introduction and held out his hand, obviously not much interested or impressed, gave a perfunctory "How are you?" and without more ado turned back to Tom to discuss a case which he and Pum were treating. At this point Pum broke in and with considerable difficulty convinced Grenville of his mistake.

Curiously, then, one of their most salient joint characteristics was their pleasure in being solitary. They both required "to be much alone," and were happiest when they were, though Pum was adamant that they were never lonely. At heart, he wrote, they were decidedly ungregarious and unsociable, even antisocial. They were undemonstrative to a fault, unusually self-controlled, self-reliant, and, he believed, tolerant. It irritated him enormously that the contemporary studies of twinship he devoured always ignored the paranormal aspect of the relationship. He was in no doubt that twinship was imbued with telepathic and other unexplained phenomena, and that a study that did not take these into account would never be thorough or satisfactory. Telepathy, even between man and wife, seemed to him to be such a universal thing that he found it hard to understand why its existence was even doubted or denied by so many, and he looked forward to the day when the paranormal would be recognized and treated as a science.

*

Pum might have agreed that any expression, any banality, dream, fantasy, linguistic tic, or physical habit could be used to explore a person's life; after all, most biographers ("biografiends," according to James Joyce) were unapologetic quasi-psychologists. In her thinly disguised, unpublished, autobiographical novel, "Love Is Not Love," Evelyn Wynn, who had a child with Pum in 1924, mused that the twins had "the same movements of their bodies, in countless little tricks and mannerisms . . . the same vibrant quality of voice, the same trick of suddenly looking up from under their heavy brows with a prolonged gaze that held and seemed to pierce their listener, the same quiver of the sensuous lips that seemed to taste, omnivorously, all chance fair things that came their way." Yet she saw a dangerous side to all this and thought "it might be that that their very similarity had set up a subtle rivalry between them, and made them enemies at heart, yet enemies that could not do without each other; and by tradition and training joined them in an alliance against the world that could never be openly broken."

Evelyn based the anti-hero of her roman à clef on Pum, describing him as "sensual, even gross, possessing a broad-based earth-bound solidity that contrasted disturbingly with something delicate and wistful and almost childlike in his character." Though his eyes had a "remote spiritual look [his] egoism was a fierce pagan thing that would not brook the laws of the herd . . . he was both a dreamer and a hard-headed man of affairs." Moreover,

> [it] was this duality of his nature that formed part of his fatal attraction . . . he would confuse not only himself but those with whom he made contact, by assuming the role of a sober god-fearing citizen. He would attend Church to please the vicar or the vicar's wife, expound his belief in public schools and the British electorate, he would worship the god mammon while in secret a slave to beauty; with secret loathing he would pay court to women of title and position; he would decide and reassemble and decide again the Protean plasm of his complex personality until [people] were bewitched by the kaleidoscope.

Pum lived many different lives within one, each distinct and separate. In simple terms, his respectable and dutiful public life had to be separate from his private life of unconventional desires and ideas. This more obvious duality had its shadow in his paranormal experiences, in his account of meeting his disembodied self in Gibraltar in 1906, for example, and in the disturbingly pleasurable negation of ego he experienced after getting lost in the African wilderness, when he failed to recognize himself in the mirror.

There were endless discussions between Pum and Tom in which they compared each other's characters, temperaments, tastes, and all that goes to make up personality and individuality. They realized that they had developed some "very odd, inconsistent and often contradictory characteristics," two of which were important: Tom had always been the more aggressive, at home and at school, up to the age of about seventeen, and, though it had waned, it only really faded out in their middle-age—luckily, thought Pum, otherwise he felt he would have suffered from a serious inferiority complex. It was such a serious influence on them both, though, that he believed if one twin might be in danger of destroying the other's individuality then they should be separated at once, schooled and brought up apart, and that there should be a branch of psychiatry to deal specifically with the subject of twinship. The intense period of Tom's dominance caused a painfully difficult schism, an inhibition between them that they both deplored, but were unable to shake off for many years. They were on good, if constrained, terms when together, they wrote regularly to each other when apart, but they didn't manage to be completely communicative again until very late in their lives, when they rediscovered mutual affinities and intimate experiences and ideas.

Pum thought there was a distinct character difference between himself and Tom, "a subtle and delicate one, doubtless inherited." Pum was more like their mother and Tom like their father, although Pum was noted as being exceptionally psychically aware as Henry had been, while Tom was "just average in this respect." When they were young, their interest in and sentiments about other people had been, he thought, comparatively normal; they had made friends easily and were popular. When they became men, however, these feelings steadily deteriorated, possibly as a result of their obsessive interest in objects rather than people, until, he was ashamed to say, even among friends and associates (with the exception of children), that they found it "hard to muster even a mild liking for people (individuals or classes)." Though they felt "sincere sorrow and pity for the afflicted or oppressed," Pum thought that the adage, "Those who don't or can't like themselves cannot like their fellow men," was probably true of himself and his twin.

Their attitude toward women was as complicated and detached as their sympathies for their fellow men, possibly more so. At school, when it was the thing to have a sweetheart, Tom and he had "shared a little school friend" of their sister Violet's and were very fond of her.

This arrangement proved satisfactory and didn't strike any of them as odd, and in early manhood, the twins "discussed with equanimity the idea of sharing a wife, when the time should come, and quite seriously agreed to try the experiment." Humphrey Spender, recalling the twins' attitude to sexuality, noted in an interview how charismatic they were in late middle age. They were "not exactly handsome but very welcoming and warm, attractive physically. Not to me, but one could see they were attractive; tubby and of medium height, sprightly and very good-mannered, so much the gentlemen. I have heard women talking about them." They occasionally exploited this sexual attractiveness and their likeness to each other to amuse themselves: "They had this trick of making love to a woman, I mean in the old-fashioned sense, and then leaving the room and the other twin going in and carrying on. The women never caught on. They thought it was great fun." Pum was trapped by his "despising yet needing women," wrote Evelyn. In fact, he "needed people . . . their praise and admiration was the invisible spring of his busy life." According to Tom, too, "all his life [Pum] had a yearning for recognition and appreciation of which he never received anything like his proper share and, though he did not complain, he felt this deeply." The powerful need for recognition was constantly brought up against his need for privacy.

All through the 1950s, after he had lost Pum, Tom avidly collected all and any newspaper cuttings about twinship, any on the new science of genetics and Julian Huxley's work that he came across. He wrote to Dr. Jacob Bronowski after his BBC "Science in the Making" program, "Like Father Like Son," which he had watched in January 1954. He wrote often to the Society for Psychical Research, sending some of his and Pum's drawings, which he believed illustrated their telepathic bond. He was particularly keen that the society should see these sketches, made during a game of "heads, bodies and legs" in the summer of 1932 in Santa Margherita, near Rapallo, where they were holidaying with their mother, Glyn Philpot, and Vivian Forbes. Pum's and Tom's drawings were almost identical. He was looking for any evidence, clue, or anecdote that might explain the roles of heredity and environment on twins and, in particular, throw light on their own relationship. Tom edited Pum's memoirs, cut out difficult passages, corrected his grammar, footnoted and commented on the text in a way that was both generous and damning—honest in the manner of someone so close that he can't see or chooses not to see the covert criticism. It seems that no other relationship rivaled that of their own, twin to twin. Consuming and complex, it often faltered so that they were frustrated by being so close yet unable to get on, much like a marriage, perhaps. Tom was the more dominant and aggressive; Pum tried to appease him but ultimately failed, he thought. Being a twin, having a mirrored life, was the inescapable fact of Pum's existence, both a blessing and a curse.

15
A Bachelor Father

F amily life had been a series of emotional bottlenecks for Pum, yet still he made an abortive attempt at it when he was in his mid-forties. Abortive because he wanted it very much, but only on a part-time basis: he was not going to allow family life to interfere with his bachelor existence in Cairo. To have a family he needed a home, or at least a house, in England, where he could install it and visit during the summer months when he found Cairo unbearable. There was also his eclectic collection to be considered, and he envisaged this being installed there, too, eventually. So, in 1924, Pum bought the fifteenth-century timber Great House, the adjoining Little Hall, and six tenement cottages in the market place of Lavenham in Suffolk, "a lovely and still unspoilt example of a medieval village of about 1,000 inhabitants." Here he planned to spend his annual leave, entertain friends, and construct some sort of domestic life.

The ancient timber Great House stands on the east side of the square by a sixteenth-century stone cross, "its steep tiled roof extending in a protective way over the roof of the adjoining cottage like the arm of a big boy thrown over the shoulder of a smaller pal." The whole formed a single block, the front of which is flush with the street and market place. Pum began renovating and furnishing it straight away and over the next few years restored the buildings to what they had once been—a small high-hall house of the fifteenth century. "Unfortunately," one of the six cottages, which he had given to Tom, was still occupied by a village couple, Old Bye and his wife, who he agreed could stay on until the old man died—but the local reputation for longevity soon made him realize that he had made a "rash promise." A walled garden ran alongside the house and formed an L shape abutting against the cottages, the plan of which forms another L. There was an outside staircase onto a small courtyard with rose-covered trellises, and the south-facing windows looked out over a spreading fig tree in the middle of the court. In its shadow stood a bronze replica of a Pompeian statue so the whole had a pleasingly Mediterranean air about it—when the sun shone.

Suffolk village life, however, did little for Pum. He thought it had a strange and ugly atmosphere about it, that the people lived under a morbid cloud of superstition, suspicion, ignorance, fear, and cruelty, a hangover of the past, something that was accentuated in isolated East Anglia. He had always found accounts of English village characters either exaggeratedly amusing or horrifying, but now, living among them, he felt that there was a great deal of truth in it all. The way in which he described the Lavenham villagers is much the same as the accounts he gave of the Egyptian fellaheen or the Sudanese women who were supposedly casting out spirits: detached, anthropological, and faintly superior. Their preoccupations, activities, and beliefs were uncivilized and slightly ridiculous to him.

Lavenham, he wrote, was a "primitive place" and full of disturbingly unwholesome old people—old age was a deeply unpleasant condition to Pum, who valued youth and beauty so very much. He spent only three months there each year and kept himself to himself, living what he called his "curious double life." The rest of the year he passed in a semi-Oriental existence at Beit al-Kretliya, unattached, socializing when necessary, and, most importantly, deeply and sensuously absorbed in his collection.

The Lavenham house was always something of a fantasy. Pum wanted to create a "happy house . . . haunted by Love." It was to be a bright home, full of young life where a child "might live and develop happily." He intended to fulfil his longing for a child and at the same time carve a place for himself in the scheme of things, to reproduce and so add weight and proof to his own existence. The key was to have a son there, to be rooted within a family once more. Since early manhood he had, he wrote, "cherished the thought of having a child of my own, it was this ambition which had nearly driven me into matrimony in 1914." This experience "had so shaken me that I dropped all idea of gaining my objective at the price of a life sentence of marriage with its frightening possibilities and so I decided that adoption would be the soundest course. So during my leave in England in 1924 I at last carried out this long cherished project and adopted a small boy, John, and arranged that he should legally bear my name."

It wasn't quite as simple as his short account makes it seem. John was actually Pum's second child, his "dream boy," born on June 10, 1924, at Buckingham Palace Road, almost as if by divine conception. Humphrey Spender revealed that he thought it true of Pum in particular, that "as with many homosexuals he wanted to carry on his family name but that he disliked ladies so much that he didn't want to be involved in the physical act. He only wanted to carry on the male line." The twins decided between them that they would "ask a lady friend if she was prepared to mother one of their children [and] tried it out with one lady," whose name Humphrey couldn't recall ("Skein, perhaps?"), who "proceeded to go through the physical contortions and produced a child." But "unfortunately the child was a girl. 'Not on,' said the twins, and the girl was rejected and sent to South Africa."

"Oh well, all's fair in love and war," Humphrey said, "and they started again and asked around in their friendships." John had a different mother, Evelyn Wynn (née Burton), the rejected wife of one of Pum's Great War friends who had been on the hospital ship at Gallipoli. Evelyn and her husband were "estranged as there was another woman in the background." They had two children already, a pigeon pair, Richard and Pauline, when Wynn left them (his new woman, in turn, left him after the airplane he had bought her crashed and he was made bankrupt). Everyone came to what seemed to be a mutually beneficial arrangement. Evelyn, according to an interview with Humphrey, was persuaded by Pum and Tom to "mother their child" and, "being very gentlemanly in their behavior, they said she must have a house and what about the house next door to the Great House, and they established her and the baby there. Evelyn had her baby, called John, known as 'Little John' because of Pum being known to his friends here as 'John.' Pum would have his son, take care of the family financially, and Wynn could go off to his new life unencumbered." Pum gave the baby the name Gayer-Anderson by Deed Poll in 1924, Tom and Mary were the boy's godparents, and in November of that year the family moved into the Little Hall.

It was a happy enough home in the early days, but it didn't last. It became "haunted" by sadness, not a "temporary lapse from happiness [but] a permanent fatality." Wynn's daughter Pauline, Humphrey said, "was made to leave because they said Evelyn couldn't look after the baby and give enough attention to her, too. This was a very bad blow to Pauline's psychology and made her resentful of her mother, who she disliked from that time on." Humphrey married Pauline in 1948, three years after he lost his first wife, Margaret ("Lolly") Low.

Each year, when Pum returned from Cairo to Lavenham, he marveled at how his "suckling babe became a wee boy, learning to walk, adventuring across the drawing room floor from his mother to me and back again to her." The twins thought Little John was a "budding genius," a "miracle of childish intelligence," and they told everyone who would listen, keen to show off the boy. But though Pum had achieved one of his greatest desires in having a son, he "did not sever his connection with the East in order to be with the child." All he could bring himself to acknowledge was a "sincere affection" for his son and an interest in his development. In 1931 he took John to Cairo with him and they cruised down the Nile, but the seven-year-old was much more keen on building sandcastles than learning about Egyptology; Pum found the real child very different from the ideal boy of his dreams. "Still I could not love," he wrote, "and I found myself incapable of sufficient devotion to enrich and maintain his love for me." Pum blamed himself and thought the root of his detachment was in his own father's inability to love or know his children, a state that was "more or less in the normal course of things."

He worried that his "double life . . . so strange a mixture" would wreck his new family, left alone in England for nine months out of every year. In Cairo, at Beit al-Kretliya, he saw himself as an "unattached and deeply occupied" man and told himself that his two lives dovetailed neatly into each other, one amplifying the other, thus "making it more vital." But every time he returned to Lavenham, he was assailed by "an uncomfortable feeling of selfishness," due, he knew, to the fact that he was "free of all the major difficulties and labours . . . the rewards that the others, John's mother, Tom, and the servants, had worked and suffered for during trying winter months." The split in two was painful, but he couldn't avoid it—and didn't want to. It was irresistible and second nature to him.

Evelyn, however, felt differently about her circumstances. After Pum's death she wrote her roman à clef under the nom de plume "Anne Somerset," faithfully detailing the story of John's birth, the collapse of the domestic arrangement, and the misery that followed. The title of the unpublished book is taken from Shakespeare's Sonnet 116, "Love is not love / Which alters when it alteration finds." Evelyn's characters are based on the Lavenham ménage and their friends; all are thinly disguised with different names. It is a terrible story of free love, betrayal, illegitimacy, idealism, double standards, the sex war, and a very bitter custody battle fought out in the 1930s. In the novel, and in her diaries written between 1939 and 1945, Evelyn describes how she had hoped to come to love Pum as she got to know him, and despite the trials of having an illegitimate baby and "living in sin" in the 1920s, she "felt that he was a man whom I would like for the father of my child . . . I knew that one day I should love him." And she says she did, at first, even though he had told her from the beginning not to expect too much, given that the "idea of marriage with any woman was intolerable to him."

In his writings on the "New Cosmology," Pum imagined that matrimonial ties would cease after death unless the married couple wished them to continue. "For many husbands and wives on this Earth," he wrote, "the chief recompense or joy in death is to break away from a wife or husband for whom there has been no real love or to whom each has been bound in a bond of mutual hate." Free love, which Pum could not (satisfactorily) find on earth, would, he hoped, be manifest in the spirit world, as sex was the "most bodily divinely and spiritually satisfying and significant manifestation of which the human being is capable." Sex would be free, open, and promiscuous, not "a means of reproduction" but a "beautiful and symbolic expression of mutual love." When it came to earthly reproducing, though, Pum was more moved, however briefly, than he might have guessed. He wrote these poems for Evelyn:

The Inevitable Chance
To E.W.
Child of mine
That is not yet,
That has not been,
That lies
Midway between,
Our lips, our eyes,
That is within
The womb of her
That cometh towards me
Unaware.
*

A Trinity
To E.
You and I, we two are one,
And in us, of us, this our son.
What holier trinity could be,
Than just we three?

What happier unity,
Than just we one?

*

Thus Life Occurs
To E.W.
I like to think,—a quaint conceit at best—
This child, unborn, umeant that stirs,
Within her womb, behind her suckling breast,
Is of my being blent with hers,
Our love this-wise made manifest.

After John's birth, when Evelyn and her three children were ensconced in Lavenham under Pum's protection, she discovered, unsurprisingly given her precarious position, that she wanted to belong to him in a permanent way. She was "[d]ocile, eager to trust him and feel his approval, eager to build up from the ruin of her marriage this new thing." She soon found, though, that he could never be persuaded to stay in England by any pleasures or commitments she provided, and resigned herself to having him for just three months of the year. Not only that, but she was a peripheral member of the household excluded from the decisions and plans that Pum, Tom, and their mother were always making. Pum's "strong aggressive personality overwhelmed" Evelyn's, and when they were together she seemed to become a "non-entity." The hope that he might come to feel romantic love for her dwindled as it gradually became clear that she was merely the vehicle.

Village life was not kind to Evelyn, either. The family arrangement was deeply unconventional and existed right in the middle of the village, under everyone's busy noses. Their easy lifestyle, the odd visitors, the naked sunbathing, all of the goings-on fascinated and appalled the neighbors. Inevitably, it became known that Evelyn and Pum were not married and that the little boy was illegitimate. Tongues wagged and Evelyn had to endure social ostracism and the "fluctuating eye-brows of the Vicar's wife." Pum, too, was subjected to the prurient outrage, and a lecture to boot. As Evelyn put it, "Christ! Did the woman want him to kneel down there and then and pour out the tale of his sexual misdeeds? She was actually panting for his confession—almost drooling at the lips like a dog—Well, if he once started on that tale, she would get more than she bargained for." Even the village church bells "remorselessly clamoured of a religion shaped to the stupidity of the minds that rang them. 'Thou shalt not! Thou shalt not! In very deed thou shalt not! . . .' over and over again, until the mind rebelled at their senseless importuning."

Outside pressures and internal dissatisfactions began to plague Evelyn. At home she was expected "to be content with the position of chief of his harem, mother of his child. But had he," she asked, "the right to expect this of any woman who was not an oriental by birth or tradition?" Then, after eight years of being alone and peripheral, she began an affair with Henning Nyberg, a Swedish artist who appears in her novel as Olof, a poet. The relationship was a "subconsciously deliberate . . . gesture of rebellion against her lonely winters," and "incredible as it might seem [a] symbol of her love" for Pum. She did it, she reasoned, "to balance the love between them, to free [Pum] from the burden of an undivided devotion which she had been forced to realize he no longer sought from her." In the spirit of freedom and honesty that Pum expounded, Evelyn wrote and told him about Nyberg; Pum, after all, had made no secret of his amorous life. At first his response was measured, even disinterested, and he seemed to brush it aside, but things changed rapidly after Tom wrote to him. Now living full-time in the Great House, cheek-by-jowl, Tom was increasingly hostile to Evelyn: she described him as an "embittered spider" waiting for her in his web; and the twins' mother was his ally against her. A sort of "business letter" arrived from Pum, full of "cold, pompous words and weighty phrases." He was severing their arrangement. He wanted the matter settled reasonably and quickly, and told Evelyn to pack up her things and leave as soon as was conveniently possible. She was shocked and scared by his brutal, unforgiving rejection of her. "He would not seek to understand," she wrote, and "he would not yield her the liberty he had taken for granted in his own life."

Far worse than this for Evelyn was the knowledge of just how dispensable she was. Pum wanted the boy for himself. "Whose child was he?" she railed in "Love is Not Love." "Is it possible to share a child?" Surely John belonged to her "by right of her body, by right of the price she had paid for him, the love with which she had cherished him since the moment of conception. What price could [be] set beside the price she had paid, not only in her body, but in her good name, the sacrifice of her reputation in 'society'?" Pum had paid for the child in money alone, and Evelyn knew that "whatever might happen to her in the future she was now, according to the world's valuing, to some extent damaged goods." It was a catastrophe.

Evelyn was distraught at Pum's behavior; all his high-flown philosophies of free love and his arguments against the blind stupidity of provincial English life meant nothing when it came down to it. She felt she had not known him at all. Their arrangement, their understanding as she had imagined it, was not rational pragmatism after all: "The intimacy of love was not knowledge, not even friendship, but an animal truce between two age old enemies, the man and the woman, and at any moment the truce might be broken, the bugle sound the alarm, and a fight bitter to death be resumed. . . . Oh Christ! the pity of it all, the infinite heartbreaking pity."

Pum refused to discuss it with her, and she was forced to pack up and leave for London, to leave her child in Lavenham. She had no means of support, nowhere to live, and no reputation. At first she stayed with her friend, the artist Edna Clarke Hall, at her home at Upminster Common, then she lived for a while with Nyberg before moving to a flat in St. George's Square, in October 1932. She moved around, from Primrose Hill Road to Church Street, Kensington, before finally settling in Cambridge, on Storey's Way, in April 1940. Alone and forcibly parted from her child for weeks at a time, she wrote countless letters to Pum begging him to be reasonable. Then, after taking the advice of a lawyer friend and discovering that their original arrangement was not legal, she wrote to tell Pum that "by English law a mother can only be deprived of the custody of her own child by an order of the Court." But, still, in practical terms she had no money and no name to give the boy, and it began to seem that it might be better for Little John if she gave him up and let Pum adopt him. Then again, she argued with herself, she should keep the boy and do her best in the circumstances because, after all, "there are men living who have not been to public schools—men who speak with authority and are heard with reverence." Pum continued to either ignore or bully her, backed up by Tom. Eventually, he presented her with legal adoption papers and a new arrangement: their seven-year-old child would be his and would be sent off to boarding school to benefit from "male influence"; Evelyn would be allowed to visit him at school sometimes, and to have him for part of the holidays. If she refused to sign the papers, he informed her that he would have no qualms in rejecting the child completely. She caved in.

By the close of 1932, the ménage had been dissolved, Evelyn dismissed, John packed off to school, and Tom and Pum moved into the Little Hall; the Great House remained empty for the next two years, until it was sold to their friends, Humphrey and Stephen Spender. Pum later wrote, with only half an eye on the truth, "Although I do not think Thomas approves, I have had a few girlfriends and one illegitimate son—John. He has taken the family name but will not inherit Little Hall." The pastoral parody of a family unit that Pum constructed at Lavenham had disintegrated.

16
The Lavenham Ménage

While it lasted, the Lavenham life was filled with daily tasks, children, and a constant succession of visitors. Among the most frequent guests were the artists Edna Clarke Hall, Dod Proctor, Glyn Philpot, Vivian Forbes, and Eric Gill. Pride and pleasure marked Pum's descriptions of these friends who came to stay. He recognized in them some of his own qualities, or those he would have liked to have had. They gave expression to the side of his personality that he most valued, but was least able to display.

Edna Clarke Hall (1879–1979) was a watercolorist, etcher, and lithographer, and had about her, wrote Pum, "the stamp of genius and of other-worldliness more strongly marked than in any other person I have met." When he talked to her, especially if alone, he got the impression that she was only partially present, with "one foot in some fairyland or other where only the supersensitive, psychic and intensely artistic" could enter, yet she concentrated on individuals with a forceful power of friendship. When Pum first knew her, she was already middle-aged, still beautiful with "girlish" features and "large perceptive and superlatively honest brown eyes, full of light and vivacity while behind them lurked the mystery of that unfathomable other-worldliness and of perpetual youth," a quality Pum had always worshiped. Her voice was low, pleasant, and very precise, and whatever she said was always original and highly characteristic. She was, he believed, essentially that rare genius, a poet-painter. Her poems were largely pictorial, often giving a sensation of color harmony; her paintings and drawings were visual poems. Clarke Hall was regarded as one of the best artists of her generation, but much of her work was destroyed in the Blitz. She was a close friend of Evelyn's, and this is most likely how Pum came to know her. The women exchanged photographs of each other and books of poems and drawings, hand-sewn and hand-written with personal dedications. One includes a poem, "The Hamadryad," about the chaos of instinct and sex, something that Evelyn had some experience of:

I know when the wild lament "Great Pan is dead!'
Made many voices one,
His gay, mad piping called you, and you fled
Across the forest with the slanting sun.

The cult of the pagan goat-god Pan was an incongruous one for middle England in the early twentieth century, but it was present in much of the contemporary English literature, in the works of E.M. Forster and D.H. Lawrence, for example. The energy, tumult, and panic it embodied revealed the carnage that lurked just below the façade of civilization, the façade that was blown away by the cataclysm of the Great War. Life and society continued, but they had been shattered for many people from all walks of life who now struggled to find a new way to exist, something that perhaps goes some to way to explain Evelyn's decision to have an illegitimate child with a man she barely knew, and Pum's attempts to rationalize established Christian values with his life of freedom and free love.

Clarke Hall herself seemed to marry childishness with adult sensibility. In the evenings after dinner, "she would talk while she smoked a cheroot or even at times, a pipe; she would play games with the children and ourselves, herself as free and happy as a child, always more one with them than any of us—indeed she would often encourage and herself lead the children into pranks and mischief." Exuberant, large folios of the children's Heath Robinson-esque drawings and plans, entered for family competitions, survive from these evenings. Or, while everyone was talking or playing, she,

> having armed herself with a small paint box and a cup of water and brushes, would wander round sketchbook in hand and standing, sitting or kneeling now in one place now in another would float on color washes here and there in the most casual manner possible. During this process she would join in any conversation that was going on, make jokes and tell yarns as though not concentrating in the slightest on her painting.

Her father, Benjamin Waugh, was a cofounder of the National Society for the Prevention of Cruelty to Children, and, for Pum, she never lost her childlike qualities.

Tom, too, nurtured a close and admiring relationship with Clarke Hall; they gave each other drawings and wrote often. Writing to her from Pune (then Poona) in 1926, Tom told her, "what lovely thoughts those are you write so filling to the hollows of my mind almost as though they were my own—I feel an unusual joy when I read or say to myself those lines—what an unusually joyous trusting friendship ours has been!—As you found and I find nothing hurting about it. I've never had anything like it before the reason being that elements which are physical in most of my friendships are intellectual in ours. I think that's it!!" And, later: "Friendship is an odd business, odder than that of 'lover' . . . you might correct me and say that friendship and love are both love.—whereas when I say 'love' I know you will know what I mean [not] this 'drag-in' of sex and bodies."

Where Clarke Hall appeared to Pum (and Tom) as childlike and fairyish, Glyn Philpot (1884–1937) was an entirely different, more real, and sexual creature, one who truly shared his own interests. Philpot was a Royal Academician who worked initially on religious and historical paintings and portraits, but in later years began to concentrate, controversially, on male nudes, painting his models, friends, lovers, and black servants, especially his long-term manservant, Henry Thomas. The tension between his established reputation and his personal life meant that Philpot, too, spent much of his time abroad, in Europe, America, and North Africa. It all came to a head when, in 1933 (he was forty-nine), he submitted his painting, "The Great Pan," to the Royal Academy and it was, in Pum's word, "banned." The painting revealed Philpot's homosexuality a little too explicitly for British mores and was summarily rejected by the establishment.

Pum first met Philpot in Cairo, at the Sharia Maghraby flat, in 1923. He had arrived with his partner Vivian Forbes, "delightful men" who had met during the Great War, each recognizing in the other a sensitive man and a reluctant soldier. They both "passionately hated life in the Army." Forbes was then a teenager, Philpot some ten years older, and when the war ended they lived together as master and disciple in a London studio. They had also adopted a child, Paul, born in 1922.

Philpot had come to Cairo to paint the portrait of King Fouad, and Pum gave him and Vivian the run of his flat while the commission was carried out. Not an easy task, as it turned out: Philpot would sit about for hours, reading or chatting, standing by for the alarm, "like a fire engine," and the summons to go to the palace to work. When the telephone rang he would shoot off in a taxi to Abdin Palace and then have to wait again until his sitter was ready. He might, if lucky, get in a quarter of an hour's work before it was time for the king to go off to another appointment, or he found that the king had already been sidetracked. When he did paint, courtiers would make helpful suggestions over his shoulder. Even the sitter occasionally took a look and either admired or protested. The "temperamental" Philpot found this almost unbearably nerve-wracking and frustrating, eventually turning out a "second-rate" work which ended up in a dim and unused council chamber of the Egyptian parliament (the place it had been destined for was occupied by Philip de Laszlo's later portrait of Fouad, a "slick and flattering likeness which possesses all the qualities proper to every Royal portrait"). By the time Philpot had finished his painting, he was thin and his nerves were frayed, so at Pum's suggestion, he and Forbes took off to Luxor for a couple of weeks. Arriving back in Cairo, he made sure he secured his fee of £3,000 and then quickly left for England before any royal complaint could be made.

Pum was not short of praise for his friend, whom he thought a "superlatively sensitive and accomplished a painter." He was also a musician, wit, bon viveur, and poet, though his talent was "delicate, if slight." But Pum's greatest accolade was that Philpot displayed "the most sensitive, unbiased and broadest sense of beauty in everything, not only artistic, literary and musical but in every sensuous activity of any man I have met." He wanted to believe that they were like-minded in every respect, "sensuous creative characters." Visiting Pum's Lavenham home, Philpot would only be moved to paint "when the beauty he saw in some village child or young person enthralled him irresistibly. Then he would borrow a pencil and a drawing block and do wonderful quick and sensitive sketches or sometimes he would use Tom's studio and make a delightful sketch in oils in an hour or so." Forbes, on the other hand, might spend a whole day painting in there and if his landscape didn't "come off" he would destroy it. Pum saw Forbes as a "younger brother" to Philpot, usually good company and full of amusing ideas and pranks, but introspective, sulky, and depressed, too, emotionally and financially dependent on Philpot and increasingly possessive of him. Pum remarked that Forbes "had a strong vein of melancholy in him which finally proved his undoing." Evelyn looked after Forbes in February 1936 when he was in court for an unstated offence, writing in her diary, "Fuss over Vivian. I went to court as witness for him with Glyn & Da on Feb 10th. Fuss all week. To court again on 17th when charge was dismissed." When Philpot died of a brain hemorrhage in 1937, Forbes was distraught, and ten days later, on the day after the funeral, he took an overdose of sleeping pills. Pum wrote that he "slipped quietly out of this world leaving it the poorer for not only was he an unusual and lovable character but an imaginative and fanciful artist who, had he lived, might have added considerably to our heritage of visual beauty." Not long before he died, Philpot had written to Pum to say that "if only extreme old age may bring us together more uninterruptedly I will look forward to it without misgivings." December 1937 was Pum's "most terrible month." His mother, Glyn, and Vivian all died within the space of nine days.

In 1940 Pum had his book, *Personae Gratae (A book of impossible people)*, privately produced in Cairo, "with illustrations by the author," and he dedicated it to "The Friends GP and VF—A David and Jonathan union." The foreword muses on friendship: "after youth, boy and young-man-hood are over—those impressionable and romantic years when every friendship is indeed a love-affair—are we capable of really friendly feeling at all? Of this emotion that is often as subtle and deep as that of love itself. Childhood, school-boy, college friendships! How dear at the time! But alas! How soon lost and forgotten as we venture out into the world, into the ocean of life beyond our depth and theirs."

Pum's own truly romantic attachment was that with Kathleen Silver, and it was unrequited. Later friendships, he wrote, seemed to "bristle with disapprovals and antagonisms, so that behind a scanty façade of regard they soon harbour such malice as turns them to those cold concealed hatreds that we so often reserve for our 'best' our most 'intimate' friends, of whom it is no exaggeration to say that in time they become, if not our worst enemies, at least those we dislike and avoid the most." They illustrated a complete loss of innocence, the purity that infused his boyhood loves; when he thought about his three best adult friendships, he couldn't understand "why he formed and maintained such unhappy relationships." It seemed that, as one got older, love became impossible: "that we can only like a little, or lust, or hate, and so too friendship, save for such as cause us no trouble, entail no expense, demand no sacrifice, inflict no deep emotions [for] we grow difficult, cynical, selfish, or, even worse, indifferent . . . the process is mutual, we as well as they are afflicted by the disease called life, the malady of living, the infirmity of age, growing old and outcast, like ancient bulls from a herd, just 'impossible people.'"

Eric Gill was one such impossible person. He visited the Lavenham ménage less frequently than Philpot and Forbes because he had his own complicated domestic arrangement at Ditchling, Sussex, and later in High Wycombe. Still, Pum felt he knew him very well, and in fact had fallen for the "extreme tolerance, honesty and perception" that made Gill seem an inspired, though difficult, Christ-like presence. Gill induced in Pum a "devotion such as I have seldom felt for any other man of about my own age." He gave him a feeling of deep confidence: "he was so obviously sure of his philosophy of life and art; his deep sense of religion showed itself in every one of his special activities as in his general life." But Gill's overt religiosity, though quite radical to many, seemed to unsettle Pum, who kept his own peculiar views on Christianity to himself. He felt Gill rather overdid things in his writings, though in day-to-day life he didn't thrust it down everyone's throats.

Pum visited Gill's homes, too, and had him stay in Cairo where, in 1938, he took him to his first *hammam*. Gill proved to be a "perfect guest, fitting into my semi-Oriental ménage as if born to it and what with his beard and his characteristic dress (a grey smock) capped by a turban or a tarbush he resembled a sage or a saint and was immediately accepted by my servants and other Mohammedan friends and treated with the greatest reverence."

When Gill stayed at Lavenham for the last time, in August 1939, he was cutting stone over the arched portals of a new building at St. John's College, Cambridge, dressed in dusty overalls and a square paper cap like those worn by Italian sculptors and stone-masons since Michelangelo's time. He spent ten days with Pum, Tom, Little John, and the Spenders, was cheerful and philosophical, refusing to believe that war was coming, though with each day the news grew more ominous. On the morning that Gill left, Pum drove him to Long Melford station and remembered him standing on the platform, "spectacled, hatless, dressed in his grey smock and smiling." He gently assured Pum that there could be no war, but "[n]ot very long thereafter, that rare and beautiful character left a world that had let him down." Some of his peers doubted that Gill had any sense of evil in the world and that this explained his surprise and shock when war as declared. The "privilege of innocence" may have been his and would have been the source of Pum's friendship and admiration. Each of them at least idealized innocence, even if—or because—they hadn't managed to retain it in adult life.

The social circle at Lavenham often included the Spenders and their wives, who lived in the Great House from the early 1930s. They were a generation younger than the Gayer-Anderson brothers, and Humphrey thought that Pum was fascinated by their lives, which "at times was quite intrusively investigative." He probably was, for the younger men were living their unconventional lives much more openly than he had ever been free to do. "Writers, painters, musicians all came to visit, wandered in and out," Humphrey remembered. "Robert Buhlers was there, he married a rather beautiful girl" (Prudence Pelham, who worked with Gill and "disentangled muddles" for him). Humphrey thought Pum was a mystical creature, not prone to "having a giggle," and "very glamorous, very glamorous. Both the twins were. They represented a world of art and culture." Still, they also cut deeply old-fashioned figures as

> they walked around the village in the 1930s, looking absolutely marvellous because of their feathered military hats and the medals . . . Egyptian medals, probably. There were lots of servants, a housekeeper who was never seen without her hat. She did all her work in a hat. They had a lot of help. An old boy in the garden who would refer to tomatoes as "them new-fangled things." And oranges, you couldn't get oranges in the winter. There was an odd-job man, Turner, who became one of Pum's . . . umm . . . great personal friends, permanently occupied doing things around the Great House and Little Hall where we all lived. He would be there for the ritualistic glass of sherry and the annual "Cleaning of the Oven" that took place in the big kitchen as they took apart the stove, marked each piece with a colored ribbon, and then set them to fizz away in tubs of bicarb. And the "Tying-up of the Roses," too. Sherry in the garden whilst we watched.

Humphrey and Stephen were very fond of Pum and Tom, a sentiment tinged with gentle ridicule for their perceived eccentricities.

The Little House was the scene of much upheaval as well as entertainment, and there was cruelty, too. In the late 1920s, Pum's parents, Henry and Mary, neither of whom liked the place, had occasionally visited, but only three or four times a year and always out of a sense of duty. They were getting very old, frail, and forgetful, and Henry "hung as a dead weight" on Mary, though she would not let him out of her sight. The husband was now entirely dependent upon the wife, like an infant. Pum described her attitude toward Henry as a "deep mother-love," something that he had been used to thinking of as belonging to himself and Tom alone.

On their last visit, in 1926, Henry insisted on bringing The Books with him, determined to square up his accounts in the quiet and calm of the country. It became a nightmare. "For some occult reason," Pum wrote later, the completion of The Books had assumed a vital importance to Henry. They filled a heavy, ominous box, and there were other boxes, too, full of large stock exchange books, files of vouchers, and receipts that he had collected throughout his life and intended to work on in his retirement. Henry spread all the papers out in a room set aside for him and began to extract and copy entries, to erase and correct and tot up. As he worked, it became apparent that the whole complicated system no longer held any meaning for the old man, yet he was compelled to continue worrying away at it. Mary, "whom he had crucified on this cross of accountancy," was called in: Did she know? Could she explain? Could she remember? He would wake her up in the night to ask if she could recollect what change he had been given from a ten-shilling note, or had their tea cost one and six, or two shillings? He would lie awake in the dark chasing the three and sevenpence, the five pounds, the fifty pounds that he couldn't account for. No matter the sum, his anxiety was the same. With the backing of the local doctor, Pum managed to persuade his father to agree that The Books should be put away for good. Henry meekly did so, but by the next day had forgotten his promise and gone back to them to start all over again. It seemed that there was only one, dreadful way out of their dilemma: The Books had to be burned; they had to be placed "out of sight, out of mind, out of existence."

Perhaps anxious about his ailing father's health, or perhaps with a keen sense of the shift of power and a timely revenge, the ritual destruction of Henry Anderson's lifetime obsession was put to him as a cruel-to-be-kind act. It was heavy with malice as well as relief. With a mixture of "diplomacy, threats, cajolings and frightenings," Pum got his father to properly take in and consent to this "terrible deed." Henry gave his permission with a pathetic smile of renunciation; he knew that this sacrifice was symbolic, and Pum tried to convince himself that Henry welcomed it as much as he dreaded it. But it would mark the relinquishment of purpose in Henry's life, the only material monument apart from his children that he had created. He made several attempts to defer the day, but Pum, Mary, and the doctor remained adamant.

Pum lit the fire in the Well Room of the Little House, in the big open hearth beneath a great oak chimney breast that smoked out the whole room when the fire was moderate, but roared fiercely when the fuel was lavishly piled on. Henry and Mary stood by to watch, even though Pum tried to persuade them not to. It was, he wrote, horribly like a cremation. It was a funeral pyre, with himself officiating, priest-like, in "a terrible fury against the deceased, a deep sympathy and pity for the bereaved who stood there forlorn with bent knees and bowed head supported by his mate." The son piled on the wood, and when the fire was raging, he ruffled out the pages of each book in turn to make it as inflammable as possible. Shielding his face with a plywood box-lid, he darted forward and placed each book carefully, one after the other, on the blaze. Soon the fierce heat had driven them all back across the room and Pum had to toss the books into the red gorge from several feet away.

Again and again, Henry tried to intervene and would ask to see a Personal Digest before it was thrown into the roaring fire, or he cried, "We mustn't let that one go, it's the Yearly Summary, it's of great interest—twenty-seven years!" He seemed prepared to dash into the flames to rescue his work as, despite his protests, Pum continued with the destruction. Pum and Mary, "deeply moved to pity," did their best to ignore Henry's distress as his life and books were "silently and relentlessly" consumed.

Long after it was over, Henry and Mary stood looking at the glowing ashes, the remains of the work that had meant so much to them in such different ways. Their son remained by the angry heat, which assailed his "red face and bloodshot eyes"; his heart, he wrote, "was torn between compassion and relief." The end of The Books was an "apogee, a supreme sacrifice on the altar of some unknown god, some Moloch, some god-devil. Would that it had happened some half a century earlier!" It was never mentioned again. Henry never visited again. He was dead within the year.

It seems, and obviously was, an extraordinarily violent act. Evelyn believed that Pum's whole character, his individualism, was a "rebellion against his father, and against an unhappy and repressed childhood that drove him to express himself at the expense of others more and more as he grew up." She believed, too, though he always declared his greatest love for his mother, that Pum "really dislikes even her, and hates to be possessed by her [so] must pretend to her and to himself and to everyone that there is no more devoted son than he in the world." In her opinion, Pum "despised all women at heart."

17
Collecting Beauty
and Beit al-Kretliya

Whenever they were in England together, Pum and Tom went off on "antique crawls," unshaven and dressed in rough clothes to fool people. Bicycling around the junk shops, they would venture across country and up to London, into the "slums" of Deptford, Greenwich, and Woolwich, picking up good furniture, pictures, and bric-a-brac for almost nothing. These expeditions had something of the Blyton-esque about them; the twins likened them to the thrill of fox hunting and extracted a secret, childish pleasure from the deals they made with the unwary and unknowing, so it was a slightly shameful game, too.

Their tastes in most intellectual and all sensuous matters were and always had been, wrote Pum, identical. Each was a highly acquisitive collector, "absorbed by a love of and a devotion little short of idolatry to man-created beauty in all its tangible forms." Pum's collection was always changing and growing, and in 1927 he offered some of it to the Wellcome Historical Medical Museum in London—for a price. Two years later, after a bit of the haggling that Pum so loved, the museum bought his "Phallic Collection" for £130. He had begun by asking £155 for this "unique" group of objects that had taken him many years to collect, "added to which on export from this country there is a 2% duty of heavy expenses of packing and transport before all the goods are safely landed in London." His emotional connection with the objects did not interfere with his eye for business, and he had obviously inherited some of Henry's accountancy skills. A second collection of phallic objects, which he offered the following year to the conservator at the Wellcome, a Mr. Malcolm, was eventually rejected. It included:

Large phallic figure of a seated man 10" on a black stand, £5.
Man and woman in relief between palm. Phallic on black stand,
    6½", £3.
Man seated holding pot. Phallic, 6", £3.10.0.
Boy squatting holding tambourine. Phallic, 6", £3.
Thirty-three phallic pieces in TC—stone, bronze and faience,
    £18.
Etc.
Total: £38

Malcolm replied that the museum only wanted a "Persian Pornographic" book, for £6.10s, but Pum had already shipped the lot to London, banking on the fact that they had bought the earlier collection. He was very much aggrieved, he wrote, when Malcolm informed that they wouldn't be taking the other items because, "the prices of the material you offer us are far in excess of the prevailing prices now obtaining in London, and further, as I told you this morning, we have duplicates of practically all the objects already in our collections." Pum answered, on December 4, that he had understood that he and Malcolm had come to an agreement, and due to the "circumstances" he deserved "special consideration." Arguing that the prices may have seemed excessive because of the financial crisis that had occurred since their earlier correspondence, he emphasized that his prices were lower than any dealer in Cairo and that the Wellcome, in his opinion, was being quite inconsiderate. "These objects . . . of ancient medico-historical material are, as you know, hard to come by and even harder to disperse and so . . . I shall be left with this collection on my hands through no fault of my own and be in consequence, very seriously out of pocket." He wanted payment or return of his phallic objects, telling them he was "decidedly hard up" and needed the cash to settle "outstanding affairs." But a Peter Johnston Saint from the Wellcome wrote back with some vigor saying, "I see from correspondence that Mr. Malcolm has already informed you that we possess duplicates of nearly everything on the two lists and since then much other material has come to light, so that I can say that we have quite a number, and sometimes many examples, of most of the objects in these two consignments."

Pum was obviously very familiar with and skilled in bargaining techniques, and had noted in his memoirs that he was quite well-off during this period. He was senior political officer in Upper Egypt and Oriental secretary to the high commissioner and was making a pretty income from acting as an agent and doing his own private deals, too. Extremely proud of his haggling, he absolutely loved to get one over on a dealer, recounting his victories at dinner parties. He and his twin could be quite aggressive and tricky when doing a deal, whether it be in Egypt, the little provincial antique shops of England, or the halls of the world's major museums, where he would put pressure on directors and bandy about 10 percent discounts for job lots.

In the 1930s his commitments on government business often irritatingly curtailed his antique hunting in Fayoum, Luxor, and the provinces, so he was more than pleased when an old friend, Percy Stout, then director of the Anglo-American Nile Tourist Company, offered him a job on the cruise boats. It would mean a yearly trip, all expenses paid, as doctor on one of the company's tourist steamers. For the next nine years, 1930–39, he made the return trip each winter from Cairo to Aswan. He could search for antiques and bargain with dealers to his heart's content, plus it took him out of Cairo for a month or six weeks of the coldest weather and gave him a complete change of scene, society, and occupation. He also searched further away, in Jerusalem, Aleppo, and Constantinople. It soon became known that fine antiques could be bought from him at prices that considerably undercut the well-known dealers, and that every object was guaranteed genuine. He held annual sales at 27 Sharia Maghraby at the height of the season. The flat was thrown open to the public for a week, the objects displayed with their prices clearly marked (to avoid embarrassment to the amateur collector), and always netted him a good thousand pounds each time. Every object of beauty that he sold gave him a pang of regret and made him feel as though he "was parting from a beloved child"—but there was, he noted, always a counter-advantage, not present in parting with people: that it produced cash, sometimes enough "to enable you to buy two or three others equally lovely."

In 1934 Pum had another psychic antique adventure, this one at a second-hand book market in Farringdon Road, London. Calling on an old friend and dealer, he was given the opportunity to pick over the stock in the store-shed where the piles of old books stood some five or six feet high. On the very top of the first heap he went to was a copy of Vivant Denon's *Voyage dans la Basse et la Haute Égypte pendant les campagnes du général Bonaparte*, published in Paris in two volumes in 1802. He put it on one side with hardly a glance, knowing that this was a unique chance and he hadn't a moment to lose if he was going to make the most of his unsupervised rummaging. There were many volumes on Eastern subjects and he added them on his pile, too, just taking a quick look at the title pages. When his time was up, he had fifty-five books for which the owner asked £8 the lot; he paid happily and immediately. Back home in Lavenham, Pum and Tom went through the haul and discovered that the Denon was heavily annotated in ink and pencil in an almost illegible hand, as were the additional plans of the battles of Aboukir and the Pyramids. The original owner's signature was also in the book, but it was hard to decipher until they found, pasted inside the front cover of the first volume, a cutting from a Sotheby's auction catalogue, dated 1823. It was the sale of the Emperor Napoleon's personal library, shipped to England on his death in 1821. Pum had found Napoleon's personal, annotated copy of Denon.

Inside the cover of the second volume was a letter to the emperor's minister of war, written and signed by Napoleon, and loose between the pages, a sheet of notepaper signed "Joseph" (presumably Napoleon's brother) and a French playing card (the two of spades), doubtless used to mark the page by the man himself. Pum gave these volumes and the letter to the Bodleian Library, Oxford, in 1943.

All through these years, Pum was advising and making acquisitions for various friends and colleagues. He helped, for example, John Drinkwater, one of the six Dymock Poets (also a playwright, actor, theater producer, and director) with his collection, and in 1935 received a grateful letter from him with a volume of his poems enclosed. Humphrey Spender remembered Pum telling him that he chose and bought antiques for King Farouk, too, and that when he and Stephen went to dine at the Little Hall, "the table would be laden with beautiful objects and each one had a story, how they were acquired by a clever stroke of swindling. They were props to be brought out and displayed." Pum devoted himself to his collecting mania, "handling, caressing, doctoring, studying (sometimes with a fervour little short of worship)," and felt "naturally and completely fulfilled." Ronald Storrs had once said of Kitchener that, "where another man would fondle a woman, 'K' gets his satisfaction from fondling an antique." Pum felt that the same might be said of him.

By far the most spectacular antique adventure of Pum's collecting career was his acquisition of the Gayer-Anderson Cat, now in the British Museum. It was his greatest and most adored find. One breakfast time in October 1934, a villainous-looking "old friend" of the tougher sort from Bakkara had *salaam*-ed his way into Pum's Cairo flat and, with a great show of drama and mystery, produced a large bundle wrapped in cloth. Instead of the assured smile he usually wore for such occasions, the man had a serious—if shifty—air of apprehension about him. Accepting and lighting a cigarette with a flourish, he asked that the servants be sent out so that Pum and he should be alone when he revealed his treasures. This was very unusual, so Pum was of a mind to humor him. The dealer squatted on a low stool beside him and very deliberately untied his bundle. Taking out a number of objects done up in newspaper and dirty clouts, he handed them reverently to Pum, one at a time. There were dilapidated bits and pieces, wooden and mummified fragments of cats, friable pieces of very little interest or value. Neither of the men spoke and it became obvious to Pum that his visitor was building up dramatic tension, a familiar technique of dealers.

There was a long pause. The unwrapping ceased. "Is that all?" Pum was constrained to say, and thus gave the man his cue. Without answering he fumbled among the wrappings and brought out another object of some size and considerable weight. He continued to carefully unwrap it and, at last, with a skillful turn of hand, he held up to him the life-size bronze statue of a cat.

Excitement robbed Pum of breath. It was no *khazook*, but a very rare, most beautiful and valuable object that would once have adorned a shrine of Basht, the cat-headed goddess who symbolized the rays of the sun. This was the first life-size bronze cat he had ever seen. Keeping outwardly calm he examined the extraordinary object. It was covered with a heavy coating of crystalline verdigris and crisp flakes of red patina, hiding much detail and subtlety of modeling. His wily dealer-friend, though, sensed his excitement and pleasure and pro-ceeded to give an over-dramatized account of its finding, saying he had come across it quite by chance on the site of the ancient Memphis near Saqqara, where he lived. It had been lying on a wooden block shaped as the Basht sign on which it had once stood (which disintegrated almost at once). After lengthy and exciting bargaining, Pum bought the lot for a hundred Egyptian pounds (equivalent to nearly a hundred pounds sterling), a ridiculously small price, but much to the dealer's relief, for the police had their eye on him.

Though Pum gazed at the cat and caressed it daily, it was not until a month later that he began to clean and restore the piece. It was a trial-and-error labor that took him over a year to complete. He chipped away at the encrusted bronze body, which was preferable to using chemical treatments or to filing the debris away because there was always his uncertainty as to when he might reach the original surface. He felt as though he, and no one else, was producing all this beauty as he gradually revealed and restored it. It was the most fascinating and satisfactory of all activities, better even than being the original artist, for Pum considered himself at a distance from the creation: he could err in his work with none of the fears and anxieties of the artist.

The cat's mount had to be replaced with one of the same wood, *lebbek*, and the cat itself bore the scars of a jagged break running around the upper part of the body and another around the neck. The head had apparently been broken off at some time and rather clumsily replaced, and the gold rings that once must have pierced the cat's nose and ears were missing; these Pum replaced with gold rings from the same period. Also missing were the inlaid eyes, which would have been made, he thought, of black and white stones. Still, their absence, in his opinion, was "probably all for the best artistically, for Ancient-Egyptian inlaid eyes are apt to give the human or animal statue a hard and exaggerated stare which detracts from their quiet dignity and repose." Soon the original surface appeared, almost unaltered and with much fine ornament, chiefly of religious significance.

A complicated "Collar of Isis," inlaid or incised with silver, circled the neck four times with a relief of the "Eye of Horus" at its center, all in silver, set against a rectangle. Below this emerged a beautifully drawn and incised winged scarab bearing between its front legs the disc of the sun god, Ra. Within each of the cat's ears there was also an incised "Feather of Truth," symbol of Maat, goddess of truth and justice, mistress of heaven and earth, and in high relief between the ears was the "Scarab of Kephron." The cat's tail curled around to the right alongside, touching the feet, and bore six rings notched around the end representing, Pum thought, lines cut in the fur of the living animal, a unique adornment. "She" sat nearly fifteen inches tall and weighed close to eighteen pounds. She had no equal—not in London, Cairo, or New York.

It was going to be tricky, he knew, getting the cat out of Egypt. In Pum's opinion, the whole system and the regulations governing the export of ancient Egyptian artifacts were "ill-conceived and ineffective in the extreme." Not only did they make life difficult for him, "they set a premium on the destruction and scattering of antiques." Sometimes the rules could be overcome, but in "very dubious not to say underhand ways, as in the case of the Nefertiti head and those unique gesso life-masks and other objects of the Akhenaten period which were smuggled out of Egypt by the Berlin Museum authorities." Pum overcame his obstacles by what he maintained were perfectly legitimate methods, the details of which "though amusing and enlightening, I am not at liberty here to disclose. Suffice to say that in the summer of 1936 I carried this treasure ashore at Tilbury with a feeling of triumph and accomplishment, unspoilt by any twinges of conscience."

During this time there was a bit of rush by collectors to see the cat, and some offered to buy her. One early buyer had been particularly persistent and had nearly got her for £2,000, on condition that Pum could have a replica made for himself, but no other should ever exist. According to Pum, he was offered as much as £3,000, but he chose not to sell (in modern equivalent prices using average earnings, he was rejecting nearly £400,000). Back in England he had three copies made, one for Beit al-Kretliya, one for his English home, and one for Mary Stout-Shaw. Mary was the wife of Pum's friend Percy Shaw and a woman who felt, most strongly, that she had been reincarnated as a priestess of the goddess Basht. The original cat he gave to the British Museum with certain conditions, one of which was that Mary Stout-Shaw be considered a joint donor, "officially accepted over the signature of the Archbishop of Canterbury," who was principal trustee. The declaration of war in 1939, before the cat could be delivered, led to Pum agreeing to keep it for the time being, but rather than put it in the bank, "which might have been rifled by German invaders," he placed it in an ancient concealed well shaft in the Well Room at Little Hall, Lavenham. There it remained, buried in the dark once more, only re-emerging in 1942 when it was felt safe enough for it to go to the bank.

In the 1930s, Pum's love of Egypt extended to wanting a piece of it that was bigger and more permanent than any antique. The governor of Aswan, another old friend of his, had been looking for an island for Pum to buy so that he could build a house there and gaze out over the Nile. He found Hassan Island, once known as Monkey's Island, directly in front of the Cataract Hotel near the west bank of the river.

They rowed out one sweltering evening to a bare rock with a just few stunted bushes. A second island behind his, belonging to a rich Copt, was bigger with a little European house and a neat garden. The Nile rose here about twenty-four feet, and it was high that day so the islands were at their smallest, though at low tide Hassan Island was, he was assured, some four acres. Despite reservations, Pum fell for it at once. There was a plinth of boulders where he could build a house, well out of high water, and a magnificent façade of rock on the south side that towered at low Nile some thirty-five feet above the river's surface; the rest of the land sloped away behind it into fertile mud. Pum was in a fever of excitement now, even though he had another major project going on in Cairo, and he set to designing a little bungalow with three domed rooms and a loggia running nearly all around it. When he next came to visit, the Nile was low and he saw to his horror that his Coptic neighbor had been manipulating the flood currents so that the channel between the islands was almost completely silted up. This was a technique perfected by Nile dwellers to increase their acreage and it meant that now the two islands were only actually separate at the greatest high water. Fuming, he resold his island to the "Cursed Copt" and never opened his "magic casements" onto the Nile.

It was 1935, and back in Cairo, he was nursing his health and spirits after a bout of virulent influenza that left him with angina. Pum was fifty-four years old, his hair was gray, thin on top, and brushed straight back from his forehead. According to Tom, he had "grown stout due to lack of exercise because of ill-health"; Humphrey remembered him as a gourmet who overindulged, and that his drinking and eating exacerbated his heart condition. Pum was thinking seriously about returning to Suffolk, of retiring there and staying for good. He began carefully packing up his personal collection of antiques, gathered over the last twenty years, and shipping them home to England where they were stored in special fireproof cupboards in the Little House.

He did not underestimate his emotional ties to Cairo, however, and desperately wanted to find a house there where he could install a smaller, permanent collection. Many old Arab houses were being demolished as a new town planning scheme got under way to open up the older, "congested native localities." Pum had already seen the potential in this project and began buying up the discarded paneling, doors, *mashrabiya*, rare, colored glass lights, wall cupboards, tiles, marble basins, and more. The flat at 27 Sharia Maghraby was due to be pulled down, too, and a cinema built in its place. Soon enough, demolition began and the walls crumbled around the tenants, who were allowed to stay on as long as was physically possible; Pum was the last to leave. He had begun viewing properties, one of which was the Round Palace, or Pavilion, that overhung the Nile at the south end of Roda Island, and it had a very rare and unusual feature: an ancient "human abattoir" for doing away with any unwanted fellow whose existence might irritate. It was a deep circular well with spikes and sword blades protruding at intervals from the walls, designed to slash or disembowel the unfortunate victim who fell, or was pushed, into the gruesome pit.

Eventually, he found a flat in Gezirah House—a once fashionable but haunted building of monstrous proportions and adornment, far enough away from the center of the city and the Turf Club to put off most visitors—and he stayed there for the next eighteen months, nursing his deteriorating health. Pum, so "particularly sensitive to psychic influence," happily moved in with the ghosts, the jinn, *afreet*, ghouls, and *marid*, spirits of every kind that haunted all old Cairene houses and privies, blind alleys, dark rooms, and corners, "since any accepted idea implicitly believed for long enough will become a fact." Oriental ghosts were courted or guarded against with spells, philtres, incantations, amulets, and charms, and seemed to Pum to be so much a part of everyday life that they ceased to be frightening and their footsteps and rattlings were accepted as just more background noise.

It was on one of his frequent forays into the ancient warren of "slummy hovels" which engulfed the seething heart of Cairo that he at last found his true home. As a young man in 1907, new to Cairo, he had first explored the Islamic quarter of the city, marveling at its colors, stifling smells, astonishing sights, and complexity. Negotiating the tightly packed lanes, he had come upon a much dilapidated but splendid dwelling of a sixteenth-century Mamluk bey—originally two, it turned out—pressed up against the wall of the great ninth-century Ibn Tulun Mosque; one house had been built by Amina bint Salim al-Gazzar in 1540, the other by a wealthy merchant, Abd al-Qadir al-Haddad, in 1670. They were like limpets attached to a great rock, just two of the domestic buildings that surrounded all sides of the mosque, most being then divided into tenements for the poorest Cairenes. He had approached the magnificent main door via a narrow lane bordered on either side by high stone walls and a finely ornamented entrance gate. The windows were filled with exquisite *mashrabiya*, the intricate lattice-work of turned wood that caught any breeze and allowed women to look out, unseen by those in the teeming streets below. The houses were joined together at a great height by a bridge stretching over the lane.

As the young Pum looked up to admire the building, a pretty, unveiled Egyptian girl stuck her head out of a window, laughed, and beckoned to him. Pum's dragoman was out walking with him and quickly let him know that it would be very unwise to accept her invitation, so all he did was peep through the dark and twisted entrance into a dirty courtyard with a very high unbroken wall on one side. On another wall was a pillared and arched loggia, and on the other two there were many doors and *mashrabiya* windows. The stone was carved and partially covered with colored decoration. Beneath an arch in one corner was a well with several ragged children playing about it among hens, cats, dogs, and a few fat-tailed sheep. It was a very strange portent, that summons from the girl, for this was the Mamluk Beit al-Kretliya—the House of the Cretan Lady—which, nearly thirty years later, would become Pum's home.

In February 1935, he visited the house again. It seemed to him that he had been neglecting an old friend and he felt him calling. Straight after his siesta he hired a horse-cab and drove leisurely through the hot and noisy streets, down the great Europeanized Sharia Mohamed Ali toward the Citadel and, bearing off to the right, dived into the "native quarter" he knew so well. At its heart was the magnificent Ibn Tulun Mosque. He found to his surprise that the decrepit old houses that had leaned up against the walls of the mosque had been demolished—all except his.

Scaffolding was up in places, workmen were coming and going, and one of them told him that Beit al-Kretliya had been acquired by the Egyptian government for renovation as an "antika," a museum-piece of Arab architecture. The building had already been cleared and its restoration begun. Pum later remembered his desire to possess it as almost ungovernable. The house looked so fine and solid and inviting—the several doors that led into the court from two sides were wide open. He could see the fabulous possibilities of the place, its fitness and rightness were exactly what he had long wanted and looked for, but had despaired of ever finding. Everything was clear to him, his "scheme of things entire" unrolled before his eyes—the "eyes of his soul and heart."

Pum didn't go into the mosque at all, but spent the remaining daylight exploring every inch of the house, planning and arranging. He could see at a glance just where his treasures would go and how each object would look, where his bedroom would be, where the kitchen, the study, the servant's rooms, and storerooms. He was galvanized, but also knew that the work would be long and hard and that his health and energy were declining. Further, the place was isolated inasmuch as he would be surrounded by and "very much at the mercy of the neighbours in this wild and unregimented" area of Cairo. His servant, Ahmed, found the plan hard to comprehend—why would his master leave a beautifully furnished and convenient flat in one of the best quarters of Cairo to make his home in so large a house, and among the "despised natives" to which he for one had the greatest aversion?

The apparent inevitability of his rediscovering the house was, Pum felt, down to occult reasons, determined by the "hand of Fate." It was magnificently grandiose of him, as he imagined the

subtle interplay of an infinite number of actions and reactions since the beginning of time: here was this house just completed in every essential of its structure, yet empty, unspoilt and undecorated—here was I who madly desired just such a place and who already possessed quantities of antique oriental fittings, furnishing and objects of every sort . . . and here, as important members of the Comité de Conservation des Monuments Arabes which had acquired the house and at great cost so perfectly restored its structure were two of my best friends, Sir Robert Greg and Sir Ian Home.

He went straight to these two friends and found them very sympathetic. They took him to see other houses they had as if they were offering him his "choice of alluring women in some hareem [sic]," but he had already chosen. A written application secured him the house in May 1935—despite some bitter opposition on the Comité—and it was handed over to him as his own for his lifetime. He undertook to complete the internal renovation and house his collection there until his death, when it would be handed back to the nation as the "Gayer-Anderson Pasha Museum of Oriental Arts and Crafts." It was returned to the care of the Egyptian nation in 1942, when Pum went to live permanently at Lavenham, and his grandson, Theo Gayer-Anderson, has undertaken some of the conservation work since.

Moving into Beit al-Kretliya was done in a characteristically piecemeal and deliberate fashion. Three donkey-carts arrived at his door early every morning, and the drivers in their blue shirts loaded up their vehicles and went off while Pum leisurely breakfasted before following on with Ahmed by tram. After unloading, each piece of furniture and each antique item was distributed at once to its allotted place in a particular room. The process took all of three weeks, nothing was broken or lost, and Pum spent his first night there on October 16, 1935. Moving in helped abate his deteriorating health and marked the end of some of his ceaseless obligatory and increasingly distasteful social duties, which had become boring and crippling to him. Not only that, but money was running a bit short, or so he told the director of the Museet in Stockholm. He wrote saying that he had "spent far more on my new house than I intended, and since I find it a constant expense I am now very much in need of money indeed especially as I have done no business this year at all, and so if the Museet can see its way to the purchase of a section [of my collection] it would be a real help and boon to me."

He left vivid descriptions of the house and the loving task of renovation. In 1939, the *Sphinx* published his series of stories about the place, which were posthumously collected by Tom and published in 1951 as *Legends of the Bait al-Kretliya as Told by Sheikh Sulaiman al-Kretli* (republished with a slightly different title in 2000). Some of the stories say that the hill on which the house stands was the scene of Noah's descent from the ark, of the sacrifice of Abraham, and of the confounding by Moses of the pharaoh's magicians. Some tell of the miracles of a saint called Haroon, whose tomb adjoins the house and is looked over by Sheikh Sulaiman, and others of the Bat King who lives in the well of the house. Beit al-Kretliya has also appeared in feature films such as the early James Bond movie, *The Spy Who Loved Me*.

Pum entertained many visitors at the house, including the king of Siam and various other royal dignitaries, Howard Carter, Eric Gill, and Freya Stark in the days when she was a modest traveler, rather than the "self-assured grande dame" and expert on Arab affairs that she later became. He made a plaster life-mask of Stark and many others for display in his homes. To cope with the visitors, Pum instituted a day on which he would personally show his guests around, for he wanted the house to function as a cultural center to encourage friendly relations between England and Egypt. It was a place that enshrined the quality he most admired in life, and above the main door a sixteenth-century inscription read: "This house gives forth beauty and was adorned for the benefit of the beholder. The praise be to God."

According to Stephen Spender, Pum was a serene man while he lived at Beit al-Kretliya, and he was never idle. Every morning at about dawn, a boy brought him his morning tea and "thereafter began what he called his 'wander round,' that is to say pottering in a dressing gown and slippers, throughout the house and roof-garden, accompanied by a boy or two, the animals and any guests who might be staying with him, arranging, planning, noting the progress of works which were always in hand." The rest of the day he would spend cataloging and restoring his antiques, seeing dealers, and visiting bazaars, always on the lookout for beauty. "His was a rare and lovable personality," Stephen continued, "made all the more lovable by the fact that he had his share of human weaknesses [though] none could be magnified into a serious blemish." Spender described Pum's "intense love and appreciation of beauty [as] the greatest incentive of his life," but it was an appreciation that "due to his warm-hearted nature was more sensuous than intellectual."

The eight years Pum spent at Beit al-Kretliya were, he wrote, the happiest, most important, and most worthwhile of his life. This place, not Lavenham, was where he belonged. He was devoted to the house and lived a life there that was "intimate, free and unharassed—the only life that appealed to me."

18
I Am Dying, Egypt, Dying

At summer's end in 1939, when Pum's annual sojourn in Lavenham was nearly over, the threat of war was ratcheting up. The world had "hardly recovered ere the whole of our tottering civilisation is again plunged into chaos," Pum wrote. Life was blighted. Waiting for the conflict to begin, Pum took to making plaster cast masks of his English household, as if to preserve the living from complete annihilation. They were almost death masks. Making casts had been really popular for the mid- to late-Victorians; it brought pieces of beauty and art to people who would not otherwise have seen them. Before the Great War, Pum had taken lessons at Brucciani's, a casting company in London's Covent Garden that had special links with the British Museum and the Victoria and Albert Museum. Now, anticipating death, he began casting again. On a "dreary ill-omened" day, he immortalized "the lyric poet of his generation," Stephen Spender's "young-Shelley-cum-Voltaire face and billowy locks" were cast in plaster. Masks of his twin, his mother, and his own face, cast in an aluminum alloy with astonishing and unsettling detail, now hang in the Little Hall as their memorial. He hid them in a secret recess in the Well Room and covered them with an oil painting so that all three could stay together forever, as though they were fetish objects that could somehow keep the subject alive. It was impossible, of course, and his poem "Life-Mask" shows his distress:

227

I cast your mask and having done
Looked to see if you were there
But no, the song-bird sure had flown
I held a cage, but it was bare.

Everything good seemed to be flying away, out of his grasp. Some refuge could be found by immersing himself in cataloging his collection of antiques, and he spent hundreds of solitary and sedentary hours fixing and pinning them down. With a dogged determination and a total disregard for his health, he slaved away, handling, repairing, sorting, mounting, and finally sending his treasures out to museums and institutions worldwide. Pum's collection of Egyptian and Saracenic antiquities now exists in museums from Oslo to Oregon. The Gayer-Anderson Cat, among other pieces he donated, is on permanent display in the British Museum, and in the United Kingdom alone there are others in the Natural History Museum, the National Gallery, the Victoria and Albert Museum, and in Manchester, Ipswich, Liverpool, Hull, Norwich, the Fitzwilliam Museum, Cambridge (which has over 7,500 objects), and the Ashmolean, Bodleian, and Pitt-Rivers in Oxford. More of his collection exists abroad, including at museums in cities such as Portland, Alexandria, Athens, Jerusalem, Toronto, Stockholm—and, of course, the Gayer-Anderson Museum in Cairo. His "small selection of pornographic Greco-Roman pieces . . . naturally a difficult collection to place but of very considerable anthropological interest," had been bought by the Wellcome Historical Medical Museum. It was a final, strenuous, self-imposed task and one that he thought of as his "cumulative act of beauty-worship!" The toll it took on him, and his sense of urgency in getting the work done, was reminiscent of his father Henry's fervid concentration on The Books shortly before his death.

No one was happy in the Lavenham houses: Pum and Tom's "sore subconscious contacts were almost at breaking-point"; Stephen Spender was troubled by domestic sorrows; Humphrey's young wife, Margaret, was already in the grip of some mysterious complaint that turned out to breast cancer; and the artist Bobby Buhlers and his wife were agonized, like many others, by the very thought of war. Humphrey said that Buhlers was a "conscientious objector but fascinated by aircraft and would go out haunting airfields. Though, with a name like "Buhler," in due course he was arrested. Stephen bailed him out." Each one of them had hidden griefs, small or great, which though unspoken were still obvious to all as they gathered at the Spenders' or at Pum's for tea or evening drinks. Little John, now aged fifteen, came to visit for part of his holidays from Sedburgh School, but Pum "could not enjoy him." In the last week of July, a long spell of heavy rain had set in. Day after day it came down, and the feeling of being slowly submerged was irrevocable, as though the world deluge was at hand.

Then came a "flight of Cockney doves auguring war!" Evacuees arrived from London, and the weather changed briefly to warm bright days with lazy cumulous clouds filling the sky, and, ironically, the fruit trees, crops, and garden all seemed to promise fulfillment and peace. At the reception center, Pum and Tom picked out and were allotted six boys, "charming little bedraggled creatures," between the ages of eight and fourteen, all from the same school in Bethnal Green, lugging battered suitcases and paper bags of belongings. They put their stuff in the great dormitory where wooden chests still bear their names: one can make out Henry [Owen], Reggie, Victor [Smith], Billy, and Terry. Their bunks were fitted side-by-side under the king-post and low, heavy oak beams darkened by five hundred years of soot and smoke that reached up to the apex of the roof. When the boys had unpacked they came down for tea and to explore their temporary home—out in the orchard, wrote Pum, they marveled to see apples growing on trees. Evelyn, who was in exile in London by this time, noted in her diary that "T.G. got 6 boy evacuees who behaved well. The Spenders had 6 girls, who threw apples & were a nuisance." Humphrey Spender remembered that Pum and Tom had "absolutely refused to have any girls. We were there when the evacuees arrived, trainloads of them. We had a lot, but the Gayers refused the girls. That would be frowned upon now. Yes, yes, and all the girls were pushed onto us. It wasn't our choice to have only girls, not at all." Tom eventually and "unofficially" adopted Henry. The portrait of another boy, Tony Maunder, who was sent to Lavenham with his brother, still hangs in the house. Papers in the Lavenham archive show that Tony knew Tom as "Colonel TG," who "wanted to paint us both, but we were too shy to agree to this"; he remembered Pum as a kindly man who told them stories about Egypt.

On the morning of Sunday, September 3, 1939, Pum and Tom summoned John and the evacuees to the study—the boys didn't want to stop their play and come in from the garden, and when they did, they stood sullenly and silently looking out of the window as the wireless was tuned in, just before eleven o'clock. There was a long pause, and then the announcement crackled over the airwaves in the "solemn voice of that self-opinionated, inefficient man," the prime minister: war was declared. The "family" stood as the wireless played God Save the King, and then Pum sent the boys to fetch wine glasses, the sherry decanter, and a bottle of their home-brewed dandelion wine. They drank to a speedy victory and "To Hell With Hitler!" before the boys rushed back outside to continue with their games.

During that night Pum was woken by a slow, gentle rending sound, almost as though the sodden, heavy earth had given a loud sigh. The luxuriant fig tree that stood in the middle of the courtyard had fallen, "weighed down by its rain-drenched leaves—wrenching its very roots out of the ground." When he saw it on the ground, its leaves flabby and disheveled, it brought to Pum's mind a gazelle he had once shot in Sudan whose eyes as they had gradually glazed over had filled him with a piercing remorse. He had mentioned to Tom one evening that the fig was listing slightly, but he had done nothing about it. Preoccupied as he was by personal and political worries, he was isolated and fatalistic, with a disturbing antipathy to the country and the company he was in—he had a return passage to Egypt already booked, and he concentrated on that escape. By failing to act, Pum believed he had condemned them all, he had somehow "connived with fate to the ruin of our house, of ourselves and of others!" It was an omen, and he felt he was to blame; he had not done enough or seen what needed to be done.

Stephen Spender, in his autobiography, *World Within World*, recounted being awoken by a great crash as the fig tree fell to the ground and he, too, saw it as a symbol—of death. It had come upon his separation from his wife of three years, the novelist Iñez Maria Pearne, who believed in socialism and free love and who had fought in the Spanish Civil War. And there was a "far worse disaster than mine . . . my sister-in-law, Margaret, was diagnosed as having an incurable disease." Pum realized that both households felt the "terrible import of this ominous thing. MS was there suffering from a fatal but unsuspected malady, S's wife had proved unfaithful, our group was about to be broken up, perhaps never to meet again forever!"

Five days later, Little John, also unhappy, went back to school, "glad to escape the evacuees." Writing to his mother in July the following year, he told her that his uncle Tom, who they referred to as "T.G.," was being "pompous" and would not let him come home to Lavenham for fear of an invasion. Instead, Tom was insistent that the fifteen-year-old John should either stay at his school or go to work on a farm in the relative safety of the north of England. Evelyn suspected that Tom's real motivation was not the boy's safety, but a mean desire to keep his nephew separated from his mother, "as they [Pum and Tom] always wanted to do." John wrote to her from Sedburgh:

> What an absolutely bloody letter from T.G. The man deserves castrating. . . . I am going to write to him (we will compose the letter together) & say that I prefer staying at 58 Storey's Way [Cambridge, where Evelyn now lived] rather than Lavenham because at the latter there are a) The whining little evacuees, b) The food is lousy, c) The mealtimes are ridiculous, d) There is no cinema within 6 miles' and, finally, 'A natural instinct [. . .] urges me rather towards a mother than an uncle.

Eventually, however, Tom won the fight and John went to stay on a farm, though he and Evelyn wrote to each other about his running away to be with her. In her diary, Evelyn cursed Tom, "That bloody T.G.—Shall never forgive him. He & Pum wrote the most awful pompous pseudo-patriotic letters to John, enough to make any boy a pacifist . . . wrote pretty straight to T.G. But it was all no good . . . . Blast T.G."

Pum succumbed to depression. Even when King Farouk of Egypt made him a *lewa* (major-general) carrying the title of pasha, in January 1943, one of the most important events in his life, he could not rouse his spirits. The illness that had hit him during the Great War returned. "I am once more oppressed by a darkness," he wrote, "a darkness that I can feel like a heavy pall—the knowledge of my approaching end." His days, he wrote, "seem to be numbered and I know myself definitely on the edge of the abyss." He was not alarmed by it, he scarcely even regretted it, but he was alive to the urgency of things and seemed to have gained "a calm height, some last dawn from which I can look back and to which my past, out of the distance, hastens pathetically to me, recalling itself in scenes that are succinct and individual with poignant definition and detail." All of his past was returning to him: "it wants to identify itself with me and I with it—we go together—we [will] cease to be at the same instant." All that was left to him now, if he were not to disappear without trace, was "to leave behind some essence, some part of me. One craves, one longs to pin some part of one's identity, of one's individual self, onto the sleeve of time before one departs with one's long-loved retinue of things past."

He made one final journey to Cairo. In November 1944, Pum was called upon to help with the handing over of Beit al-Kretliya and its treasures to the Egyptian people. The following January, Little John was posted to Cairo, where he visited his father and trekked around the bazaars with him, "bathing in his glory." They worked together at the house, Pum writing in a letter to the Stockholm Museet that "my time here, which draws to a close, has been almost entirely devoted to antiques—at first the Museet's and Cambridge's collections and then organising and putting this place [Beit al-Kretliya] into perfect arrangement and working order after these years of great neglect . . . the great relief of having the war over will make the whole world lighter of heart."

John's time in Cairo was brief, ending suddenly when he broke his leg in a motorbike accident, colliding with a buffalo in the street. But while he was there he formed a different view of his father and wrote home to his mother with newly opened, adult eyes asking, "Why has Pum no real friends out here—they all seem to hate each other like poison. . . . Oh, but Mummy, it is tragic, isn't it. Why is he such an escapist at his age?" Pum had not expected to return from Egypt. He had thought he might die there, but he endured an arduous trip back to England, by sea via Cape Town, owing to the continuing fighting in the Mediterranean. He arrived back in Lavenham in late May 1944 and, soon after, on June 9, he suffered a severe heart attack and died a week later.

On June 18, in a letter to his mother, John told her about the cremation in Ipswich at which he "read a little eulogy by T.G.—Very maudlin but soon over." On the 23rd "a little thing of ashes is to be buried in the Churchyard," he wrote, saying that he "felt extremely odd when I got [to Lavenham] knowing there was a body in the studio (but did not look)." Evelyn had refused to go to Pum's funeral—there would be too many people there she didn't want to meet again—but she did go to the Little Hall for the day on the 27th, fourteen years after she had been told to leave. She and John went upstairs to see Tom, ill in bed in a narrow room "like a coffin." The house was still haunted by Old Bye, she felt, and was the same "mass of staircases, doors, rugs, beams and shadows, very constricted." The three of them sat and talked before Evelyn and John were able to escape the stuffy little sickroom and get out into the garden, but "what a ruin" she thought it had become. The Great House, too, was "an absolute wreck, tiles slipping, windows broken and wrenched off, floors sinking . . . haunted, haunted everywhere by children's voices. Oh God what a wreck after so short a time—the Spenders had spoilt it too with daubs of paint here and there." The whole place, once and for such a brief while a happy house, was now even "more poignant, more haunting, more insistent."

When Pum had made his final trip to Cairo he was "at half time as it were (or, to be more exact, at three-quarter time)" in the work of writing his memoirs. He was sixty-two, in poor health, and no longer leading the active life he once had, but unwilling to give it up. Thinking about how best to do this led him into reviewing his life and then, naturally it seemed, to the writing of it. He soon became engrossed and was surprised at the clarity of his early memories, something he decided must be a phenomenon of getting older. It all came as a bit of a shock that, from his middle age on, he just "grew out of self-searching"; he had neglected the customary self-analysis that had marked his introspective younger days. The pleasure of his recollecting, whether good or bad, exciting or placid, was a balm to him, "all the more poignant because the memory of the sadder ones was tinged with a shadow of regret or even a faded remorse." Incidents, feelings, and thoughts crowded his brain, one leading kaleidoscopically to another, "jostling to get out onto paper" until he could collect the haphazard jottings and notes into some chronological order. He had inherited the family habit of doing most of his thinking, reading, drawing, and writing (always in pencil) propped up on cushions in bed, and when the memories clashed with sleep, he took to working more intensely in the mornings and evenings. In the space of a few days he had a hundred headings and impressions from every period of his life, many he had thought long-forgotten until he started "living" them again, and he strove to be as candid as he could bear.

The memoir, "Fateful Attractions," constituted "an up-to-date and final appraisement of myself which I believe could not have come about without the actual discipline of its writing." Moreover, the work "combined itself with an already existing literary source of self-expression": the verse he had been composing since his adolescence, his "Obsessions," poems devoted to self-revelation in a very private and personal way and which, until the end of his life, he had kept strictly to himself. Remembering and rekindling had refreshed his troubled mind.

Pum's mother, Mary, had also written down her memories and left some diaries, but she felt less sanguine about their benefits.

"Oh! what are the strange folds of the brain," she asked, which receive and retain the impressions of a life, "*everything* that happens . . . what are the mysterious impulses which open them again, after long long sleep?" . . . "I think I have written all these things already—but where? in what? and why do I write them? who but myself can possibly care about them! To what ultimate consummation, to what result is it all tending? Is it to ruination and obliteration or to some 'One far off divine Event to which the whole creation moves'?"

The mother's anguish is so different to her son's sense of release at his careful organizing, collecting, and recording of memories. He had no such anxieties: he had been able to structure his own life and thoughts as far as he could, and had left his collection of beauty to the world.

*

Pum's ashes were buried beneath a stone carved by his friend Eric Gill. His name and titles are engraved in English and Arabic, the inscription presented by King Farouk, and around the stone's edge runs the epitaph Pum eventually chose for himself:

> Here lieth that which scattereth and yet remaineth,
> The immortal body of a man:
> It to the whole, the true, the beautiful pertaineth
> Which is "God".

This was more than a little different to his early "Cosmic Epitaph," included in one of his volumes of poetry, of which he wrote: "I would wish this epitaph inscribed on my stone when the time comes."

> AGE
> I sigh when I behold and see
> The beauty of my body gone,
> What youth made fair to look upon
> No longer fair and yet still me—

When, turning to my glass, I view
With anxious eyes, my anxious eyes,
And mark the lines that advertise
The tragedy of life come true.

Pum had wanted grace for himself, and for the world. As a child he had been aware of his own prelapsarian beauty and innocence and had wanted to preserve it against the odds. Failing that, almost inevitably, he sought it out in unchangeable artifacts and in boys. Beauty became the only reality, the only thing of substance worth preserving. "The strongest incentive in his life," Stephen Spender wrote, was "the beauty which [he] prized above all other values in this life." The obsessive urge to collect that had gripped him from an early age was perhaps a substitute for intimacy, an attempt to channel his "devious devotions," a way of bringing order to a chaotic interior world. It allowed him to step outside his personal history and upbringing, to stop time and overcome his horror of aging and decay. A collection of beauty preserved at least something from the fragility of existence and made some sense of the world.

Pum had spent a lifetime searching out beauty and meaning, but he cannot be pinned down. His life and writing are filled with contradictions, parallel feelings and attitudes to himself and to other people and races. Love, desire, and admiration constantly rubbed up against disgust and a conservative condemnation of behaviors that he himself was sometimes guilty of. He was as fallible as any other, but had always struggled to understand why he did what he did, thought what he thought.

"I have, from early manhood," he wrote,

considered that precept of Greek Philosophy, 'know thyself,' to be an essential to all right understanding. It implies the revelation of oneself to one's self rather than to others; to which latter form of exhibitionism I have a morbid aversion which has, I fear, led amongst other traits to a serious lack of demonstrativeness in my make-up. Till middle age my intro-spective tendencies led me, through much self-investigation, to a close self-acquaintanceship.

Such intimate contemplation, he knew, was impossible without honesty and concentration. The ideas that Pum had grown up with, inculcated by Henry and Mary and so influential on his childhood character, were not, it turned out, ultimate truths at all, and he questioned the idea of predestination. He realized that, though his life had conformed to a certain pattern, he had, "like some sentient leaf borne upon a river's face, been swept, pushed or pulled along a course which he has had to follow willy-nilly." Such external "guidance" had been "exercised through a series of attractions (each with a plus or minus sign in front of it) very personal to himself. Such are the 'Fateful Attractions' of each one of us!"

As a young man he had recognized a "still centre" of being within himself, one of his strongest and most insistent "fateful attractions, the oracular edict, the signpost which said, 'Turn to the East.'" Contemplating his life's career, adventures, and obsessions, he formed "the impression (quite new to me) that mine has been an eventful and in some ways an unusual life and that its chronicle may have some interest even for the general reader, I hope that may be so."

He had been attracted irrevocably to Egypt, that "most entrancing of all Eastern lands, with its endless variations, age-old traditions, its child-like fickle yet loveable people!" It was the "land of my heart's desire, where meet the crossroads of civilisation," and it had possessed him completely, become his adopted home where he felt accepted, free, and in the midst of affection and beauty. His lot had been cast in and around Egypt, in the Anglo-Egyptian Sudan, Uganda, the Congo, Arabia, Turkey, Syria, Palestine, Libya, and Morocco. Most of Pum's fabulous adult life, more than forty years, had been spent "in the service of the last of the Khedives, the first Sultan and the two subsequent Kings of Egypt [and] this country of Pharaohs has become more my own than is my native land—I more of its 'teen wa tibn' [sand and chaff], it more of my flesh and blood than is any other part of the earth's surface." Egypt had possessed him, it was "the land of [his] heart's desire, where meet the crossroads of civilization . . . the land of [his] adoption." In and around Egypt, he wrote, had his lot been cast.

Appendix:
Tonbridge School Register,
Michaelmas Term, 1894

ANDERSON, Reginald D'Arcy. 1894-8. Day boy. Eldest son of Henry Gayer Anderson. *b.* 1880. Gazetted to the R.A., 1900; Lieut., 1901; transferred to the Army Ordnance Dept., 1905; Capt., 1912; Major, 1914; served in the 1914-18 War with the R.G.A.; died at sea on 14 Aug. 1917 while *en route* for Mesopotamia.

ANDERSON, Robert Grenville (changed his name to GAYER-ANDERSON by deed poll). 1894-8. Day boy. Second son of Henry Gayer Anderson. *b.* 1881. Guy's Hospital; M.R.C.S., L.R.C.P., 1903; House Surgeon, Guy's Hospital. Fellow of the Society of Tropical Med.; Physical Society's Prize Essay, 1904. Gazetted to the R.A.M.C., 1904; Capt., 1908; Major, 1914; seconded to the Egyptian Army, 1907-17; served in the Tagoi Punitive Expedition, 1910 (in Dispatches); Sudan medal with clasp and 4th Class Turkish Order of Medjidie). Member of the Sudan Sleeping Sickness Commission, 1908-9; Kordofan Leprosy Mission, 1910. Served in the 1914-18 War in Egypt, Gallipolli, Turkey and Arabia; Political Officer, Red Sea Littoral (in Dispatches; 3rd Class Egyptian Order of the Nile, 3rd Class Hedjaz Order of El Nahda; wounded). Promoted Miralai (Col.) and Adjt.Gen. (Recruiting) Egyptian Army, 1914. Senior Political Officer, Upper Egypt, on the outbreak of the Egyptian Revolution,

1919; retired, 1920, on appointment as Senior Inspector, Ministry of the Interior, Egyptian Govt., Oriental Sec. to the High Commissioner for Egypt, 1921; retired, 1923, to devote himself to Egyptology and Saracenic Archaeology. Procured a mediaeval Cairo house, which he restored and furnished with his collections as a show place and museum of Oriental crafts and arts, which he presented to the Egyptian nation on his leaving the country in 1942. Granted the honorary rank of Lewa (Major-Gen.) with the accompanying title of Pasha by H.M. King Farouk of Egypt, 1943. In 1942 he and his brother, Col. T. G. Gayer-Anderson, O.T., bequeathed their country house at Lavenham, Suffolk, to the Surrey County Council to be a hostel for students. Died at Lavenham, Suffolk, 16 June, 1945.

ANDERSON, Thomas Gayer (has changed his surname to GAYER-ANDERSON by Deed Poll). 1894-8. Day boy. Third son of Henry Gayer Anderson. *b.* 1881. Royal Military Academy, Woolwich, 1898. Gazetted to the R.A., 1899; served in the South Africa War, 1901-2 (in Dispatches; Queen's medal with five clasps); Lieut, 1901; Capt., 1908; served in the Mandal-Sabai Expedition (Sudan), 1913 (in Dispatches; medal with clasp); Major, 1914; Bt. Lieut.-Col., 1918; Lieut-Col., 1921; Col., 1922. Served in the 194-18 War (in Dispatches four times; C.M.G., D.S.O., Bt. Lieut.-Col., 4th cl. with Swords Serbian Order of the White Eagle, and 3rd cl. Greek Military Cross), and with the Constantinople and Black Sea Forces, 1919-20. Staff Coll., 1921; afterwards G.S.O.1, Poona District, India; retired, 1929. 1939-45 War:- Chief Liaison, Home Guard, at the War Office, 1940; cmdg. Cambridgeshire Sub-area, 1940-1. Club: Naval and Military. (The Little Hall, Lavenham, near Sudbury, Suffolk.)

Bibliography

Publications and Other Sources

Blomd, Philipp. *To Have and to Hold: An Intimate History of Collectors and Collecting*. New York: The Overlook Press, 2003.

Cameron, Hector Charles. *Mr. Guy's Hospital 1726–1948*. London: Longmans, Green, 1954.

Dalby, Richard. *The Golden Age of Children's Book Illustration*. London: Michael O'Mara Books Ltd., 1991.

Dellamora, Richard. *Masculine Desire: The Sexual Politics of Victorian Aestheticism*. Chapel Hill: University of North Carolina Press, 1990.

Dowling, Linda. *Hellenism and Homosexuality in Victorian Oxford*. Ithaca: Cornell University Press, 1994.

Freud, Sigmund. *Three Essays on Sexuality*. New York: Basic Books, 2000.

Fussell, Paul. *The Great War and Modern Memory*. Oxford: Oxford University Press, 2000.

Galton, Francis. *Inquiries into Human Faculty and its Development*. London: Macmillan, 1883.

Gayer-Anderson, Robert Grenville. *Legends of the House of the Cretan* Woman. Cairo: The American University in Cairo Press, 2001.

———. *Christeros and Other Poems. With a Preface to the Poems by Stephen Spender*. Shrewsbury: Wilding & Son, 1948.

———. "Some Tribal Customs in their Relation to Medicine & Morals of the Nyam-Nyam and Gour Peoples Inhabiting The Bahr-el-Ghazal." *Wellcome Tropical Research Laboratories, Khartoum*, rep. no. 4, vol. B, pl. XVIII no. 1, 1911.

———. "Fateful Attractions—The Autobiography of R.G. 'John' Gayer-Anderson Pasha." Unpublished memoir (1940s). Version held by Theo Gayer-Anderson.

———. Letters, notebooks and sketches. Gayer-Anderson family papers. Little Hall, Lavenham, Suffolk, England.

Gayer-Anderson, Thomas. Letters, notebooks and sketches. Gayer-Anderson family papers, held by Theo Gayer-Anderson and at Little Hall, Lavenham, Suffolk, England.

———. "He/She: The World's Sweetheart" (1941). Bodleian Library, Oxford, England.

Gillam, John Graham. *Gallipoli Diary*. London: George Allen & Unwin Ltd., 1918.

Handler, Clive E., ed. *Guy's Hospital 250 Years*. London: Guy's Hospital Gazette, 1976.

Hankey, Julia. *A Passion for Egypt: Arthur Weigall, Tutankhamun and the 'Curse of the Pharaohs'*. London: IB Tauris, 2007.

Hart, Peter. *Gallipoli*. London: Profile Books, 2013.

Hatton, Edward. *A New View of London; or, an Ample Account of That City*, 2 vols. London: John Nicholson, 1708.

Higgins, Patrick, ed. *A Queer Reader*. London: Fourth Estate Ltd, 1993.

Houlbrook, Matt. *Queer London: Perils and Pleasures in the Sexual Metropolis, 1918–1957*. Chicago: University of Chicago Press, 2005.

Hyam, Ronald. *Empire and Sexuality: The British Experience*. Manchester: Manchester University Press, 1990.

Ikram, Salima. "Pasha's Pleasures: R.G. Gayer-Anderson and his Pharaonic Collection in Cairo," in *Offerings to the Discerning Eye: An Egyptological Medley in Honor of Jack A. Josephson*, edited by Sue D'Auria, 177–85. Leiden: Brill, 2010.

———. "Some thoughts on the mummification of King Tutankhamun." *Institut des Cultures Méditerranéennes et Orientales de l'Académie Polonaise des Sciences, Études et Travaux* (2013), xxvi.

Inglis, Brian. *The Paranormal. An Encyclopedia of Psychic Phenomena*. Boulder, Colorado: Paladin Press, 1986.

James, Robert Rhodes. *Henry Wellcome*. London: Hodder & Stoughton, 1994.

Jung, Karl. "The Syzygy: Anima and Animus," in *Aion: Researches into the Phenomenology of the Self: The Collected Works*, translated by R.F.C. Hull. London: Routledge and Kegan Paul, 1968.

Kipling, Rudyard. *Barrack-Room Ballads and Other Verses*. London: Methuen, 1974.

al-Kretli, Sulaiman. *Legends of the Bait al-Kretliya*. Translated by R.G. "John" Gayer-Anderson. Ipswich: East Anglian Daily Times, 1951.

Lane, Christopher. *The Ruling Passion: British Colonial Allegory and the Paradox of Homosexual Desire*. Durham, North Carolina: Duke University Press, 1995.

Lanver, Mak. *The British in Egypt: Community, Crime and Crises, 1882–1922*. London: I.B.Tauris, 2012.

Luckhurst, Roger. "Unwrapping the Mummy's Curse." *New Humanist*, vol. 127, no. 5 September/October 2012.

Lycett, Andrew. *Rudyard Kipling*. London: Wiedenfeld & Nicolson, 1999.

MacCarthy, Fiona. *Eric Gill*. London: Faber, 1989.

The Marlborough Express. "The Deirut Murders." Vol. LIII, Issue 174, July 25, 1919, page 2, http://paperspast.natlib.govt.nz/cgibin/paperspast?a=d&d= MEX19190725.2.4

Milton, John. *Paradise Lost*. London: Penguin Classics, 2014.

Muensterberger, Werner. *Collecting: An Unruly Passion: Psychological Perspectives*. Princeton, New Jersey: Princeton University Press, 1993.

Robinson, Ronald, John Gallagher and Alice Denny. *Africa and the Victorians: The Official Mind of Imperialism*. London: I.B.Tauris, 2015.

Rodenbeck, Max. *Cairo: The City Victorious*. London: Picador, 1998.

Rohan, Thomas. *Confessions of a Dealer*. Bournemouth: Richmond Hill Printing Works, Ltd., 1936.

Royle, Trevor. *The Kitchener Enigma*. London: Michael Joseph, 1985.

Smith, Sydney. *Mostly Murder*. London: Harrap, 1959.

Smith, Timothy d'Arch. *Love in Earnest: Some Notes on the Lives and Writings of English 'Uranian' Poets from 1889 to 1930*. London: Routledge & K. Paul, 1970.

Spencer, Neal. *The Gayer-Anderson Cat*. London: British Museum Press, 2007.

Spender, Humphrey. "National Life Stories Collection: Artists' Lives." Archival sound recordings (15 of 39). British Library Sounds. https://sounds.bl.uk/ View.aspx?item=021M-C0466X0101XX-1600V0.xml.

Spender, Stephen. Preface to *Christeros and Other Poems*, by R.G. Gayer-Anderson. Shrewsbury: Wilding & Son, 1948.

Souter, Nick, and Tessa Souter. *The Illustrator's Source Book*. London: MacDonald Orbis, 1990.

Stoler, Ann Laura. *Race and the Education of Desire: Foucault's History of Sexuality and the Colonial Order of Things*. Durham, North Carolina: Duke University Press, 1995.

Taylor, Anne. *Annie Besant: A Biography*. Oxford: Oxford University Press, 1992.

Thomas, Martin. *Empires of Intelligence: Security Services and Colonial Disorder after 1914*. Berkeley and Los Angeles: University of California Press, 2007.

Turner, Helen. *Henry Wellcome: The Man, His Collection and His Legacy*. London: The Wellcome Trust & Heinemann, 1980.

Warner, Nicholas. "Collecting for Eternity: R.G. Gayer-Anderson and the Egyptian Museum in Stockholm." *Världskulturmuseerna*, 2016.

Weeks, Jeffrey. *Sex, Politics and Society: The Regulation of Sexuality Since 1800*. Harlow: Longman, 1989.

Wynn, Evelyn. "Love Is Not Love." Unpublished novel, from the 1940s. Humphrey Spender family papers. Little Hall, Lavenham, Suffolk.

———. Diaries, 1939–45. Gayer-Anderson family papers. Little Hall, Lavenham, Suffolk.

Archival Sources

Bodleian Library, Oxford, England. MS. Res. d. 366/367/368/369.

————. MS. Res.b.38, "Virginibus Puerisque Vol.I."

————. MS. Res.b.39, "Virginibus Puerisque Vol.II."

————. MS. Res.b.40, "Virginibus Puerisque Vol.III."

————. MS. Res.b.41, "Vive Le Sport No.4."

————. MS. Res.b.42 & 43, "Queer Animals."

————. MS. Res.b.44, "Childish Nudes Vol. I."

————. MS. Res.b.45, "Childish Nudes Vol. II."

————. MS. Res.b. 46, "Childish Nudes Vol III."

————. MS. Res.b. 47, "Childish Nudes Vol IV."

————. MS. Res.b.48, "Seldood Morf Dnalmaerd Vol.I."

————. MS. Res.b.49, "Seldood Morf Dnalmaerd Vol.II."

————. MS. Res.b.50, "Seldood Morf Dnalmaerd Vol.III."

————. MS.Res.d.360, "Poems I with illustrations by the author and TG." Privately produced, Cairo, 1940, Bayt-El-Kredlea, Ibn-Tulun.

————. MS.Res.d.361, "Poems II with illustrations by the author and TG." Privately produced, Cairo, 1940, Bayt-El-Kredlea, Ibn-Tulun.

————. MS.Res.d.362, "Poems III with illustrations by the author and TG." Privately produced, Cairo, 1940, Bayt-El-Kredlea, Ibn-Tulun.

————. MS. Res. d. 363, "Poems IV 'Quaint Conceits' another vol of poems." Privately produced, Cairo 1940, Bayt-El-Kredlea, Ibn-Tulun.

————. MS. Res.b. 364, "Personae Gratae (A book of impossible people)" by RG "John" Gayer-Anderson Pasha with illustrations by the author. Privately produced, Cairo.

1940, Bayt-El-Kredlea, Ibn-Tulun.

————. MS.Res.d.365, "Poems VI with illustrations by the author and TG G-A." Privately produced, Cairo, 1940, Bayt-El-Kredlea, Ibn-Tulun.

Public Record Office of Northern Ireland. Mary Anderson memoir (1925). File = 51-01-01, T3258/4/1.

Public Record Office of Northern Ireland. Mary Anderson letters: Letter One. File = 51-01-02, T3258/4/2.

————. Letter Two. File = 51-01-03, T3258/4/3.

————. Letter Three. File = 51-01-04, T3258/4/4.

————. Letter Four. File = 51-01-05, T3258/4/5.

————. Letter Five. File = 51-01-06, T3258/4/6.

————. Letter Six. File = 51-01-07, T3258/4/7.

————. Letter Seven. File = 51-01-08, T3258/4/8.

————. Letter Eight. File = 51-01-09, T3258/4/9.

————. Letter Nine. File = 51-01-10, T3258/4/10.

————. Letter Ten. File = 51-01-11, T3258/4/10.

————. Letter Eleven. File = 51-01-12, T3258/4/12.

————. Letter Twelve. File = 51-01-13, T3258/4/13.

Index